PEN & SWORD MILITARY CLASSICS

We hope you enjoy your Pen and Sword Military Classic. The series is designed to give readers quality military history at affordable prices. Pen and Sword Classics are available from all good bookshops. If you would like to keep in touch with further developments in the series, including information on the **Classics Club**, then please contact Pen and Sword at the address below.

Published Classics Titles

Forthcoming Titles

PEN AND SWORD BOOKS LTD

47 Church Street • Barnsley • South Yorkshire • S70 2AS

Tel: 01226 734555 • 734222

E-mail: enquiries@pen-and-sword.co.uk • **Website:** www.pen-and-sword.co.uk

John Ellis

CAVALRY

The history of mounted warfare

PEN & SWORD MILITARY CLASSICS

To Tom Bowden and Mike Beames
and all other veterans of the Central Ref. Light Horse.

First published in 1978 by Westbridge Books.
Published in 2004, in this format, by
PEN & SWORD MILITARY CLASSICS
an imprint of
Pen & Sword Books Limited
47, Church Street
Barnsley
S. Yorkshire
S70 2AS

ISBN 1 84415 096 8

A CIP record for this book
is available from the British Library.

Printed and bound in Great Britain by
CPI UK

For a complete list of Pen & Sword titles please contact:
PEN & SWORD BOOKS LIMITED
47 Church Street, Barnsley, South Yorkshire, S70 2AS, England.
E-mail: enquiries@pen-and-sword.co.uk
Website: www.pen-and-sword.co.uk

Contents

The story of the horse began some 60 million years ago, though what was to come was far from obvious. When the early ancestors of the equids, known as *Eohippus* in America and *Hyracotherium* elsewhere, first appeared on earth they were a mere 10in high and had three or four toes on each foot, each toe having a tiny hoof. During the millennia of pre-history these animals went through the snakes and ladders of evolution, and approximately one million years ago there appeared the *Equus caballus*, much bigger than its predecessors and with only four hooves. This animal first evolved in America, slowly moving northwards until it finally crossed the frozen-over Bering Sea and moved into Asia and Europe. Had it not made this journey the history of mankind would have been very different, for the *Equus* became extinct in the Americas, probably as the result of some virulent disease.

Four main types have been indentified, known to zoologists as Pony I and II and Horse III and IV. The former came in the earliest waves from America. They were only thirteen hands high (a hand is 4in) and they slowly moved right into Europe. The latter were a good couple of hands higher and, having come from America much later, were only found in the Asian heartlands when man first began to try to harness the horse to his own purposes.

At first they were merely hunted for food, a habit that persisted much longer in Europe than farther east because the horses there seemed far less suitable for any other role. But during the third millennium BC, in the vast Asian steppelands, there emerged peoples who had eschewed the settled life of the narrow coastal areas and adopted a nomadic style of life, constantly moving from one area to another in search of better hunting. For such people the horse became valuable as a provider of milk and food and many were domesticated, it being easier to handle reasonably placid herds which could move along with their owners. These first herds consisted exclusively of mares; the stallions proved completely intractable, and anyway they did not produce milk. The herds were kept up to strength by staking mares out away from the rest so that stallions might mount them. Not all the steppe peoples carried on their nomadic way of life. Some, particularly around oases, developed a settled agricultural existence and did not develop horse-rearing beyond the provision of draught and traction animals. Those on the fringe of the oases, however, dependent almost exclusively upon hunting, saw the potential of the horse as an aid to mobility, to match the speed of their prey. These marginal people developed into the mounted steppe nomad of central Asia and southern Russia.

For a thousand years or more, however, riding was unknown to most owners of domesticated horses. Lack of incentive was not the only reason. To catch the horse in the first place most herdsmen used crude rope traps, which almost crippled the animals for good. On the whole the domesticated horse was by definition an unridable one. Eventually, however, nomadic practices spread and one of the first references to riding is a drawing on a bone found at Susa, in the Euphrates Valley and dating from the third millennium BC. Similar finds in central Asia show that riding was established there at least by the second millennium. A neolithic Prussian amber sculpture of the third millennium seems to depict someone riding, but as far as is known riding was not common this far west until the last thousand years before Christ. Amongst the earliest written references to man on horseback are the Chagar Bazar tablets of 1800 BC, whilst a letter of 1750, written by Samsulluna, says that extensive movements of nomads took place in Mesopotamia at this time, and such people almost certainly brought the horse with them, probably into Egypt as well.

However, the first impact of the horse on war was not a result of its being ridden. In about 1500 BC a wave of invasions poured in from the steppes. But these warriors drove in chariots rather than on horseback, probably because they came from the more settled steppe communities, driven from their homeland by some kind of agricultural calamity. The first chariots known to us are those depicted on the Standard of Ur, found in that ancient Sumerian city and dating from the third millennium. What is represented is a ponderous four-wheeled cart, drawn by onagers, and it is difficult to believe that it was more than a means of simply bringing men on to the battlefield. The classic light two-wheeled chariot was an innovation of the Asian hinterland, from where it spread to most other parts of Europe and Asia. The Aryans took it through Persia to India, the Hittites and Mittani to Mesopotamia and Syria, the Kassites into Babylonia, the Hyksos into Egypt, and the Celts and Germans into Europe.

This book is essentially a history of mounted warfare but certain points about the chariot are worthy of mention in that they raise issues relevant to the whole history of the horse in war. One of these is the exact use to which the speed and mobility of the horse is put. In the following pages attention will be drawn to the continual oscillation between the use of the horse as a shock weapon, to pierce the enemy lines by the momentum of its charge, or as a means of getting within range of the enemy, loosing off a missile and getting away again as swiftly as possible.

The chariot civilizations of the Middle East knew proponents of both schools of thought. The ancient Egyptians saw chariots as essentially mobile weapon platforms. Their axles were mounted well to the rear of the chariots to maximize the speed, though this also meant that the vehicle was much more likely to overturn if driven too fast. But this was not a vital consideration because the Egyptians never intended actually to charge at the enemy and close with them, but only to get within javelin or bow range and launch a shower of missiles before galloping off again. The Hittites of Anatolia, however, had a central axle to keep their chariots more stable as they charged right into the enemy's ranks. To this end also, although the chariots were very light, each carried three men armed with short spears to provide a reasonable force in the hand-to-hand struggle.

But the history of war is not simply a matter of mere tactics. There are broader social ramifications, for no form of military activity takes place in a historical vacuum, but is at the same time both a consequence of and an influence upon the type of society in which it is undertaken. The story of the horse in war reveals this just as clearly as any other aspect of military history, and the story of the chariot provides a foretaste of one of the most basic of these social considerations.

Horses and their equipment are expensive. In ancient armies it was possible to expect that most citizens would be able to equip themselves with a primitive wickerwork shield and some sort of pointed stick, and be ready to fight when called upon to do so. As long as this mass infantry levy was adequate it was possible to maintain a state in which most men were equal, at least in economic terms. But a chariot and a pair of horses were quite beyond the capacity of ordinary men to provide. The horses needed feeding and skilled attention. In this regard it is noteworthy that the first piece of writing to come down to us entirely devoted to horses is a Hittite manual, written by a Mede, Kikkulis, for King Sepululiumas in about 1360 BC. In it he envisages a very sophisticated regimen for the horses, based entirely upon hand-feeding and housing for most of the year. His stipulation that on Day Two of the training cycle the horses were to be 'annointed all over with butter' might also have involved considerable outlay. Also the chariots themselves were very expensive. They were built by teams of specialized skilled craftsmen who had to be paid high wages. Chariots were so prized by Babylonian kings that they were regarded as being on a par with infant princes, harem women and royal officers. They were often used as diplomatic gifts when it was vital to

Assyrian charioteers. The war chariot was first brought to the Middle East by invading nomadic peoples from the north, in the second millennium BC.

9

Rameses II in his chariot, late
thirteenth century BC. The chariot
was first brought to Egypt by the
nomadic Hyksos. However, unlike
the Assyrians or the Persians, the
Egyptians never went on to
develop an effective cavalry force.

make an effect. The crews too had to be trained, which meant that the state or a large household had to pay for their upkeep.

Thus, to be able to provide battle-worthy chariots it was necessary to find the money to create and maintain such lavish weapons. This was done in two ways. Either the king himself used the taxes and booty from his raids to maintain a palace-bound chariot force, as was the case in Egypt, Babylon and Assyria, or he granted land to certain of his followers so that they might use a share of the harvest or a part of the taxes to provide a chariot of their own in time of war. Such was the practice amongst the Hittites and the dependent lords of the Shang and Chou dynasties in China, in the last two millennia BC. Thus were there created elite groups with considerable political and economic power, whose main, or at least original function, was to provide horses and chariots for the king's wars. The chariots vanished in time, but this integral relationship between the war horse and political power remained as a basic feature of all kinds of nations and empires for thousands of years. The horse meant more than mere battlefield mobility or impetus; it was a foundation of power and prestige and long remained as a potent symbol of that pre-eminence. This relationship will be one of the fundamental themes of this book.

From about 1000 BC the chariot began to decline in importance. The chariot-borne invaders had themselves left their original grazing grounds in response to pressures from other peoples further inland, who were adapting themselves to life on horseback. Over the years these peoples roamed wider and wider and their skills were transmitted further and further afield. The fusing together of the Medes and the Bactrians in 900 BC was very important in transmitting their knowledge of horses and riding further west. Riding had appeared in Babylon in 1200 BC and cavalry appeared in their armies some time later. Certain Syro-Hittite reliefs of the tenth century BC, as well as those of Tell Hulaf at about the same time, also give evidence of military horsemanship. The Etruscans, in Italy, had horses for riding around 700 BC and the Persians, under Cyrus, introduced cavalry into their armies in 500 BC. In China, though riding was known from well before the last millennium BC, the chariot took rather longer to disappear. Its swansong was at the battle of Lake Ulan in central Mongolia in 125 BC. There the Chinese fought the nomadic Hsiung-nu, magnificent horsemen who forced the chariots into a completely defensive and fairly ineffective posture. After this the Chinese swiftly increased their cavalry at the expense of the chariots. Indeed, by the end of the first century AD they had almost completely disappeared throughout the world, living on only in such primitive backwaters as Britain and Ireland.

The military superiority of the individual horseman was the reason for this demise. The chariot was really effective only against infantry, either by virtue of its momentum in close-quarter fighting or its superior mobility. Opposing horsemen, on the other hand, could simply move out of the way of a chariot charge or out of range of any chariot-borne spearmen or archers. Moreover, most of the early horsemen were archers, using the short but powerful Scythian reflex bow. Thus there was never any question of actually engaging chariots in face-to-face mêlées, but simply falling back and saturating them with a deadly hail of arrows, to which the horses were particularly vulnerable.

The military superiority of the horseman could also be had much more cheaply. A cavalry force was much more cost-effective than a small number of chariots, and less of an economic strain on the palace bureaucracy or the individual landholder. But this is not to say that the advent of cavalry meant a democratization of warfare. Horses were still very expensive. In ancient Greece, the famous cavalry commander and historian Xenophon sold a horse for 1000 drachmae, the equivalent of a brigadier's pay for a whole year, and even very inferior animals cost around 300 drachmae. Horses remained the monopoly of the social and economic elite and in all ancient civilizations one finds a close identification between cavalry service and political privilege.

One of the very first political theorists, Aristotle, noted this about his own country. Throughout Greece, he recalled, 'the earliest form of government . . . after the abolition of kingship, was one in which the citizen body was drawn exclusively from the warrior class, represented at first by cavalry'. Speaking of the early Athenian constitution under Draco he said that 'the franchise was extended to all who could afford military equipment . . . the Generals and Hipparchs [cavalry commanders] were to be elected from those whose unencumbered property was worth at least 100 minae'. Later, under Solon, the state was divided into four classes, one of the most important of which was the knights. Etymological evidence indicates that those who were knights were those whose property holding enabled them to keep a horse. In Thessaly the cavalry were synonymous with the aristocracy, who maintained a vigorous rule over the half-serf majority responsible for working on their vast estates and looking after the herds of horses. The Thessalians, with their large plains and abundant pasturage, were the first to use cavalry in Greece and, together with the Thracians, continued to supply the bulk of the Greek cavalry up to the time of Alexander the Great and beyond. The social prestige of the horseman remained even in those states that did not have much truck with cavalry. They had appeared in the Spartan army in 424 BC but were always a much despised arm. Yet the Spartan elite, though they fought as heavily armed infantry, referred to themselves as knights, a title that indicated their ability to provide horses for others to ride.

Unfortunately not much is known about how these Greek horsemen fought, at least until the age of Alexander the Great. The extant Greek authors tell us little. Aeneas the Tactician and Onasander mention cavalry hardly at all, whilst the work of Asclepiodotus reveals a philosophical formalism which often leads one to doubt its basis in practical military experience. What is clear is that the cavalry was definitely a subordinate arm, leaving the brunt of the fighting to the heavy-armed infantry. As Asclepiodotus points out:

> The cavalry force is stationed . . . sometimes before the phalanx, sometimes behind it, and at other times on the flanks, for which reason this arm of the service is called a supporting force, as in the case of the light infantry, and not a phalanx, because it is attached to the phalanx according as need for it arises.

He says that Greek cavalry used to fight in square, wedge, oblong or diamond formation. Of the latter, presumably going back to an old tradition, he remarks:

> It appears that the Thessalians were the first to use the rhomboid formation . . . and this with great success both in retreat and in attack, that they might not be thrown into disorder, since they were able to wheel in any direction; for they placed their crack troopers on the sides and the very best of these at the angles.

We are on surer ground with the army of Alexander the Great. Moreover, it continued to reveal the link between cavalry service and social status in Greek society. Its elite was the Companions, a regiment of noble horsemen established by Alexander's father, Philip. Macedonia had a typically European climate and offered plenty of grazing land. This was divided among the great landowners, as was much of the land that Philip managed to conquer to the east. It was said that just 800 of the Companions enjoyed estates as vast as those of the 10,000 richest men in Greece as a whole. By the end of his reign Philip had increased the Companions to 4000 men and they constituted the central shock force of his and his son's army. Most of Alexander's battles comprised a concerted infantry push in the centre to create the opportunity for a decisive cavalry charge on the right. The Companions charged in a wedge formation, first driving off the enemy's cavalry and then smashing into the flank of the infantry. This wedge formation seems to have first been used by the Scythians and later the Thracians, many of the latter being impressed into Alexander's service. Though this reliance upon

11

One of Alexander the Great's Companions, c 330 BC. Alexander was the greatest cavalry commander of antiquity and the charge of the Companions, albeit riding without saddle or stirrups, was the decisive act of all his major battles.

shock action was clearly most successful, the modern horseman might fairly wonder how it was ever achieved. For the Companions had no saddle or stirrups to keep themselves in place. Nor did they wear any armour other than a leather or metal breastplate and a peculiar fluted helmet. They carried a sword but no shield and wielded a 6ft lance that was very light and often shattered on impact. To hold this steady they often used both hands, and thus to control their horses they had to rely completely upon the pressure of their thighs and knees. But, as one historian has judiciously remarked, 'what writing has done to memory, stirrups have done to riding; without them, men simply had to grip harder and ride better than they mostly do nowadays'. These lances were not used to impale the enemy but rather as a sort of quarter-stave with which to prod or swipe him to the ground. The Companion then swiftly dismounted and dispatched his adversary with sword or dagger, or left him to the mercies of the light infantry, who usually came up behind the cavalry.

Arrian gives an interesting insight into how novel this insistence upon shock action must have been to the armies of the day, and for a long time afterwards. Of the cavalry fight that ended the battle of Gaugamela (331 BC) he says:

The ensuing struggle was the fiercest of the whole action; one after another the Persian squadrons wheeled in file to the charge; breast to breast they hurled themselves on the enemy. Conventional cavalry tactics – manoeuvering, javelin-throwing – were forgotten; it was every man for himself, struggling to break through as if in that alone lay his hope of life.

But the Companions were not the only cavalry employed by Alexander. He also used light horsemen armed with javelins or bows and arrows to be used as scouts or skirmishers in the manner hinted at above by Arrian. Such troops were the basis of the flying columns that he was very fond of, sent out to obtain information or harry small bands of the enemy. Two regiments in particular were used in this role. These were the Paiones, from the borders of Macedonia, under a fierce head-hunting chief of their own, named Ariston, and the Thracian Prodromoi, or 'Fore-runners', in other words, Reconnaissance Regiment. Both carried a very long lance, similar to the pike of the phalanx warrior, and often referred to by the Greeks as a 'barge-pole'. Alexander also had some troops known as *dimachi* who moved around on horseback yet fought on foot. They were not really comparable to modern dragoons, however, in that they were just as heavily armed as the infantrymen of the phalanx, and each had a personal attendant with him. They were meant to provide a mobile defence rather than to surprise the enemy flanks or rear. Yet, in the Macedonian army at this time, one has seen many of the types of cavalry, and their different uses, that were to be the subject of such fierce debate and 'innovation' in the centuries to come. Two thousand years before European generals were even beginning to realize that cavalry might act as skirmishers or shock troopers, scouts or reserves, Alexander of Macedon had built an army that made full allowance for all of these functions.

The tradition of shock action lived on after Alexander's death, even though he himself had been obliged to break up the Companions just prior to the invasion of India. They had suffered so many casualties that Alexander formed many small 'hipparchies' that were to be the nucleus of mainly Asiatic regiments. In the second century BC, however, Polybius noted that other Greeks still fought in much the same way: 'The Thessalian cavalry are irresistible when in squadrons and brigades, but slow and awkward when dispersed or engaging the enemy single-handed as they chance to encounter them.' At about the same time, a young Greek general, Philipoemen, persuaded the Achaean League, at war with Rome, to reorganize their armies on the Macedonian model. He paid particular attention to the cavalry. Polybius has left a brief description of his training methods:

They were to practise charging and retiring in every kind of formation until they could advance at a tremendous pace but without falling out of line or column, keeping at the same time the proper distances between the squadrons, as he considered that nothing was more dangerous or ineffectual than cavalry which have broken their order in squadrons and choose to engage the enemy while in this state.

Alexander the Great's major enemies were the Persians, and in many ways this war was a great clash of ancient horse cultures. It has already been seen how Alexander's homeland was ruled by semi-feudal nobles, whose livelihood was based on horse-breeding and whose familiarity with riding was second to none. The Persian Empire was based on that established by the Medes at the end of the seventh century BC. The Medes, who included Scythian and Bactrian nomads, were also brought up with horses and rode more easily than other men walked. It was their light, mounted archers that helped destroy the Assyrian Empire in 612 BC, and the empire that they in turn established was defined by that area they could cover in their ceaseless raids and *razzias*, pursuing slaves and plunder. Though they employed foreign spearmen and archers as well, the Median cavalry, with their leather trousers and long pointed shoes, were the core of the army set up by Cyaxeres in 650 BC. When the Persian, Cyrus I, rebelled against the Medes in 556 BC, he incorporated these cavalry into his own forces and they remained a vital element of his successors' armies. Both Darius and Xerxes spent much money breeding larger horses for the cavalry, to provide mounts for the now armoured bowmen. Darius built cadet schools in which the major stress was upon the two great themes of oriental warfare – riding and archery. Mercenary cavalry were also employed; Sargatians armed with lassoes and daggers, Caspians with bows, arrows and scimitars, and heavily armed Cissians. As with the Companions and the Thessalian cavalry, most of the native horse was supplied by the petty nobility. Much administrative power was wielded by centrally appointed satraps, but they had no military responsibilities. War was the province of the mounted rural aristocracy, tribal chiefs who went to battle with their band of vassals and companions. Their sole duties were to devote themselves to horsemanship and war and to superintend cattle-breeding or farming within their estates. Even after the overthrow of the Achaemedian Empire by Alexander, these men soon regained their primacy within the army and were the mainstay of the Seleucid and Parthian forces.

However, though the Persian Empire owed its existence to the mounted skills of various nomadic peoples, and though such skills remained an important part of the way of life of the ruling groups, it does seem that the rejection of a truly nomadic existence involved some deterioration in the standards of horsemanship. Certainly, during the reigns of Cyrus and Darius, the Persians showed themselves unable to meeting other horse peoples on equal terms. In 516 BC, Cyrus set off to overthrow

Croesus, king of the Lydians, of whom Herodotus wrote: 'In all Asia there was not at that time a braver or more warlike people. Their manner of fighting was on horseback; they carried long lances, and were clever in the management of their steeds.' In his second encounter with them Cyrus realized that his cavalry was outmatched, and so he placed camels in front of his army, the smell of which so upset the Lydians' horses that they refused to charge home.

Even more ironic was Darius' expedition against the Scythians, in the Balkan hinterland, in 511 BC. Though supposedly superior in all respects to their primitive, nomadic ancestors, the Persians proved completely incapable even of bringing their enemy to battle. Herodotus has left an admirable account of the Scythians' tactics:

> They have so devised that none who attacks them can escape, and none can catch them if they desire not to be found. For when men have no stablished cities or fortresses, but all are house-bearers and mounted archers ... how should these not be invincible and unapproachable ... [They] resolved not to meet their enemy in the open field ... but rather to withdraw and drive off their herds ... The Scythian horse ever routed the Persian horse and the Persian horsemen falling back in flight on their footmen, the foot would come to their aid; and the Scythians, once they had driven in the horse, turned about for fear of the foot. The Scythians attacked in this fashion by night as well as by day.

Eventually the Persians were forced to withdraw without having once been able to get to grips with the elusive horsemen.

The incident is important in two respects. On the one hand it introduces us to a tradition of mounted warfare quite different from that of organized national armies, be they ancient Macedonians or nineteenth-century regular cavalry. But it is a tradition that crops up again and again throughout the centuries. In later chapters we shall meet Tatars, Sikhs, Comanches, Ni'en, Boers and Mexicans, all of whom practised this guerrilla mode of combat, using their horses purely to remain mobile rather than to charge into their enemy. For such peoples, as for the Scythians, the essence of war was to avoid battle because they knew they did not possess the horses, arms or equipment to stand up to their enemy in hand-to-hand fighting, particularly against heavy cavalry or infantry with pikes, bows and arrows, or gunpowder.

The Scythians are also important as being the first of the nomadic horsemen about whom we have much written knowledge. Here too is a topic that will much occupy these pages, the struggle of more settled peoples against the eruptions of mounted nomads from the heartland of the Russian and Asian steppes. Their story begins in the Middle East. It has already been seen how one dramatic movement of populations from this area, with their mastery of the chariot, swept out in all directions and revolutionized the conduct of war. In the ninth century BC, another such explosion occurred, sending forth true horsemen this time rather than charioteers. Their main drive was northwards where they came into contact with pastoral peoples settled in their steppe villages. The newcomers' mastery of the horse made their military victory a mere formality and they began to merge with these new subject peoples. Out of this meeting of cultures emerged mounted nomadism, whose culmination was the Mongol Empire, that almost came to cover the whole of the world from France to Japan.

The first of these peoples were the Cimmerians, who were based in the south Russian steppes from about 800 BC. A little over a century later the Scythians emerged and the Cimmerians were driven down into Asia Minor and then Anatolia, which they dominated until 680 BC. The Scythians demonstrate many of the essential features of the nomadic way of life. They wore clothes suitable to a mounted people; not robes but woollen trousers and a short hooded tunic. Their main weapon was the bow, short, because it had to be handled on horseback, but double-curved and very powerful. They used an improved saddle, one of the first that genuinely merits the name. The Persians and Greeks, and the Romans after them, used a simple cloth pad secured by a girth. The Scythian saddle consisted of two cushions, well stuffed with deer's hair, which, connected with cross-straps, rested on either side of the horse's spine. Thus the rider's weight was carried by the horse's dorsal muscles and ribs, rather than by the whole back and spine. This vastly improved the Scythians' mobility in that their horses could be ridden for great distances without the risk of saddle sores.

The bow and arrow was the archetypal weapon of the mounted nomads, and their usual tactics were successive *gallopades* in which they launched a continuous hail of arrows and then wheeled away before actual contact was made. But this was not their only method of fighting. Writing in about 100 BC Asclepiodotus distinguished between three different types of cavalry, one of which he characterized as that 'which fights at close quarters [and] uses ... a very heavy equipment fully protecting both horses

Assyrian mailed heavy cavalry, c 750 BC. Regular cavalrymen were first used by the Assyrians in the ninth century BC, though they were unarmoured archers who probably dismounted to fight. Mail-clad spearmen did not appear until the reign of Tilgath-Piteser III, one hundred and fifty years later.

and men with defensive armour, and employing, like the hoplites, long spears'. Such horsemen had first appeared long before this particular passage was written and were to re-emerge several times before they reached their heyday in Europe, in the Middle Ages. They were adopted by several of the nomadic peoples, but first appeared in Assyria. Regular cavalry were first used in the Assyrian army during the reign of Assur-nasir-apli II (883–859 BC) as a counter to the Iranian nomads. At first the horsemen were virtually carbon copies of the nomads themselves, simple unarmoured archers. Later, probably because the Assyrians found themselves at a considerable disadvantage when fighting on equal terms, the archers began to wear mail shirts. Under Tiglath-pileser III (745–727 BC) another type of armoured horseman began to appear. These were spearmen, wearing mail shirts made up of metal plates sewn on to their tunics. In origin these were simply mounted infantrymen and at first probably fought like Alexander's *dimachi*. By the reign of Sennacherib (705–681), however, these two types had merged and the Assyrians were able to field large numbers of authentic heavy cavalry, equally adept at firing arrows at a distance or charging home at spearpoint.

The Assyrians never protected their horses with armour, but by the fifth century BC certain nomadic tribes came to prominence and they did protect both rider and mount. The first of these were the Massagetae, a Sacian people who lived to the east of the Sea of Aral. According to the Greek geographer, Strabo, 'they put bronze breastplates on the chests of their horses', their first armoured cavalry appearing in the sixth century BC. A related people to the south, the Chorasmians, also developed similar equipment,

A nomadic saddle of the fifth century BC. Found in South Russia, it is typical of the Scythian style of saddle. The Scythians formed one of the most important early nomadic groups and are generally credited with the introduction of the saddle.

probably in response to the threat of Alexander the Great and his armoured infantry phalanx. The most famous armoured nomads of all were the Sarmatians, not, incidentally, a homogenous people. The word is something of a catch-all for various tribes, notably the Aorsi, Siraces, Iazyges, Roxolani and Alans. Certain authorities have claimed that the Sarmatians first adopted this kind of equipment when they were overrun by the Chorasmians in the fourth century BC, but recent burial excavations have shown that it was fairly common a hundred years before. Cuirasses made of bronze scales have been found in Sarmatian graves dating from the fifth century BC, but these were probably only worn by a few chieftains; not until after the Chorasmian invasion did they become more widespread, as the Sarmatians began to adopt their tactic of charging home, shoulder to shoulder. The main weapons were a long lance with an iron head and swords which Strabo described as being of an 'enormous size which they wield with both hands'. The armour varied enormously. Sometimes it was merely a thick leather cuirass, with a similar covering for the horse. Sometimes small iron plates were sewn on to the leather. Other groups supplemented this with broad battle belts similarly made of small bronze or iron plates, or of long narrow strips sewn on to leather. There is also a strong tradition that certain tribes made the armour from small scales sliced from horses' hooves. Ammianus Marcellinus, writing in the fourth century AD, tells us that the Sarmatians have 'cuirasses made from smooth and polished pieces of horn, fastened like scales to linen shirts.' This is corroborated by Pausanias, who claims that he had actually seen such armour, made from small slices of hoof which look like clefts of pine cone.

The Scythians, too, did not stand still as regards tactics and armaments. Under pressure from other nomadic tribes, notably the Yueh-chi, various Scythian elements, known as the Sacae or Saka, moved into north-west India and carved out an empire for themselves in the Punjab. Temples in the Hindu Kush oases give a vivid picture of the new type of horse soldiers that evolved. In the army of King Chroroes heavy horsemen played a significant role. They wore coats of mail and a breastplate; the horses too had protective armour. Their weapons varied, the sword being supplemented by a shield and lance or battle-axe, or sometimes two bows and a quiver of thirty arrows. The archers also had two spare bow-strings hanging from the back of their helmets. A fragment from Tragus speaks of 'the fierce tribe of the Scythians, very swift in battle on the level ground, their bodies encased in amour, [who] protect their legs with iron, and wear golden helmets upon their heads'.

But it should not be thought that any of these nomadic peoples relied exclusively upon such armoured cavalry. Certainly riding was practised by a much greater percentage of the male population than in Macedonia, say, or Persia, but this is not to imply that their societies were an egalitarian frater-nity of horsemen. Many of the Sarmatians, for example, and after them such tribes as the Alamanni or the Goths, fought on foot, and of the horsemen only a small number fought as armoured shock troops. Nomadic societies were very hierarchical, with the chiefs and their nobles wielding absolute authority and taking the lion's share of captured booty, slaves and horses. Probably only these men could afford the equipment of the heavy cavalryman and the superior Turanian horses (from possibly as early as the seventh century BC, and certainly by the fifth, heavier horses had been systematically bred in the Turan, that portion of west Asia to the north of Iran) needed to carry them. I do not wish to join in the argument as to whether it is meaningful to speak of 'nomadic feudalism' but it is certainly clear that cavalry service was just as much a social divider in nomadic societies as it was in the more settled nations that have been referred to above. Whilst there is not the same gulf between those with horses and those without, the type of horse and equipment was still a crucial determinant of authority and prestige.

India has already been mentioned with regard to the armoured cavalry of the Sakas, and the general history of that subcontinent reveals many themes that are already familiar. At first chariots were the predominant arm, with the rather unusual addition of large forces of elephants. The elephants, in fact, remained for hundreds of years, though they tended to be as great a menace to their users as to their enemies. Any soldier today could point to the dubious merits of employing tanks with minds of their own. The chariots were introduced by the Aryans who moved into India in about 1500 BC. They were still important in the Puranic and Epic periods and did not completely disappear until the seventh century AD. They were present in the army of Chandragupta I, the founder of the Mauryan Empire, in the fourth century BC, but already cavalry had taken over the main role. The *Arthashastra*, a manual written by Chandragupta's loyal adviser, Chanakya, lays much stress on cavalry training, though some of it sounds rather fantastic to modern ears. The true art of horsemanship, *sannayham*, included being able to execute at least four different types of trot, the *gambade*, as in the Viennese Riding School, and seven different types of jumping, includ-ing *bhekapluta*, jumping like a frog, and *kokila samchari*, leaping like a cuckoo. In the first of these the horse was supposed to hop forwards like a kangaroo, this being judged a particularly efficacious way of attacking elephants. The horse's ability to do this must have been considerably impaired by the Indians' habit of giving their mounts a copious draught of wine before battle. Indian battlefield ability has never been very highly regarded. In this era it could have resembled surrealistic farce.

In fact, it seems fair to assume that these particular movements represented a theoretical level of excellence rather than the practicalities of combat. The *Arthashastra* goes on to give a much more prosaic list of the cavalry's duties, in which drunken hopping would not have played much of a part. The horsemen were to be capable of 'running against, running round, running beyond, running back, disturbing the enemy's halt, gathering the troops . . . clearance of the rear . . . protection of the defeated and retreating army, and falling upon the retreating enemy'. At this time the Indians did not employ mounted archers. Arrian has described their horsemen as being 'equipped with two javelins and with a smaller shield than that carried by the foot soldiers. They do not saddle the horses . . .' Their main role was probably to harass the enemy rather than to close in for hand-to-hand fighting.

The cavalry of the Mauryan era do not seem to have occupied the same privileged social position that they occupied elsewhere, and were to attain in India at a later date. Horses were a royal monopoly, private citizens being expressly forbidden to own either them or elephants. The soldiers formed a separate and esteemed caste of their own, the *ksatriyas*, but they were paid by the state, in peace as well as wartime, and did not have the economic power, based on land, of the great nobles or rural *petite noblesse* of other ancient kingdoms.

Nomadic horsemen have dominated much of the discussion in this chapter and they are crucial to the military history of China, the last great power to be dealt with in this chapter. Under the Shang and Chou dynasties chariots were the key weapon, but during the latter years Chou rule, in the so-called Warring States era, from 402 to 221 BC, many northern states, notably Chao in northern Shansi, had introduced light cavalry into their armies. By the end of the period they were standard in all states. The main impetus for this change came from the nomadic Hsiung-nu, regarded by many scholars as being the predecessors of the Huns, with whom many of the northern states were constantly at war. The main advocate of this adoption of the enemies' tactics was Wu Ling of Chao in 320 BC, and it seems that one of his most difficult tasks was to persuade the Chinese horsemen to adopt trousers and short jackets instead of the long gown which was regarded as an essential sign of status. The eventual dominance of Chin, who provided a short-lived dynasty until 206 BC, was facilitated by their being a northern frontier people who had fully absorbed Hsiung-nu methods of warfare.

By the time of the Han Dynasty, which ruled until AD 221, cavalry were the standard battle arm. One of their generals, Ma Yuan, had a statuette of a horse made on the base of which was carved these words: 'Horses are the foundation of military might, the great resource of the state.' With them the Han were able to turn the tide against the Hsiung-nu who, under their great king, Maodun, from 209–174 BC, had almost suceeded in overrunning China. But they were contained and after the last major expeditions against them, in 36 BC, under Ch'en Tang, their dominance in the East was shattered. A bare eighty years later they were driven from their homelands by those people we now refer to as Mongols.

But the Chinese never took whole-heartedly to the use of cavalry. The conservative opposition to Wu Ling has already been noted, and it is indicative that certain sources have named General Li Mu, in the following century, as the man who introduced horse archers to China. What seems most likely is that the arm knew various waves of popularity as the Hun threat ebbed and flowed. Certainly, as late as 140 BC, the Chinese general, Huo Ch'u-ping, had to override considerable opposition to have mounted bowmen reinstated as the prime arm. Nor, as we have seen above, was the chariot finally abandoned until after 125 BC (see p. 121 for a Tang statesman's view on Chinese reservations about the use of cavalry).

Indeed, adopting their own tactics was not the only way to defeat the nomads. In 99 BC General Li inflicted a decisive defeat on the Hsiung-nu using infantry only. They were armed with crossbows, which had first appeared in China in the fourth century BC, soon becoming complicated and very effective pieces of military technology. In the *Han-Shu*, a Chinese historian has left a very good account of the decisive battle:

At the Chiun-chi mountains he confronted the Shan-yu directly, and his army, which was situated between two hills, was surrounded by 30,000 enemy cavalry. Li Ling had his wagons formed into barricades. He drew up his forces on the outside, the front ranks armed with halberds and shields and the rear ranks with bows or crossbows. His orders were to discharge at the sound of the drum and to hold the shooting when the bells were struck.

A Chinese representation of a Hsiung-nu horseman, from the Chou period. The Hsiung-nu were the scourge of the Chinese frontiers until the last century BC. They are commonly thought to be the ancestors of the Huns, who almost overran Europe four hundred years later.

Most things seem to have been done in China long before the rest of the world, and this is a particularly striking example. It was not until the thirteenth century AD that Europeans began to meet the threat of cavalry by using bowmen, and later musketeers, protected by defensive works. The English bowmen behind their rows of pointed stakes or the Hussites in their wagon *laagers* were hardly military originators. However, it does not seem that this type of battle array was a common Chinese expedient. To be effective it needed suitable defensive terrain and a prodigious supply of arrows (see p. 37 below on the Parthian general, Surenas, who was another to realize how important was an adequate supply of arrows. The point may seem crashingly obvious, but ancient armies were very much defined by what the individual soldier could carry on his person). Excellent discipline was also a prime requisite. The three rarely came together so decisively.

A final point to notice about the Chinese is that for the bulk of the period dealt with in this chapter they managed to avoid being dependent on the nobles to provide their key military forces. Under the Shang Dynasty military power was in the hands of a landowning chariot-aristocracy, but thenceforth Chinese rulers were able to raise their forces as standing armies. The Han Emperor, Wu Ti devoted himself to breeding horses for the state, and all able-bodied males were obliged to serve for at least two years in the Han armies, though one historian has suggested that cavalry service was still reserved for the socially privileged. There was also a great reliance upon mercenaries, particularly as cavalrymen. The historian Fan Yeh recorded one expedition in AD 88 in which 56,000 assorted nomads were recruited. A hundred years earlier, Chao Ch'ung-kuo presented a memorial on ways to prevent tribal raids and recommended that 'such a force should include 1000 cavalrymen from the commanderies and 1000 non-Chinese volunteers . . . with two auxiliary horses being provided for every ten head of horse in the force'.

What are the fundamental themes that have already emerged by the end of this first period? Firstly there has been the transition from chariots to horsemen. In the second millennium BC, Mari records contain the following advice from King Limri-zin to his son: 'My lord should not ride upon a horse. Let my lord ride on a chariot or even on a mule and let him know his royal status.' Yet by the end of the pre-Christian era, and much earlier in most places, the chariot had been completely superseded and it was the horse alone that was the truly royal steed. The same peoples who had introduced the chariot in the first place went on to tame the horse for riding and their subsequent raids across the Middle East and Asia soon showed that charioteers were no match for individual horsemen with their superior speed and manoeuvreability.

There were two quite different ways of organizing cavalry armies. On the one hand there were the complex palace bureaucracies that tried to retain a monopoly of horses and keep a standing army. The Mauryan Empire in India, and certain of the early Chinese dynasties were organized in this way. In Assyria it is revealing to note that when the heavy archer lancers began to appear in large numbers, during the reign of Tiglath-pileser III, the annual levy of peasant infantrymen was abolished in favour of a standing army.

But other peoples did not simply incorporate cavalry into their armies as a technical expedient. Theirs were authentic horse cultures in which either the bulk of the population, as among the mounted nomads, or the social elite, as in Macedonia, Thrace or Persia, were born and bred on horseback. It was not necessary to maintain central barracks and stables; large forces of cavalry could be mobilized either by a *levée en masse* of much of the population, as among the Scythians, the Sarmatians or the Hsiung-nu, or by summoning the rural aristocracy and their retainers.

Yet in both types of nation the horse was a very powerful symbol. For all peoples it represented great power; the man on horseback was almost a different species from the humble foot-soldier. Mauryan kings recognized this when they forbade the private ownership of horses. Babylonian kings esteemed their horses greatly. Their Wisdom Literature contains one passage spoken by a horse: 'Without me neither king nor governor nor prince races through the streets . . . next to the king my box is placed.' For other societies they had great religious significance. Horse sacrifices were common amongst nomadic peoples. For the Aryans they defined political power; they used to let one roam loose for a year and wherever it roamed the king or chief in that region was called upon to pay tribute or give battle. In Greece and Persia the noblemen were defined as such largely because they owned horses, and even in nomadic societies, where most men owned at least one horse, a rigid sense of hierarchy was maintained by the chiefs and nobles having much greater herds, stronger horses and more elaborate equipment. In the Ancient World cavalry was not simply just another military arm; it was the bedrock of social and political power, its outward manifestation and its omnipotent weapon.

Technical Note: Bits and Bridles in Ancient Times

What is especially remarkable is that this was achieved without all but the most rudimentary riding equipment. Only the Scythians seem to have had any kind of recognizable saddle during this period. Moreover, no one rode with stirrups. Their impact has been greatly overrated. The Companions and the Sarmatians, the Assyrians and the Saka seem to have developed extremely effective shock tactics simply by being able to control their horses with their legs. The level of horsemanship is even more remarkable when it is recalled that all these peoples used the lance, which they were obliged to wield with both hands. Even bridles were a luxury to many of these peoples. There were, however, some very important developments in this sphere. At first the horse was controlled by tying a piece of rope or thong around its head, above the mouth, but it was soon realized that the mouth itself was the best place on which to exert pressure because it was so sensitive. Thus there appeared the bit. First came the snaffle, examples of which have been found dating from 1400 BC. This is a metal bar lying over the tongue and resting on the toothless area of the gum between incisors and molars. The bit usually has a cheekpiece at each end to prevent its being pulled to one side through the horse's mouth. Soon the metal mouthpiece was split into two or three jointed sections which made it more difficult for the horse to immobilize the bit by getting it between his teeth or rolling his tongue over it.

It was the Celts, who settled in Galatia, in Asia Minor, in the third century BC, who made the last important innovation in the technique of bitting. They produced the curb-bit, which is basically a snaffle with the addition of a bar, chain or thong which fits into the groove along the horse's chin. The reins are attached to the bottom end of the cheekpieces, the cheekstraps to the top. When the reins are pulled, the chin-curb acts as the fulcrum of a lever which makes the mouthpiece press downwards, rather than upwards into the corners of the mouth. This causes the horse to bend his neck at the pull and slow down, the result being achieved by gentle pressure and not sudden infliction of pain.

2 Rome and her Enemies 750 BC to AD 476

'There is only one way in which cavalry have an
advantage over us, and that is that it is safer for them
to run away . . .'
Xenophon

'They rely especially on the valour of their cavalry, in
which all the nobles and men of rank undergo hard
service.'
Ammianus Marcellinus on the Persians c AD 370

In 401 BC, the Greek cavalry commander, Xenophon, the author of one of the first treatises on horsemanship, led an expedition of Greek mercenary infantrymen to fight in Persia for the pretender Cyrus. On the latter's defeat the Greeks found themselves abandoned in a foreign country and spent many months trekking back to their homeland. In the *Anabasis* Xenophon has told the story of their adventures. At one stage the Greeks were beset by an enemy force that included many cavalry and their leader gave a stirring speech in which he bravely attempted to minimize the danger:

> If any of you feel disheartened because of the fact that we have no cavalry while the enemy have great numbers of them, you must remember that ten thousand cavalry only amount to ten thousand men. No one has ever died in battle through being bitten or kicked by a horse; it is men who do whatever gets done in battle. And then we are on a much more solid foundation than cavalrymen, who are up in the air on horseback, and afraid not only of us but of falling off their horses; we, on the other hand, with our feet planted on the earth, can give much harder blows to those who attack us and are much more likely to hit what we aim at. There is only one way in which cavalry have an advantage over us, and that is that it is safer for them to run away . . .

Clearly Xenophon was mainly concerned with encouraging his men, who *were* afraid of the enemy. He deliberately underestimated the potential of the very arm that was his first love. Yet this speech is a very good summary of a concept of war that slowly gained ground in the Ancient World. In some states, notably Sparta, Athens and Etruria, infantry service lost the stigma that was attached to it in other countries. Infantry ceased to be an ill-armed rabble, completely secondary to the charioteers or the horsemen, and became the decisive battlefield arm. The half-naked peasant, with his pointed stick and wickerwork shield, was replaced by the heavily armed hoplite, a free citizen of some means who was now proud to come forward and fight for his country. The reasons for the transition are rather open to debate. Two seem fundamental. Firstly terrain; in the three states just mentioned there were few areas suitable for either the rearing of horses or the large-scale deployment of cavalry. Secondly political and social organization; both ancient Greece and Etruria were little more than national ideals, the only real cohesive unit being the various small 'city-states'. (The term is, in fact, very misleading. These states were predominantly agricultural, based on a class of middling, 'yeoman' farmers. Such men would have found it economically unproductive to keep horses. For that it was necessary to have the ranch-like estates of Thessaly, Thrace and Macedonia.) City-states could field only relatively small armies though even these represented a high proportion of the available able-bodied citizens. Each of these men had to pull his full weight though the resources were not available to put each one on horseback. Therefore, though they served on foot, they were given heavy armour, shields and helmets and there developed, hand in hand with this, a strict emphasis upon the value of tight formations and discipline. Because it was impossible to field more than a paltry force of cavalry such states had to create an infantry arm that had sufficient weight and cohesion to be able both to withstand cavalry attacks and to provide the decisive shock action that was usually left to the horsemen.

In such states cavalry lost the social exclusivity that they had had in other countries. The ability to provide horses was still a sign of great prestige, but it did not denote the same absolute superiority to lesser men. For the Spartans and the Athenians, for example, the ability to 'provide armour' was now the basic sign of status. Xenophon, again, noted this in a short pamphlet on the Athenian constitution when he described, and regretted, the gulf between 'the commons who row the ships and give the city its power – they and the petty officers and shipyard workers' and the 'armoured troops and the gentry'. This development did lead, however, to a relatively more democratic form of government. There were still wide social divisions, but because a larger proportion of the population were called upon to serve in the elite military units, those soldiers were able to demand for themselves a greater say in public affairs, and the ability to retain at least a sufficient livelihood to provide themselves with arms and armour. Cavalry states, on the other hand, based as they were upon large-scale feudal estates or a complex palace bureaucracy had felt no need to make such political concessions. Great landowners or central administration could by themselves supply the expensive elite units. It would not do to try to push this link between the types of army and political organization too far, or to insist upon a simple casual relationship. The Greek states had once been governed by a horse-owning aristocracy and the reasons for its decline are far from clear. The Etruscans, on the other hand, though they were an infantry state, were governed by a small but powerful nobility and other classes, as far as we know, did not have much political power. Nevertheless, it is possible to posit some kind of correlation between military matters and more general social considerations. The development of societies is a dialectical process in which military institutions do have a part to play.

Many of the points made above are relevant to the history of the Roman Republic and Empire. For much of their history the Roman armies were based upon the infantry rather than mounted soldiers. Though there was always some sort of cavalry component available, the most important part of the army, at least until the late Empire, was always the legions. Moreover, whatever cavalry there was, was rarely composed of native Romans but of foreigners serving for plunder, either bound by the conditions of a short-term treaty, or because they had been conquered by the Romans.

The Romans first came to rely on infantry for rather mundane reasons. On the one hand the early tribes were not very well endowed with horses, and on the other their greatest battles were with the Etruscan hoplites. At one stage they were ruled over by an Etruscan dynasty and soon adopted similar equipment and tactics. Thus, whereas at the beginning of the sixth century BC the Roman 'army' had been a band of a few hundred horsemen armed only with flimsy javelins and no shields, by the end of the next century, particularly after the reforms of Servius Tullius, hoplite tactics were the standard practice.

This transition to an infantry-based army brought with it the same kind of political developments that were noted above, though remnants of older traditions survived. Just as with the Greeks, the earliest tribes had been ruled over by those owning horses. Even after the Servian reforms the cavalry, six centuries of them, were to be manned by the principal men of the state, their standing to be assessed by the amount of property they possessed. These six centuries had a bloc of votes in the assembly, but it is revealing to note that the aristocrats only voted after the hoplite *classis*, to whom they were clearly regarded as being of secondary importance. Because Rome had come increasingly to rely upon an infantry army, the rulers were forced to make political concessions to the class that was to provide the armoured hoplites. Servius probably saw this more clearly than most because he had come to power in rather dubious circumstances and found it necessary to rely on the ordinary citizens for support rather than the traditional aristocracy. If this citizen army was to be a reliable support it had to be given some sort of political representation. Whatever the exact facts of the matter there are clearly parallels with the development of the Greek city states. In both cases the relative unimportance of the cavalry was linked with new political and social forms.

The codification of the Servian reforms created an army that was to remain essentially unchanged for hundreds of years. Under Camillus, at the turn of the fourth century BC, the traditional hoplite lance was exchanged for a throwing spear or javelin and the solid phalanx was replaced by a chequer board of mutually supporting maniples. In 107 BC Marius took the dramatic step of abolishing property qualifications and throwing the army open to all, relying on voluntary recruitment rather than the periodic levy of one class. For Marius was a professional, a man of obscure origins who, as tribune of the plebs, created an army of his own, trained it himself and won a decisive victory against rebellious tribesmen in North Africa. His ideal was a professional army, made up of men who actually chose the military life and could be moulded over the long years of their service. So the army ceased to be such a direct reflection of the social composition of the Republic; military service to be synonymous with a certain stake in society. The protection of the state was no longer a duty, but just one more job amongst others. The barracks and garrisons became self-contained little communities, cut off from the world outside and concerned only with the military trivia of tactics, pay, food and promotion. In other words, military service and the forms it took is no longer really explicable in terms of group interests and there is no longer much value in linking emphasis upon infantry or cavalry with more general underlying pressures. Most of the story that follows is the study of a fairly inert organization rather than a dynamic social organism. Military service was a matter of technique rather than social process.

For the next three hundred years or so, the history of the Roman cavalry is easily dealt with. Even before Marius the basic features had become apparent. The cavalry was divided into two types: the horsemen attached to the legion itself, about 700 of them, and those serving in independent units of foreign mercenaries. The latter wore whatever uniforms was their national custom and were allowed to equip themselves and fight according to their own traditions. Often they were officered by their own chiefs and nobles. The legionary squadrons were a more homogenous force and are often referred to as the 'regular' cavalry. They were organized into ten squadrons and from about 150 BC were equipped with a metal helmet, cuirass, shield, sword, javelin and heavy *hasta*, or throwing spear. On the march and on garrison duty, these cavalry were to act with their respective legions, but in a large battle they were often brigaded together, usually placed on both wings of the battle line.

Under Marius the legionary cavalry was considerably increased, a move made possible by the new availability of good horses. Tolerably good horseflesh was available in Italy itself, particularly in Apulia and Tarentum in the south. But once the Romans had taken over Spain in the wake of the Carthaginian Wars a whole new source of mounts became available. During the Carthaginian occupation, the garrison had included 2000 Libyan horsemen whose stallions – they only rode mares – were available for crossing with local breeds. North African horses were also crossed with Italian during the alliance with Massinissa, king of the Numidians.

After the Social Wars, however, the legionary cavalry was abolished, though the reasons for this are unclear. Under Augustus, who became emperor in 29 BC, they were re-established as part of the new Imperial standing army. Now each legion only had 120 cavalry, divided into four *turmae*. But the foreign mercenaries, known as *auxilia*, were expanded, being organized into *alae*, or wings, or sometimes forming part of an *equita*, a cohort made up of both cavalry and foot soldiers. The *auxilia* were recruited from almost every tribe or people with whom the Romans came into contact and a bewildering array of different types of horsemen fought with the Roman eagles at one time or another. The most consistent element was the Gauls, but other important units were the Batavians from Germany, the Numidians from Africa and the Pannonians from the middle Danube. From AD 193 the Emperor Severus made special efforts to increase the complement of horse archers, recruited from Mesopotamia and Syria. Later, from the reign of Hadrian, the Romans began to make increasing use of heavily armoured cavalry, *à la* Sarmatian, but I will leave discussion of this development until later. Let me first deal with what might be called the 'light-cavalry period', through a discussion of the various wars against other cavalry powers. In this way it will also be possible to examine the development of cavalry tactics in other parts of the world.

Probably the deadliest threat to the Roman Republic came from Hannibal and the Carthaginians in the fierce war fought between 218 and 206 BC. More than any other campaigns, except those against the Parthians, the Punic Wars showed how dangerous could be the Roman reliance upon a predominantly infantry force. For one of Hannibal's most important units were the Numidian cavalry under the dashing generalship of Maharbal. These

North African horsemen, of nomadic stock, were the very epitome of light cavalry, relying not so much upon the shock of the charge as upon swift forays, throwing their javelins and then wheeling away out of range, or making feint attacks, hoping to stretch and break up the enemy formations. Livy has left us one of the best descriptions of these elusive warriors. In one passage, actually describing a Numidian detachment fighting with the Romans, during the honeymoon with Massinissa, he gives a clear insight into the Numidians' absolute familiarity with their horses and the almost contemptuous way in which they were able to taunt their flat-footed adversaries:

> The Numidians mounted their heavy horses and began to ride up to the enemy outposts, without attacking anyone. At first they presented an appearance beyond anything contemptible. Horses and riders were tiny and lean; the horsemen were without armour and without weapons, apart from the javelins they carried; their mounts were without bridles and even their movement was ungainly as they trotted with stiff necks and outstretched heads . . . The Numidians kept riding up, then retiring, but gradually bringing their horses closer to the outlet, making out that they were incapable of controlling their mounts, and were being carried along against their will. Finally they put spurs to their horses and burst through the midst of the enemy's outposts and rode out into more open country, where they set fire to all the buildings by the road. They went on to kindle a blaze in the nearest village and to start a general devastation with fire and sword.

This seeming formlessness and continuous movement was the very essence of Numidian tactics. Of one battle Polybius wrote that 'the Numidians easily scattered and retreated, but afterwards wheeled round and attacked with great daring – these being their peculiar tactics.' Appian left a more detailed description:

> [They] were trained . . . to hurl showers of javelins, advancing and retreating and again advancing. These . . . are the tactics which they always employ, alternate flight and pursuit. These Numidians also know how to endure hunger. They often subsist on herbs in place of bread, and they drink nothing but water. Their horses never even taste grain; they feed on grass alone and drink but rarely.

But they were not merely harassing troops. Contemptible though they might have looked to some observers, they were consistently Hannibal's battle winners, ready to close with the enemy at the vital moment. At the crushing victories of Trebia, Lake Trasimene and Cannae the commitment of the Numidians decided the day. On each occasion Hannibal showed himself a master of timing, a specialist in the *coup d'oeil*, knowing just the right moment to throw in the cavalry and tip the scales. At Trebia, the last act was when 'Mago and his Numidians, once the line had – all unawares – moved forward beyond their place of concealment, appeared suddenly in the [Roman] rear with almost shattering effect'. At Lake Trasimene the cavalry and light infantry were concealed behind low hills before being thrown on the rear of the Romans to bottle them up between lake and mountains. At Cannae it was the cavalry that made possible the swift encirclement once the legions had been drawn in towards the weak Carthaginian centre.

Hannibal had other, heavier cavalry contingents, but these too were used more as skirmishers and flying columns than as shock troops. In one revealing aside, and his remarks apply equally to the Romans, Livy observes how rare it was for cavalry to meet head-on in close combat. He is speaking here of an incident at Cannae:

Soon the Gallic and Spanish horse on the Carthaginian left were engaged with the Roman right. Lack of space made it an unusual cavalry encounter: the antagonists were compelled to charge head-on, front to front; there was no room for outflanking manoeuvres, as the river on one side and the massed infantry on the other pinned them in, leaving them no option but to go straight ahead. The horses soon found themselves brought to a halt, jammed close together in the inadequate space, and the riders set about dragging their opponents from the saddle, turning the contest more or less into an infantry battle. [cf the passage from Arrian on p. 12 above where a hand-to-hand engagement is similarly regarded as being outside the scope of 'conventional cavalry tactics'.]

During this period, then, cavalry tactics were very different from those of the earlier armour-clad nomads or of Frederick the Great's cuirassiers almost 2000 years later. Cavalry rarely charged flat out against the enemy line, be it mounted or on foot, but limited themselves to attempting to break up the line by constantly moving in and out of range and keeping up a hail of missiles. Even when they did find themselves involved in hand-to-hand combat there was no question of having built up sufficient impetus to smash through one's opponents. Instead both sides became locked in a confused *mêlée* in which it

was often easier to abandon one's horse completely and fight on foot. Polybius' description of the Roman cavalry in the third century BC and before applies equally to most of their enemies at this time and indicates a style of mounted warfare in which the horse was a convenience rather than a weapon in itself: 'In old times they had no cuirasses but fought in light undergarments, the result of which was that they were able to dismount and mount again at once with great dexterity and facility, but were exposed to great danger in close combat, as they were nearly naked.'

Hannibal was finally defeated at the battle of Zama, in 202 BC, largely because the Romans were able to recruit Numidian cavalry of their own and because Hannibal's contingents were overwhelmed by his own elephants. But this was not the last time that the Romans were to fight against them. In 109 BC, the Romans went to war against Jugurtha, in the Numidians' home territory, and found that their adversaries had gone beyond positional skirmishing tactics and developed a strategic role for their elusive horsemen. Because they were not now just a part of Hannibal's conventional army, but were fighting by themselves and for themselves, they fell back on guerrilla tactics, refusing the Romans the chance to bring them to battle. Our prime source for this campaign is Sallust's history and his rather erratic narrative contains an excellent résumé of the Africans' method of fighting:

Even the men who resisted with the most dogged courage were disconcerted by this irregular manner of fighting, in which they were wounded at long range without being able to strike back or come to grips with their foe. Jugurtha's horsemen had been given careful instructions beforehand. Whenever a squadron of the Roman cavalry began a charge, instead of retiring in a body in one direction, they retreated independently, scattering as widely as possible. In this way they could take advantage of their numerical superiority. If they failed to check their enemies' charge they would wait until the Romans lost formation, and then cut them off by attacks in their rear or on the flanks; and when any of the Numidians found it more convenient to retreat to the hill than to keep to the plain, their horses, being used to the ground, made their way easily through the thickets, while ours were impeded by their inexperience of such rough country.

This is classic guerrilla warfare. The incumbent forces know that they cannot stand up to their opponents in open battle and so limit themselves to harassing raids, retreating into inaccessible hideouts as soon as there is any danger of a local defeat. Sallust notes another typical feature of the guerrilla army in his observation that 'With the exception of the royal bodyguard, no Numidian, after a rout, returns to his post in the King's army; every man goes off where he pleases, and this is not regarded as a shameful thing for a soldier to do, because it is the custom of the country'. The writer's prejudices are very apparent here. Accustomed as he was to living in a state with thousands of men constantly under arms, he is unable to understand that this rapid dispersal of the Numidian forces was one of their strengths, that in so doing they denied the Romans an obvious target to strike at. The Romans, in turn, were driven to typical counter-guerrilla methods. Instead of trying to catch his enemy, the Roman commander in the first campaign, Metellus, took to destroying villages and crops, seeking to decide the issue by terror rather than open fighting. Later, the Numidians seem to have more or less abandoned their original mode of warfare and taken to meeting the Romans in pitched battle. Once they had taken this course, the issue was no longer in doubt. Without a Marbalus or a Hannibal to direct them, and without a solid centre of heavy infantry to hold the pressure of the legions, the light horseman had little of hope of breaking up the Roman formations. The war ended in 105 BC.

From around this time it is possible to discern a dual theme in Roman attitudes to their cavalry forces. For a long time they continued to employ large numbers of lightly armed *auxilia*, but they also started to incorporate units of much more heavily armed horsemen, largely in response to the type of cavalry against which they had to fight. Polybius tells us that as early as the mid-second century BC the Roman horse – one assumes that he is referring to the legionary cavalry – re-equipped themselves in the Greek fashion. This was probably a result of the battles fought against the Greek king, Antiochus III, at Magnesia, in 190 BC, and against the Macedonians and their allies at Pydna, in 168 BC. On both occasions the Romans were faced with substantial cavalry forces which included numbers of heavy lancers. In the first battle, Appian speaks of 'mail-clad Galatians', whilst Livy refers to these as *cataphracti*, though it is unlikely that they wore the full armour that later characterized this type of rider. But they were effective enough to make the Romans reassess their own cavalry. They soon, according to Polybius, 'learnt to copy the Greek arms; for this too is one of their virtues, that no people are so ready to adopt new fashions and imitate what they see is

better in others.' The main innovations did not involve extra armour but the adoption of a heavier lance, which did not shatter at the first impact, and had points at both ends, and the Greek shield, which was much more durable than the old leather-covered wooden one. With such weapons there came a new stress upon the necessity of closing with the enemy and trying to push through his formations.

But the lesson was not learnt overnight. In 180 BC, fighting in Spain against the Celtiberians, the local commander made it clear that the legionary cavalry was not accustomed to relying solely on the impetus of the charge. During one dangerous enemy assault, Flaccus was obliged to order the cavalry specifically to 'close up the squadrons . . . and give your horse their head against the enemy wedge . . . Your charge will have greater force if you ride your horses into them without reins.' Clearly Roman horsemanship at this time was not founded upon the ability to urge the horse into a breakneck gallop. The only way that this could be achieved was by the rider completely giving himself over to the horse's natural instincts. (Flaccus cites an old Roman tradition in his speech to his troopers but the only previous occasion where mention is made of this ploy was against the Veii, in 426 BC. Interestingly, the same idea crops up in the American Civil War, where too the cavalry were not accustomed to breakneck charges. The Confederate general, John Hood, maintained that if the reins could be cut before they set off all cavalry charges would be irresistible.)

But the Romans had to try and familiarize themselves with the new techniques. They were now beginning to meet heavy cavalry even in the West. As soon as the Jugurthine War was concluded Marius was called into southern Gaul to meet the threat of a massive nomadic invasion. Prominent among the enemy tribes were the Cimbri, whose cavalry presented an awesome sight. According to Plutarch these latter were descendants of the Cimmerians, one of the earliest nomadic tribes. If this is correct they seem to have evolved like the Scythians and developed an elite heavy cavalry, most likely of chieftains and other nobles. According to Plutarch:

Their cavalry, 15,000 in number, were a splendid sight as they came riding out. They wore helmets like the heads and gaping jaws of terrible wild beasts and other strange creatures, and these, heightened with great feather plumes, made them look even taller than they were. They had iron breastplates and shining white shields. Each man carried two javelins for throwing, and for fighting at close quarters they used large, heavy swords.

Unfortunately we do not know what part these cavalry played in the campaign, though clearly they were expected to rely upon shock action after the first volley of javelins. Plutarch had little to say about the conduct of the major battle, except that it was a crushing Roman victory. The latter seem to have rolled up the enemy infantry before the cavalry could be brought to bear.

But such horsemen were not really typical in the west until the first appearance of the Frankish armoured knights, out of the debris of the Roman Empire. The horses of this area were not of the quality of the great battle-chargers bred in Turan and elsewhere to the east, and the dominant cavalry tradition remained one of harassment and swift withdrawal. As the Republic entered its last years, it was the Gauls who emerged as the most adept horsemen in this part of the world. Plutarch wrote: 'The Gauls are particularly formidable at fighting on horseback, and in fact they have the reputation of excelling in this arm above any other.' Julius Ceasar was not slow to notice this during his expeditions against them, and he soon supplemented his own forces with large cavalry contingents from the various tribes he had subdued. Even after the private armies of the Civil Wars had been broken up, the Gauls remained as an important part of the Imperial forces. Writing in the first century AD, the geographer, Strabo, reported that the Gauls 'are better as cavalry than as infantry; and the best cavalry force the Romans have comes from these people'.

Certain German tribes also had mounted warriors, though in the main they fought on foot. Caesar, however, has left us some quite detailed descriptions of German tactics and they offer a useful insight into the type of mounted warfare that was prevalent in the European parts of Rome's dominion. For one thing, the German horses were 'undersized and ugly' which meant that they could only be used as a conveyance rather than as an adjunct to shock action. Thus the Suebi, 'in cavalry battles . . . often dismount and fight on foot, training the horse to stand perfectly still, so that they can quickly get to them in case of need [in battle] . . . following their usual practice, they jumped down and unhorsed a number of our men by stabbing their horses in the belly.' Amongst the Harudes, on the other hand, it was the practice for the horsemen to remain mounted, even during the mêlée, but each mounted man had with him a picked foot-soldier, who was to come to his companion's support if necessary. According to Caesar they 'acquired such agility by practice, that in a long advance or a quick retreat they could hang on to the horses' manes and keep pace with them.' The most famous of the German horsemen were the Batavians, who at one stage were the backbone of the *auxilia*. It is not known, however, how many of these troops were native Germans, for the term 'Batavian' came to be synonymous with foreign cavalry in general and men from all nations were recruited into their ranks. But there was definitely some kind of indigenous tradition. Tacitus tells us that 'in the home country they . . . had a picked cavalry force specially trained for amphibious operations. These men were capable of swimming the Rhine while keeping hold of their arms and mounts, and at the same time maintaining perfect formation.'

Certain historians have asserted that as Roman attention switched more and more to her eastern empire her cavalry forces underwent a profound change. Contact with the Sarmatians and the Persians, for example, necessitated a transition to heavier, more comprehensively armoured horsemen to counter the mailed knights of these nations. There is much truth in this but one must be careful not to overstate the changes involved. At no time did the Romans completely abandon their light horse. Pompey, at the battle of Pharsalus, in 48 BC, used mainly oriental cavalry but they were mounted archers and skirmishers whose characteristic tactics were to 'surround troops at a distance, employ sudden assaults, and retire after throwing their opponents into confusion; then they would attack them again, turning now to this side, now to that.' For his part, Caesar found it appropriate to adopt German tactics and he 'ordered young from a picked corps of front-line men, specially selected for agility, to fight among the cavalry'.

From the reign of Vespasian, beginning in AD 69, Pannonian horse began to figure prominently amongst the *auxilia*. Though from the easternmost parts of what is now Europe, they do not seem to have evolved any of the usual nomadic armoured formations, and their tactics were based upon precipitate rushes and retreats. As with most of the auxiliary cavalry, they did not wear metal breastplates but were protected only by their helmet and oblong shield.

In a unique operational order, written in AD 137 by the prefect of Cappadocia, Arrian, concerning a campaign against the Sarmatian subtribe of the Alans, there is no indication that the Romans intended to counter the enemy's initial charge with heavy cavalry of their own. It was hoped to overwhelm the nomads with artillery and infantry fire, but even if this failed the legions were to bear the brunt of the charge and 'the attacking horsemen will

be confronted with an unbroken and immovable hedge of spear points at the level of a horse's chest'. Only when it was clear that the enemy were in full retreat were the infantry to open their ranks and allow the cavalry, supplemented by foot-archers, to set off in pursuit. A little over seventy years later, one of Caracalla's most important military reforms was to supplement the auxiliary cavalry with large numbers of mounted archers from the recently annexed province of Osrhoenia. In 258, Valerian created an elite unit, ranking in seniority with the Praetorian Guard, of Dalmatian horsemen, whose tactics and equipment hardly differed from that of earlier *auxilia*. These men remained the nucleus of the Roman cavalry during its great expansion under Gallienus and Diocletian, in the second half of the third century. The cavalry's main function now was to form a mobile striking force that could be used to buttress those forces permanently tied to the frontier garrisons. As late as *c* AD 390, Vegetius tells us that the Roman cavalry was of two types. As well as the 'heavy horse, that is cuirassiers and troopers armed

with lances' there were large numbers of 'light cavalry, consisting of archers and those who have no cuirasses'.

Vegetius' description of the Roman 'heavy horse' is in fact very representative, even at this late date. The rather indiscriminate use by classical authors of the terms *cataphractus* and *clibinarius* can easily give the impression that the Romans went over to using fully armoured cavalry, on mail-clad horses, in large numbers. Though they frequently fought against peoples using this type of equipment, the Romans

Roman *auxilia, c* AD 50. During the Republic and the first centuries of the Empire, the Romans relied on their infantry legions. What cavalry forces they did put in the field were recruited from foreign allies and subject peoples, notably Gauls, Batavians and Dalmatians.

(*this page*) A charge by mailed
Roman cavalry, *c*AD 325. A detail
from the Arch of Constantine.

themselves only adopted it very late in the Empire,
and that only sparingly. In the main, what distinguished their different types of horsemen were
their weapons. Thus, although the *contarii*, (a *contus*
was a long spear) introduced during Vespasian's
reign, were clearly regarded as being a new species of
cavalryman, more adept at decisively closing with
the enemy, there is no reason to believe that their
armour was any more than a metal breastplate,
helmet and perhaps greaves. There were innovations, however, in their weapons, particularly the
lance, which had become even longer and heavier
than the earlier 'Greek' model. It is almost certainly
Vespasian's army that Josephus is describing when
he speaks thus of its cavalry component: 'The
trooper carries a long sword on his right hip and an
enormous pike in his hand, a shield slanted across
his horse's flank, and in a quiver slung alongside,
three or more darts, broad-pointed and as big as
spears. Helmets and breastplates of infantry pattern
are worn by all arms.'

Forty years later Hadrian raised a regiment of
auxilia known as the *ala* I *Galliorum et Panniorum
cataphracta*, but it is not certain how they were

(*opposite above*) A Greek charioteer
driving a four-horse team, from an
Attic red-figured vase of *c* 410 BC.

(*opposite below*) Warriors of the
Greek and Persians Wars.

32

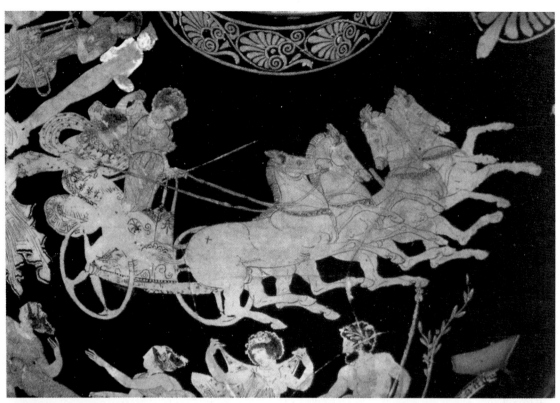

equipped. Technically the word *cataphracta* means 'covered all over with mail', but the Romans were probably not using it in this exact sense. More than likely it merely signified that these horsemen were relatively more armoured than was normal, perhaps wearing thigh-length chain-mail shirts, and it is certain that their horses had no protection. The fact that we know nothing more about mail cavalry until the third century is likely to indicate that there had been no significant innovation in cavalry technique.

Only by the fourth century can we be certain that quite new types of horsemen had appeared in the Roman armies. Ammianus Marcellinus gives us an excellent picture of them in his account of the battle of Strasbourg, against the Alamanni, in AD 357:

> The full armoured cavalry (whom they call *clibinarii*) [were] all masked, furnished with protective breastplates and girt with iron belts, so that you might have supposed them statues polished by hand . . . Thin circles of iron plates, fitted to the curves of their bodies, completely covered their limbs, so whichever way they had to move their members, their garment fitted, so skilfully were the joinings made.

Even at this date, however, it does not seem that the horses had protective mail as well. In describing the course of the battle, Ammianus tells how the Alamanni mixed light infantry with their own cavalry so that they could 'creep about low and unseen, and by piercing a horse's side throw an unsuspecting rider headlong'. Nor were the cataphracts particularly successful. Perhaps because they had encountered this Alamanni technique before, they attempted to flee the field at the first enemy assault, being rallied only by the Emperor Julian himself.

Rome's enemies, also, found that troops of this kind were a mixed blessing. So it was with the Sarmatians, who were still known for the type of cavalry described in the previous chapter. Tacitus is an important source for their role in the early Empire and his account of one battle with the Parthians shows that their tactics were still based upon the momentum of their attack. Faced with Parthian mounted archers they shouted to their commanders that 'this must not be a bowman's engagement . . . better to rush matters by a charge and then fight hand-to-hand!' In another account Tacitus has much to say about the shortcomings of their heavy cavalry and he paints a picture very reminiscent of

A Greek warrior on horseback, *c* 550 BC.

the later discomfiture of European feudal knights when they were unhorsed. The battle in question is one fought between Otho and the Rhoxolani, who had attempted an invasion of Moesia. It was fought in the middle of winter and the Sarmatians found it very difficult to keep their horse's footing in the deep slush:

> It is indeed curious to observe how completely the formidable Sarmatians depend on extraneous aids. An engagement on foot finds them utterly ineffective, but when they appear on horseback there is scarcely a line of battle that can stand up to them. But this particular day was wet, and a thaw had set in. Neither their lances nor their enormous two-handed swords were of any use, because the horses lost their footing and the dismounted warriors were weighed down by their body armour. This protective clothing is worn by the chiefs and notables and consists of iron plating or toughened leather. Proof against blows, it is cumbersome when a man tries to get up after being unhorsed.

Tacitus makes explicit here that only a few of the Sarmatians wore the heavy protective equipment. The same was true of the Persians, both during the domination by the Parthians, and under the Sassanid kings, from AD 226. Ammianus tells us that they relied 'especially on the valour of their cavalry, in which all nobles and men of rank undergo hard service'. The Parthians were the result of the mixture of populations after the invasion of the Parni in the late third century BC. The invaders were Scythian nomads, also including Saka elements, but they swiftly adapted themselves to mesh in with the structure of the Achaemenid state. As has been seen above, this was an essentially feudal state in that it was the aristocracy that supplied the cavalry, the core of the army. The new rulers took over this system and allowed most of the petty nobles to remain on their estates, as long as they undertook to abide by their military obligations. A new group of Parthian great lords also emerged, with the right to collect taxes throughout whole provinces, provided that they too fought for the king in time of war.

This division between grand and petty nobility was reflected in the structure of the Parthian army. Both provided the cavalry – indeed, during the first century BC the Persian infantry almost completely disappeared – but this was made up of two quite distinct types of horsemen. On the one hand, there were the mounted archers, lightly armed on nimble mounts, who were supplied by the lesser estate holders. Most of these were from eastern Iran, where

Roman soldiers of the second century AD. The horsemen are completely unarmoured. The Romans did not begin to use significant numbers of mailed cavalrymen until the fourth century, when they began to imitate their mounted enemies to the east, particularly the Sarmatians and the Parthians.

(*below left*) A mail-clad Sarmatian warrior. The Sarmatians, though a nomadic people, were the first horsemen to make extensive use of heavy armoured lancers. However, only the social elite were equipped in this way, the ordinary warriors fighting as normal unarmoured bowmen.

they lived in small castles and block-houses, and evolved a typical feudal culture centered round jousting, hunting, war, and a chivalric code that emphasized the virtues of personal honour and the protection of women. The grandees, on the other hand, supplied a new type of horseman, a development of the Sarmatian and Saka knight, who encased both himself and his horse in mail armour and armed himself with a great bow, lance and sword. Here, upwards of a thousand years earlier, are most of the basic elements of western European feudalism. Moreover, under Chosroes, who came to the throne in AD 531, the Sassanids foreshadowed the later development of European feudalism when they attempted to lighten the financial burden on the aristocracy by giving financial assistance and regular pay when they were called out to fight.

A late Sassanid horse-archer, of the seventh century AD. The Persians always relied mainly upon mounted bowmen to supply the bulk of their armies. They first began to use horses for war after their contact with the Medes. During the Parthian dynasty they also fielded large numbers of heavy lancers.

The first Roman contact with the Parthians was in 53 BC and was a typical fiasco. About 34,000 legionaries were wiped out at the battle of Carrhae and their general, Crassus, committed suicide to avoid capture. Plutarch has left an excellent account of the campaign. In it he describes the two types of mounted warrior known at first to the Romans only by rumour: archers who fired 'a new type of missile which travels faster than sight and pierces through whatever is in the way'; and 'armoured cavalry [which] has weapons of offence capable of cutting through everything and defensive equipment that will stand up to any blow'. Crassus chose to ignore these warnings and marched recklessly into Parthian territory, seeking to bring them to battle. This he succeeded in doing, but not on the terms he would have wished. The Parthians simply sur-

rounded the legionaries from a distance and rode back and forth pouring a never-ending hail of arrows into the packed ranks. If the Romans 'stayed in their ranks they were wounded one after the other; if they attempted to come to close quarters with the enemy, they were still unable to do the enemy any harm and suffered just as much themselves. For the Parthians shot as they fled, being, indeed, more adept at this than anyone except the Scythians'. The reason the Parthians were able to keep up this constant stream of missiles was that their general, a great landowner named Surenas, had taken the hitherto unknown precaution of bringing with him a train of camels, one for every ten horsemen, loaded with spare arrows.

So effective was the fire from the archers that Surenas never actually had to commit his heavy cavalry. Instead he merely stationed them in front of the Romans to hold them in place whilst 'the rest of their cavalry, in loose order, rode all round them, tearing up the plain with their horses' hooves, and raising great masses of sand which fell from the air in a continual shower'. In desperation Crassus threw his own Gallic cavalry forward but they were contemptuously pushed aside for 'the small light spears of his Gauls came up against tough breastplates of raw hide or steel, whereas they, with their unprotected and lightly armoured bodies, had to face the thrusts of long pikes.' After this there was nothing to be done except wait to die.

The paladins of the dying Republic were nothing if not ambitious. Less than twenty years later Mark Antony led another expedition against the Parthians, but he too suffered ignominious defeat. The disaster was not quite as all-embracing as that of Crassus, although one whole section of the army, under Statianus, was surrounded and wiped out in exactly the same way. The Parthians treated the main body of the army more cautiously, contenting themselves with harassment from a distance until the Romans were forced to turn back, having achieved precisely nothing. The retreat took exactly the same form as the confident advance, the Parthians never coming to close quarters but picking off men from a distance or falling on isolated stragglers and foragers. Antony did gain something from the experience, however, and Plutarch describes the tactical lessons learnt: 'He now covered not only his rear but his flanks with strong detachments of javelin-throwers and slingers, and arranged his order of march in the form of a hollow square. He also gave orders to the cavalry that they must drive off the enemy when they attacked, but that, after routing them, they must not pursue them far.' This passage is well worth citing if only because it describes tactics remarkably similar to those used by the Crusaders against the Saracens, the very people, in fact, who finally overthrew the Persians, in the seventh century, and whose methods of fighting were extremely similar. After the Sassinids had finally expelled the Parthians there was little change in the composition of the army. The split between light and heavy cavalry remained and still rested upon the same social divisions. If anything, however, the armoured cavalry became even heavier, fully meriting the Roman name *clibinarius*, derived from a word meaning iron box or oven. Horsemen equipped as Ammianus describes below must have indeed felt that they were locked inside an oven as they toiled through the hot sun. The historian is referring to the Persian cavalrymen encountered during Julian's wars against them in AD 358. They were drawn up in 'serried ranks of mail-clad horsemen . . . [their] bodies covered with closely fitting plates of iron . . . while the throng of horses was protected by coverings of leather . . . All parts of their bodies were covered with thick plates, so fitted that the stiff joints conformed with those of their limbs; and the forms of human faces were skilfully fitted to their heads . . . [with only] tiny openings fitted to the circle of the eye [and] the tips of their noses.' This description is largely corroborated by that of Heliodorus, who also mentions that greaves were attached to the mail coat to protect legs and feet. In the latter description the horse is even better protected: the head is covered by a metal plate, the legs have greaves, and back and flanks are protected by a blanket of thin iron plates. In fact, though both authors agree on the mask-like helmet, our only pictorial evidence for the Persian *clibinarius,* a third-century graffito, shows an almost conical headpiece with a chain-mail veil completely covering the face. Bearing in mind the climate, the latter would seem to be a much more practical idea.

The major points that emerge from this survey of the cavalry of Rome and her enemies concern the various styles of mounted warfare. One can, in fact, discern a triple tradition of horsemanship. On the one hand, there are the light horsemen of Africa, Europe and the East. These can be subdivided into the javelin throwers and skirmishers of Africa and Europe, to whom cavalry action was more a question of manoeuvring and harassment than of charging straight at the enemy, and the oriental horse-archers who strictly avoided any sort of physical contact, using their horses only to keep themselves within arrow range. But the eastern peoples also devised another form of mounted combat, based upon techniques and equipment that originated amongst certain nomadic peoples. Very heavily armoured horsemen appeared, who used their weight and their enormous lances, basically the phalanx on horseback, to smash through the enemy ranks.

In Persia this mode of fighting was easily wedded with the existing social structure, the mailed knights being supplied by the great landowners and provincial governors who could afford the necessary horses and armour. The Romans, too, began to maintain their own regiments of *clibinarii*, but this was only as a technical response to oriental warfare. Because the Roman Empire had a long-standing tradition of employing mercenaries, and a competent administration and centralized taxation system, they were able to keep a standing army, the cost of whose elaborate equipment was borne by the state. The Romans had their great landlords but they did not need to rely upon them as a military class. After the first two or three hundred years, cavalry service in Rome was never again a direct reflection of political and economic power.

Technical Note: Horseshoes

It remains only to touch upon the advances in the art of horsemanship made during this period. The key development, though far from fully realized even by the fall of the western empire, was the appearance of horseshoes. These became necessary as the practice of riding spread in north-western Europe. In the East and the Mediterranean area it was quite possible to ride horses unshod. The ground is very dry and hard, and while the dry atmosphere helps to preserve the wall of the hoof, the ground wears it down, keeping it to the correct length and shape. In damp countries, however, the wall of the hoof grows soft and too long, causing it to break away or split, which in turn places excessive pressure on the fetlock. The metalled Roman roads were no answer, for the northern ponies were born with soft hooves and these were soon worn to nothing. At first the Romans made what were known as hipposandals, a sort of iron-soled slipper which was strapped under the hoof. But they were difficult to adapt to the individual hoof and it was quite impossible to keep them firmly in place. The horseshoe proper, shaped while red hot and nailed to the hoof, was invented in northern Europe and the earliest examples yet found came from British burials of the first century AD. But it must be stressed that this was not a sudden technological revolution. The horseshoe did not immediately spread over the whole area, let alone the rest of the world. So little impact did these first horseshoes make that they had to be re-invented in the East about three hundred years later. From there they slowly spread west and have been found in the tomb of the Frankish king, Childeric I (458–81), though they are not mentioned in any extant documents until as late as the ninth century.

3 From the Ruins of Empire 476 to 1071

'. . . ut pagenses Franci qui caballos habent, aut habere possunt, cum suis comitibus in hostem pergant.'
Decree of Charles the Bold

'The commander who has six thousand of our heavy cavalry and God's help needs nothing more.'
Nicephorus II Phocas

Even before the end of the period just covered, the Roman emperors had realized the centre of gravity of their vast *imperium* had moved to the east. At the end of the third century, Diocletian introduced the Tetrarchy by which he and three other co-rulers divided the Empire between them. Diocletian himself took responsibility for the East. In 330, Constantine, though he made himself sole ruler, removed the capital to Byzantium, which he modestly renamed Constantinople. After the death of Theodosius in 395, the Empire was irrevocably divided into two, the capital of the western half being moved to Ravenna.

The history of the western empire as such need not long detain us. It finally fell in 476, after years of pressure from various German peoples, notably the Franks, Alamanni, Burgundians and Vandals. The Franks will appear again in this chapter as key innovators in western cavalry technique, and France and Italy will feature as important battlegrounds, but by that time the centre of attention was switched to the East, to what became known as the Byzantine Empire. Though many have followed Gibbon, and his contempt for Byzantine *mores*, in believing that the deposition of Romulus Augustus in 476 did constitute the fall of the real Roman Empire, it was in fact no such thing. The Empire lived on for hundreds of years as a politically and militarily dynamic force. Nor is the collapse in the West of any particular military significance, least of all in the terms of this book. The German people were singularly devoid of any tactical or strategical acumen, and moreover they fought on foot. It was their sheer numbers, and the impossibility for the Romans of manning the whole of the western frontier, that obviated the decisive advantages to be had from their cavalry and the superior discipline of their infantry. The Germans did not outmanoeuvre the Romans or decisively crush them on the battlefield; they simply kept on coming and wore them down.

The picture in the East is quite different. There too the Empire was subject to heavy pressure on its borders – from Goths, Arabs and Turks – but intelligent economic and military reforms enabled the Byzantines to withstand these onslaughts for hundreds of years. It is here that we find the focal point for discussion, here that we can discern advances in military technique and a real synthesis between war and socio-political considerations.

Huns, Goths and Lombards

One of the first threats to the eastern portion of the Empire came from the Huns, a nomadic people who had first appeared on the borders of China. There

they were defeated and at the very end of the pre-Christian era they began slowly moving westwards. In AD 375 they destroyed the Ostrogothic kingdom in southern Russia and under Attila, eighty years later, advanced into Thrace, forcing Valentinian III to recognize them as equal partners. From Constaninople's point of view it was perhaps fortunate that Attila had set his eyes to the West for he never attempted to advance into Greece or Asia Minor. The Huns were an awesome military force, the latest in the succession of fierce nomadic horsemen who seemed able to ride around more ponderous conventional formations with ease. Even before the advent of Attila they had struck terror into the hearts of more settled peoples. Of events in 375, Jerome wrote: 'Swarms of Huns . . . filled the whole earth with slaughter and panic alike as they flitted hither and thither on their swift horses . . . They were at hand everywhere before they were expected; by their speed they outstripped rumour.' One of their main weapons was the Hunnic bow. Though similar to the classic Scythian reflex bow, it was much more powerful, being made up of a complicated series of wooden and bone strips whose combined tension gave the arrow a much greater velocity. It was this weapon, it is thought, that finally marked the end of the dominance of heavy Sarmatian cavalry. Otherwise their tactics were exactly those of the orthodox horse-archer of the steppes. Ammianus Marcellinus has left a justly famous description:

They enter the battle drawn up in wedge-shaped masses, while their medley of voices makes a savage noise. And as they are lightly equipped for swift motion, and unexpected in action, they purposely divide suddenly into scattered bands and attack, rushing about in disorder here and there, dealing terrific slaughter; and because of their extraordinary rapidity of movement they are never seen to attack a rampart or an enemy camp . . . They fight from a distance with missiles having sharp bone . . . joined to the shafts with wonderful skill; then they gallop over the intervening spaces and fight hand to hand with swords . . . and while the enemy are guarding against wounds from the sword thrusts, they throw strips of cloth plaited into nooses over their opponents and so entangle them that they fetter their limbs . . .

It should be noted from this account that the Huns were always ready to come to close quarters after the first volley of arrows; to this end they carried special close-combat weapons such as heavy swords, lassoes and sometimes nets. In other words they were not content, like the Scythian or Parthian bowmen, to rely solely upon their archery, pinning the enemy down and slowly annihilating him. Nor were they familiar with the later Mongol combination of bowmen and heavy lancers (see below pp. 117–19). It is this perhaps that explains their eventual defeat at Châlons, in 451, when the Roman heavy cavalry, supplied by certain Gothic allies, was able to smash through Attila's horsemen. But little is known of the battle and it is still unclear why the Goths fighting for Rome were able to achieve what they had never been able to do during the initial Hunnic drive from the Russian steppes. Most probably the presence of experienced Romanized commanders, such as Aetius, meant that the timing of the decisive charge was well calculated, taking the Huns in flank or rear while they were disorganized and embroiled in hand-to-hand fighting. Whatever the reason, Attila's power was severely shaken and he retreated into the centre of his original empire, on the plains of Theiss, in Hungary. There his realm slowly fell apart, to be finally destroyed by Arderic and the Gepids in 454. The dissolution of the Hunnic state could well be attributable to a particularly anarchic social structure, reflected in the lack of any distinction between the various horse-soldiers. Without the rigid sense of hierarchy that underlies the Sarmatian and Saka division into light and heavy cavalry, the Hunnic peoples lacked the beginnings of an authentic state and never produced effective groups who could coordinate policy, either by virtue of their administrative competence or of a general deference to their authority.

The Goths, who were so instrumental in Attila's defeat, were one of the few German peoples to take to the horse in any numbers. They came originally from Scandinavia, but by AD 230 had moved to a region to the north west of the Black Sea where they came into contact with various Iranian tribes, from whom they learnt to ride. By the beginning of the fifth century a portion of them, the Visigoths, had moved to France and a hundred years later down into Spain. There they established a kingdom, centred upon Toledo, which survived until the Arab invasions of 711. It is assumed that the Goths came into contact with horses *via* one or other of the Sarmatian nations, because they never adopted the bow, except as infantrymen, and all their mounted warriors fought with sword and lance. At some stage these horsemen began to wear armour. During their rule in Spain the cavalry were equipped with a chain- or ring-mail shirt, a round shield and a crested helmet which was open above the forehead but tapered down at the back to protect the neck. It seems likely that these armoured riders were

provided by the Gothic noblemen and their retainers, although the military laws of King Erwig, of 681, stipulated that landowners must bring one-tenth of their slaves to war and there are indications that at least some of these slaves were provided with horse and armour.

Another Germanic people who took to horse at an early stage were the Lombards. They are first mentioned on the Elbe, around AD 200. In the sixth century they moved into the Danube plain where the Avars taught them to ride. In 568 these latter drove them out of Pannonia and a little over a hundred years later they arrived in Italy. There they finally obliterated the old Roman aristocracy and established their own noblemen on the estates. As elsewhere, these landowners provided the heavy horsemen. All freemen were obliged to answer the call to arms but these were subdivided into three separate classes. At the bottom were the ordinary freemen, who were to serve as infantry with shields and bows and arrows. The rest came mounted, armed with a lance and a shield, but a distinction was made between those who could provide themselves with a mail shirt and those who were unarmoured (many of the Lombard elite also wore greaves, and were the first of the German peoples known to have had this item of equipment). Whether this implied a distinction within the aristocracy, as in Persia, or whether the unarmoured cavalry were not nobles at all is unclear. What is certain is that possession of a horse was of considerable economic significance; one with full trappings cost upwards of 100 *solidi*, two-thirds of the value put upon the life of a low-born free Lombard. Perhaps the lighter horsemen were the noblemen's retainers, for by the end of the seventh century we hear of the *gasindii* – war bands sworn to protect their lords.

In the interim between western Roman collapse and the Lombard invasion, Italy had been ruled by the Ostrogoths and it is through them that the story returns to the Byzantine Empire and the unending struggle to protect its frontiers. In 535, Justinian sent his great general, Belisarius, to invade Italy and to try to regain the Roman homeland. By this time the Roman army had almost completely abandoned the old infantry legion. Ever since the brief reign of Theodosius, 394–5, mercenary cavalry regiments of Goths and Huns had formed the main striking force. But such troops were not just blindly thrown into the fray, trusting to their native abilities and techniques. The lessons of the Persian Wars had also been learnt, and the cavalry of Belisarius was a well thought-out amalgam of the best of non-Roman horsemanship. Most of our knowledge of this period comes from the

43

Histories of Procopius. In his first few pages he makes clear what type of soldier formed the backbone of the Byzantine armies. He attacks those who bemoan the passing of ancient days, when men were men and such modern fads as armour and regimental discipline were unknown. In fact, he suggests, the modern horseman is a far more efficient soldier than Homeric heroes could ever have been.

> The bowmen of the present time go into battle wearing corselets and fitted out with greaves which extend up to the knee. From the right side hang their arrows, from the other the sword. And there are some who have a spear also attached to them and, at the shoulders, a sort of small shield, without a grip, such as to cover the region of the face and the neck. They are expert horsemen and are able without difficulty to direct their bows to either side while riding at full speed, and to shoot an opponent whether in pursuit or in flight.

In the wars in Italy Belisarius relied almost completely on cavalrymen of this sort. Though he always had an infantry force with him it played almost no part at all in any of the important engagements. At one stage, in fact, they 'refused to remain in their usual condition' and used captured horses to try to turn themselves into cavalry. One doubts whether they were of much use on the battlefield but it must have been a considerable boon on the march to have almost the whole force on horseback. We are especially fortunate in having an account by Procopius of the exact way Belisarius used his cavalry and his awareness of their particular advantages when facing the traditional Gothic lancers. In an address to members of his staff, of whom Procopius was one, he pointed out:

> Practically all the Romans and their allies, the Huns, are good mounted bowmen, but not a man among the Goths has had practice in this branch, for their horsemen are accustomed to use only swords and spears, while their bowmen enter battle on foot . . . So [their] horsemen, unless the engagement is at close quarters, have no means of defending themselves against opponents who use the bow, and therefore can easily be reached by the arrow and destroyed; and as for the footsoldiers, they can never be strong enough to make sallies against men on horseback.

In other words, even though Belisarius' cavalry was just as heavily armoured as the earlier Roman *contarii*, for example, they adopted quite different tactics. Many of them eschewed the lance completely and all relied on the famous Parthian tactic of loosing off hails of arrows from a distance, rather than trying to charge their enemy head-on.

The Byzantine Empire and the Wars on the Frontiers

Though some Byzantine military manuals have survived, it is difficult to extract much precise information about the changes in Byzantine military equipment. It does seem, however, that the cavalry after Belisarius did not put much emphasis upon the bow alone. The lance became standard issue and the horsemen's armour was increased, as well as that of some of the horses, all of which helped lead to a revival of the charge. For 400 years and more, until the eleventh century, the heavy cavalry were the only important unit in the army. They wore a steel skull-cap with a small tuft on the top and a mail shirt reaching down to the thighs. Their legs and feet were protected with greaves and steel shoes, their hands with metal gauntlets. Officers' horses and those of the men in the front ranks were equipped with steel frontlets and poitrails, and all mounted men used stirrups. They had a linen surcoat to be worn over the armour in summer and a large woollen cloak for winter and the cold nights. Their arms were a heavy sword, a bow, and a lance with a small pennant attached. The surcoat, helmet tuft and pennant were all of the same colour, depending on the squadron to which the rider was attached. The Emperor Leo (886–912) pointed out in his tactical manual that if mail shirts were not available in sufficient quantity, resort had to be made to horn-scale armour or thin steel plates sewn on to buff-leather coats. On this basis it seems reasonable to assume some kind of distinction between front-rank shock troops, the cataphracts proper, and the rather more orthodox armoured horse-archer as described to us by Procopius.

But one feature of this Byzantine cavalry that has no equivalent in the earlier period was the method of recruitment. From the reign of Maurice (582–602) onwards a determined effort was made to escape the old reliance upon foreign mercenaries and to recruit an army of native troopers. On the one hand this would make the emperor less at the mercy of individual war lords, responsible for recruiting their own contingents, and on the other it would give both army and state more resilience if citizens were made responsible for the defence of their own country. To this end there evolved, through the seventh and eight centuries, yet another example of the ownership of land being predicated upon the provision of cavalry service. But the Byzantine emperors did not rely upon an already existing aristocracy, most of whom lived at court, or upon creating new large-scale landowners. They tried rather to form a broad-based group of small soldier-farmers whose property should only be sufficient to equip themselves for war. Certain historians, indeed, refer to these men as free peasants, but the following remarks of Leo make it clear that they were persons of some standing within the community: '[These farmers must be] provided with means, so that, whether they are in garrison or on an expedition, they may be free from care as to their homes, having those left behind who may till their fields for them. And in order that the household may not suffer from the master being on service, we decree that the farms of all soldiers shall be free from all exactions except the land tax.' These troopers were organized into regiments and brigades, to which they were to report as soon as the alarm was given about an enemy raid. A number of brigades were under the command of a *strategos*, who was the military and civilian governor of a province, or theme. An individual theme could put approximately 4000 cavalry into the field

But even as Leo was writing those words the system was beginning to break down and more traditional patterns of military landholding were emerging. Some farmers began buying up the land of less fortunate neighbours and came to form a small group of powerful frontier magnates who insisted on prestigious military commissions. As they became more powerful the small farmers entered into agreements by which they were guaranteed the great lord's protection in return for abdicating the freehold of their land. Nicephoras Phocas[1] (963–9) trebled the value of the soldiers' allotments in order to make them more economically independent, but this only served to reduce their numbers and transform such as did remain into minor nobility. In the eleventh century the theme system was swept away entirely and the new nobility were offered huge landholdings, known as *pronoia*, with full right to all taxes and dues that had previously been paid to the state. In return the estate owner had to provide his own force of cavalry. At first such estates were not hereditary but this was changed by Michael VIII (1259–82). Then the nobles began to pay money to the crown in return for exemption from their military obligations. There are many parallels here with medieval Europe, as will be seen below, but the Byzantine emperors were not able to use the monies thus received as effectively as in England and France, for example. The feudal array which had replaced the thematic levies was not in turn superseded by a strong force of mercenaries, paid

for by the crown, and the army as a whole simply withered away. By the reign of Andronicus II (1282–1328) the whole Empire was only able to field a meagre 3000 horsemen.

But this whole process took hundreds of years. Between the accession of Maurice and the death of the last great Macedonian emperor, Basil II, in 1025 the Byzantines showed themselves able to deploy their army of soldier-farmers to great effect. Their campaigns and theoretical writings show a flexibility of mind, a willingness to experiment and adapt their methods to a particular enemy, that was far superior to western methods until well into the sixteenth century. Just as Belisarius had worked out the best way of dealing with the Gothic onslaught, so did later generals take the trouble to study their enemy before risking everything in battle.

So it was against the Arabs. The latter's greatest asset was the speed with which they moved. The Byzantines soon recognized that it was impossible actually to prevent an Arab raiding force from crossing the Taurus Mountains and penetrating into the frontier themes. What they could do, however, was to ensure that few of these raiders ever got back. Watch-towers were set up all along the frontiers, garrisoned by the thematic cavalry or by light Turkish auxiliaries from Trebizond. As soon as an Arab incursion was spotted, messages were flashed from tower to tower and the whole area was alerted. The heavy cavalry rode off to their assembly points, the civilians fled into the walled towns, and some of the light horse were assigned to hang on to the tail of the enemy. These were instructed to travel with their weapons covered so that the glinting of metal might not betray their presence. The main force should do as much as possible to minimize the invaders' depredations. If they were in small numbers the commander might well fall upon them at once. Otherwise he had to be sure to keep his main force intact, awaiting reinforcements from other themes, and to block all roads, fords and passes that were easily defensible. If he could locate the main enemy camp, he was to attack any lesser raiding parties that set out, and if the whole force issued forth he was to avoid it and fall on the camp. Only when a commander was sure that his forces were strong enough, and particularly when the enemy were slowly making their way back, laden with plunder, to one of the mountain passes through which they had originally come, should he think of attacking. By this time an infantry force should have assembled to block the most likely exits, to hold the pass and force the Arabs to turn to meet the main body of cavalry.

By this time the Byzantine forces should be strong

Seljuk Turks, depicted by a Byzantine artist, in 1048. The Turks were yet another fierce nomadic people. They were the most dangerous enemy of the Byzantine Empire and inflicted a crushing defeat upon its forces in 1071, at the Battle of Manzikert.

enough to risk an open battle. The Arabs were excellent fighters on horseback but were no match for the heavier cataphracts. Again the Imperial tacticians had taken note of the enemies' weaknesses. As one officer wrote: 'They are very bold when they expect to win: they keep firm in their ranks and stand up gallantly against the most impetuous attacks.' But if their original charge failed or if their own line was once broken, they swiftly dispersed, every man looking to his own safety. Byzantine tactics were designed to ensure that their line did break, for they made provision for a whole series of assaults rather than just one all-out rush. The horsemen were drawn up in three lines, each eight to ten men deep, and each line charged in turn until their opponents finally broke. In addition, there were squadrons posted away from the main group, to either turn the enemy flank during the main assault or to fall upon his retreating troops. Here is a concept of cavalry action that was far in advance of even that of Hannibal or Alexander the Great. For them the great potential of horsemen was the furious mass onslaught when the enemy line was beginning to waver and lose formation. For Maurice and Leo it was constant pressure and, above all, the use of reserves that was decisive. There is not much, indeed, that Gustavus Adolphus or Cromwell could have taught the Byzantines about the use of cavalry.

The other great enemies of Byzantium were the Turks, the various nomadic tribes who had moved westwards from central Asia and were eventually to overthrow the Arab Empire in Persia. They were mounted bowmen 'given to ambushes and stratagems of every sort'. Their tactics are already familiar to us. They did not advance into battle in a solid line, but in small well-spaced groups that galloped along the enemy's front, loosing off streams of arrows, and only charging home if they detected a gap in the line or a small party cut off from the main army. The Arab historian, Masudi, has described the campaign of 934:

> The engagement began with the horsemen of the right wing attacking the main battle of the Byzantines, showering it with arrows and taking up a new position on the left. Then they of the left wing likewise advanced and shot against the Byzantine main battle, changing over to the right of the line. So the mounted bands kept wheeling across the Byzantine front, grinding away at it like millstones, while the Turkish main body was still not engaged. As the hail of arrows came shower after shower, the Byzantines in open order charged the Turkish main body, which till then had made no move. The horsemen did not impede them, but the Turks received them with such a shower of arrows that they recoiled.

According to Leo, a general should not hesitate to give battle at the first opportunity, for the Turks, even more than the Arabs, were helpless in the face of the consecutive disciplined cavalry charges already described. Nevertheless, great care was necessary in choosing the field of battle and in the disposition of one's forces. It was above all necessary to protect the flanks so that the more mobile Turks could not sweep round and fall upon the rear. Physical obstacles such as a river or marsh made ideal anchors for one's line, and it was sometimes advisable to split the cavalry into two and place them on either flank. For, against the Turks, the Byzantines usually placed a contingent of foot-archers in the centre because their longer bows could outdistance those of the nomads. But even when the Byzantine cavalry had ridden over the Turks it was not deemed advisable to carry the pursuit too far as their retreat was often merely a ruse to draw the enemy into an ambush of fresh groups of horsemen, or to lay bare the flanks of the infantry. The validity of such counsels was tragically underlined at the battle of Manzikert, in 1071, when the Emperor Romanus' army was annihilated by the Seljuk Turks of Alp Arslan. The whole campaign got off to a bad start when one Imperial division was lured into an ambush by a Turkish reconnaissance party. Later, Romanus did succeed in driving the Turks before him and capturing their camp. But the battle had been fought in open, rolling country and when the Byzantines turned for home after this seeming victory, and their line became fragmented, the Turks closed in again, creeping through the gaps and round the flanks. Soon the individual groups were all completely encircled and the Turks were able to pick them off at their leisure, even managing to capture the emperor himself. (In this chapter I have limited myself to discussing only those aspects of Arab and Turkish warfare that help to illuminate Byzantine practice. For a more detailed summary of the role of cavalry amongst these peoples see below pp. 111–17.)

Frankish warrior. Note the distinctive crested helmet, with the open front and long neckpiece. This type of headgear was also found among the Lombards, the barbarian conquerors of Italy.

The Franks

Belisarius was not the last Roman warrior to fight in Italy. The Byzantines long maintained a presence there in the Cabrian and Langobardic themes and sent many expeditions across to repel the attacks of the Franks and Lombards. The Franks were another Germanic tribe and they had entered Gaul in the fourth century AD. There they were employed by the Romans as *feoderati*, military allies who were allotted territories of their own in exchange for military aid against other barbarian invaders. Originally, their native loyalties were to their own various tribal chiefs, but one of these, Clovis (481–511), succeeded in gaining total dominion over the whole Frankish people.

At this time they were predominantly infantry warriors. Procopius wrote of them, referring to a force in Italy in 539: 'There were but few horsemen and these the king kept about him.' Horsemen were present at the battle of Tolbiac, in 496, against the Alamanni, and a royal edict of 507 made the explicit point that the army's provisions must include some food and water for the horses. Nevertheless, it would be wrong to think of the Franks at this stage as being a cavalry people. Their traditions were those of other Germanic nations, to whom horses were a rarity and the idea of actually fighting on horseback was an absurdity. It is most unlikely that the king's retainers mentioned above regarded their mounts as anything

A Gallo-Roman or early Frankish cavalryman. He is not using stirrups, though the Franks are generally regarded as being the first European people to adopt this aid. The extra stability they afforded enabled the Franks to charge at their enemy with their lances couched under one arm.

more than a means of transport and a way of emphasizing their superior social status.

How then did they transform themselves into highly respected cavalry? It is first of all important to realize that the Franks were not 'Frenchmen', and when they arrived in Gaul the native population did not simply disappear. Even as their power grew under the Merovingian kings and their frontiers spread wider and wider, they were nothing more than foreign overlords extracting whatever surplus they could from the Gallo-Roman population. In many respects the indigenous civilization was far in advance of that of the Franks, not least because of the Gallo-Roman familiarity with riding. It has already been shown how important were the Gallic cavalry in Roman armies and this was still true in the West, even during the campaign against Attila. The more the Franks merged with the native population, particularly the aristocracy, the more likely it is that they began to recognize the advantages of fighting on horseback and the role of the horse as a mark of prestige.

The other impetus to the Frankish adoption of cavalry was the simple fact that almost all the other peoples against whom they fought, especially the Lombards and the Frisians, were expert horsemen. The Saracens in Spain are often cited in this context but it is worth noting that the first regular Arab cavalry units did not arrive in Spain until 740. This was eight years after the famous battle of Poitiers, and here the Franks fought on foot even though they had ridden to the field itself. It would seem that the campaigns to the east gave the Franks the first indication that they must take to horse, rather than those against the infidel in the south. Indeed, the first mention of an actual cavalry charge comes in the reign of Clothar II, in 626, whilst he was fighting against the Saxons. Their tactics at this time left much to be desired and the Byzantines clearly looked upon these barbarian horsemen with much contempt. Leo wrote of them, presumably referring to earlier historical experience:

> The Frank believes that a retreat under any circumstances must be dishonourable; hence he will fight whenever you choose to offer him battle. This you must not do until you have secured all possible advantages for yourself, as his cavalry, with their long lances and large shields, charge with a tremendous impetus . . . You will find him utterly careless as to outposts and reconnaissances, so that you can easily cut off outlying parties of his men, and attack his camp at advantage. As his forces have no bonds of discipline, but only those of kindred or oath, they fall into confusion after delivering their charge; you can therefore simulate flight, and then turn on them, when you will find them in utter disarray.

But it was the Arabs who dictated what *kind* of cavalry the Franks would become. The former were fairly light horsemen, relying on speed rather than weight, and this obliged their adversaries to adopt much heavier equipment and horses to enable them to ride the Arabs down in the first onslaught or at least give them some protection against the more nimble foe. From a fairly early date they wore steel helmets, very like those of the Lombards, and a mail shirt of metal rings or plates. They were armed with a long lance with a narrow, leaf-shaped head and a cross-piece beneath the point to prevent its becoming too deeply embedded in the victim's body. They also carried a heavy, two-edged sword, a shorter one with only one edge, and a round shield, painted red or blue, with a heavy central boss. Under Charlemagne (771–814) two additions were made. The Merovingians had not worn any kind of protection for their legs, having only embroidered linen trousers over which 'long leather thongs were cross-gartered . . . in and out, in front and behind'. From Carolingian times, however, leg armour was introduced, some men wearing just greaves, others having the entire limbs covered. The variation here stemmed from the problem of riding without stirrups, so that 'for greater ease of riding, other men

kept their thighs bare of armour'. Yet, whatever the exact details of their armament, the Carolingian array presented a formidable sight. When it marched against the Langobards, in Italy, a turncoat Frankish nobleman who had sought refuge there 'was terrified for in happier days he had been in close contact with the strategy and the military equipment of the peerless Charlemagne . . . [He warned] "When you see the fields bristle as with ears of iron corn, when you see the Po and the Ticino break over the walls of your city in great waves which gleam back with the glint of iron, then indeed you can be sure that Charlemagne is at hand." '

Charlemagne's other major innovation was to insist that his armoured cavalry also carried with them 'a bow, two bowstrings and twelve arrows'. No doubt his model was the Byzantine horsemen, but unfortunately we have no details about what place archery had in Frankish tactics. Perhaps the bow was just a homage to 'civilized' traditions, for Charlemagne was certainly very conscious of his people's murky past. If it did have a real military significance, was the bow used as a prelude to the charge or as a last-ditch defensive weapon if the terrain was unsuitable for mounted action? The very paucity of references to this weapon leads one to assume that it was not much used. Contemporary chronicles tend to base their imagery and metaphors around the weight and extent of the armour and the mighty hewing of the swordsman. For the Franks cavalry was above all a shock weapon.

By the end of the ninth century the horsemen were the basis of the Frankish forces. At the battle of the Dyle, in 891, the Norsemen had taken cover behind entrenched field works. The Franks would have to attack on foot, but before King Arnulf could persuade his men to dismount he had to overcome their grave misgivings that 'the Franks were not used to fighting on foot'. Even so one can often detect a certain diffidence about fighting on horseback. Riding for them was still not the automatic reflex that it had been in the East, in Macedonia or Persia for example. This in 864, Charles the Bold had to reiterate in writing that when his vassals were called to war they must appear on horseback. The explanation lies partly in the different cultural background, but there are also more prosaic reasons. Chief among these was the sheer expense of the thing. By Charlemagne's time the mount and complete equipment of an armoured knight cost between 36 and 40 shillings. This was equal to the value of 18 or 20 cows, a very considerable sum when one bears in mind that even the royal domain of Annappes could only boast a herd of 45 cows.

This exorbitant cost had profound social repercussions. It has already been noted more than once how the pattern of land ownership, and consequently of political power, was dictated by the king's need to raise charioteers or mounted soldiery, always expensive commodities. So it was amongst the Franks. It had long been their tradition that the chiefs and nobles each assembled around them a war band of retainers, sworn to defend their person and to die with them if necessary. As long as these men fought on foot it was feasible for their lord to feed and shelter them under his own roof. But as the Franks were obliged to take to horse and their equipment became increasingly elaborate, it became impossible for these lords – or the king, the greatest chief of all – to provide his men with the necessary battle gear. The only way was to have them provide it for themselves, and they could do this only if they had their own piece of land from which to exact the wherewithal to purchase horse and armour. The income from such an estate also brought them the leisure in which to practise the arts of the mounted knight. They started very young. An old Carolingian proverb maintained: 'You can make a horseman of a lad at puberty; later than that never.' From that time forth the rider was constantly engaged in looking after his arms and armour, training his war horses, and perfecting his skill with lance and sword.

Of course there are many features of Frankish feudalism that pre-date the coming of cavalry, such as the reciprocal oath between lord and retainer to protect and to serve (Germanic traditions – the *comitatus*, the *gasindii* – are in evidence here as well as Gallo-Roman – the *buccellarii*), but the move to purchase a man's service with a grant of land seems to be inextricably linked with the provision of cavalry service. To this extent Western European feudalism reveals exactly those connections between military requirements and the allocation of land that have been noted in previous chapters and that will constantly reoccur in other parts of the world. The warrior on horseback becomes the landowner and eventually the lord and master of all on his estate. The ability to ride and the possession of a great warhorse and full suit of armour become inseparable from social privilege and economic and political power. An Arab emir in Spain, Ousama, put the whole thing in a nutshell when he observed of his Frankish opponents: 'All pre-eminence belongs to the horsemen. They are in truth the only men who count. Theirs is to give counsel, theirs to render justice.'

Technical Note: The Stirrup

The problem of the stirrup is far from being resolved. It recently came into prominence in a book about the wider implications of medieval technological develment (see Lynn White Jr in the Bibliography).

An early example of stirrups being clearly depicted. This is on a Korean statuette of the fourth century AD. It is generally conceded that stirrups first appeared in the east, probably among nomadic peoples. The earliest wooden or leather examples have almost certainly perished.

(*opposite*) Eleventh-century French knights from a fourteenth-century manuscript.

ensoin acomer tt
oc sa copaignie. 7 reto
al roi ban oc benoye.
le roi booit oc gauncl

a benoye engrant io
leefoe. 7 furent auec
eft qui milt estovent

There it was argued that the introduction of the stirrup into the West allowed the full development of the armoured horseman. The extra support they offered, the argument runs, allowed the cavalry to charge with their lances couched between elbow and side, held in one hand, and to absorb the shock of impact through their legs. There is obviously some validity in this assertion. Common sense, even Hollywood costume 'epics', shows that the stirrup simplifies the lancer's task. But the point should not be overemphasized. As has been seen, extremely effective heavy cavalry appeared which managed perfectly well without the benefit of stirrups. Assyrians, Sarmatians, Parthians, Sassanid, Persians and Roman cataphracts all managed to stay on their horses in heavy armour, wield their huge lances, and even, so it would seem, charge straight at the enemy's line without any support for their legs. So, though the stirrup might have speeded up the development of Frankish tactics, particularly in view of their original unfamiliarity with riding, it would be unreasonable to suppose that they could never have succeeded without them. As has been seen, even when heavily armoured, many of them rode without stirrups. It is certainly the case that their introduction brought no overnight revolution in cavalry technique and we know of no sudden transition amongst the Franks from techniques and equipment without stirrups to new, suddenly viable, shock tactics. Whereas we do know that those Franks who did adopt the stirrup at an early date long carried on using their lances in the old two-handed grip, though at no great cost to their effectiveness. On the whole, given the length of time it took for the stirrup to percolate through their society, it would seem that it was regarded as being a useful aid rather than a decisive breakthrough.

No one is certain who first invented the stirrup. The usual story is that they came to Europe *via* the Avars who were certainly using them in the sixth century AD. They were copied by the Persians – we know of their presence in Iran by 694 – and Viking traders brought them from there to western Europe and Byzantium, where they were fairly common by the ninth century. Another theory is that the Byzantines copied the stirrup from the Franks, but it seems scarcely credible that they would not have been aware of this development when it first appeared on their own doorstep. But none of this explains who first invented the stirrup. Our first written reference is in the memoirs of a Chinese general, in AD 477 and he claims that they were invented by the Huns. Archaeological evidence seems to point to even earlier origins. Chinese statuettes seem to depict stirrups around AD 300, whilst miniature stirrups – that at least is the most common interpretation – have been found in Minusinsk that date from the first two centuries after Christ. Professor Rostovtzeff claims that those found in Sarmatian graves in the Kuban date from the first century AD, whilst S. W. Bushell is of the opinion that certain bas-reliefs in Shantung, from a century earlier, show riders using stirrups. India too has its supporters. In his *Guide to Sanchi*, Sir John Marshall says that Mauryan bas-reliefs clearly depict the use of stirrups by these people in the last century BC.

It is most unlikely that the question will ever be satisfactorily resolved. We shall probably never find the first examples for it seems reasonable to suppose that they were made by one of the nomadic steppe peoples and were probably made of wood or simple leather loops that have long since perished. What is clear is that they did not make any dramatic impact on horsemanship or cavalry technique. Ancient peoples first learned to ride without stirrups or saddles and centuries of experience, and individual lifetimes of practice, bred a competence that did not have to depend on artificial aids. In fact, the rather haphazard history of the stirrup leads one to believe that they were adopted wholesale only when they were taken up by Germanic 'foot-sloggers', for whom riding was rather a precarious experiment.

(*above*) Norman knights depicted on the Bayeux Tapestry.

(*centre*) Italian men-at-arms of the thirteenth century, from Uccello's 'Rout at St Romano'.

(*below*) Thirteenth-century knights giving battle.

4 The Medieval Knight 950 to 1494

'For above the people must sit the knight. And just as
one controls a horse and he who sits above it leads it
where he will, so the knight must lead the people at
his will.'
The Romance of Lancelot

'Armour protects the wearer, and prevents him from
injuring others.'
Twelfth-century German emperor

The Knight in Society

In many ancient societies, usually those without a strong centralized government and bureaucracy, the cavalry component of the armed forces was invariably the ruling elite on horseback. The horsemen, omnipotent on the battlefield, were the very men who held the reins of power in society as a whole. The beginnings of the Carolingian era offers yet another example of this correlation. Land, almost the sole determinant of wealth and prestige at this time, was apportioned to certain members of the warrior group so that they would be able to serve their king as armoured riders. The surplus that they could extract from the labours of their peasants enabled them to obtain horses, equipment and the free time in which to practise their skills. To this extent, cavalry service was at the very root of the feudal system. The point is underlined by the fact that continued possession of the land was explicitly contingent upon the satisfactory performance of the military obligations. If the holder of the benefice, the grant of land, refused to come to war when summoned, then that land was to be handed to his lord until a more amenable vassal could be found.

Feudal relationships are obviously basic to the history of Europe in the medieval period. It might be thought that these centuries will also offer another close parallel between cavalry service and political dominance whereby the mounted masters of the battlefield are also the arbiters of society. In fact this soon ceased to be the case, and all kinds of factors combined to qualify the strictly military features of the feudal relationship.

Even in France the basic Carolingian obligation to provide armed service was soon ignored except at the lowest levels of the hierarchy. Though the theory was that the failure to give military aid in person should result in the loss of one's land, in practice this was very difficult to enforce. After the death of Charlemagne and the division of his kingdom, central power virtually collapsed, and the individual lords held on to their estates by dint of their personal efforts rather than by virtue of the performance of certain duties. Even after the accession of the first Capetian king, in 987, it was many years before the French monarchy could begin to assert their authority over those who were supposedly their vassals. And even when that task was accomplished the interpretation of what did constitute feudal responsibilities, as we shall see, was very different from the absolute commitment to personal military service that had once prevailed.

In other parts of Europe, notably England, the feudal system was more of an artificial creation. The necessity of obtaining mounted troops was still basic but the element of personal service, the notion that the great enfeoffed lords themselves should fight was greatly diminished. The king granted the land because he wanted heavy cavalry but he was not particularly concerned how the knights themselves were obtained. Under William of Normandy's settlement after the Conquest, the country was divided among 200 barons who between them were to provide the services of 4000 knights (the Church was to provide 780 knights). Each baron's multiple quota was to be supplied by their own vassals and the latters' sub-vassals. Recent research has shown that in fact the tenants-in-chief and many of the intermediate fief-holders used this system as a means of escaping their personal military obligations and leaving those at the lowest end of the scale to do the actual fighting. The fiefs of these authentic knights were rarely more than one to one and a half hides (a hide was 120 acres), not much more than the holding of a middling peasant. Their lowly status is amply demonstrated by the derivation of the actual word 'knight' which comes from the Anglo-Saxon word *cnihtas*, 'serving youth'. For their superiors land-holding was already regarded as having little to do with mere military service. The provision of the fighting men was used as a convenient means of maximizing income for purely personal use. Thus a middleman might receive 18 hides from his lord and the attendant duty to provide three knights, whereas the knights he enfeoffed would receive fewer than two hides each. The middlemen were quite happy to accept the services of men of very lowly or even unfree origins as long as they in turn would be satisfied with the absolute minimum of land.

In the following centuries it is possible to discern all kinds of ways in which the large English land-owners sought to divorce their rights of tenancy from their military obligations. There was, for example, a continuous struggle to make their estates hereditary. They sought to make the very fact of possession the basis of their legitimacy and quietly gloss over the original notion that a fief was held on condition of the performance of certain duties. In the twelfth century there was a tendency at all levels for landholders to eschew their military responsibilities. Henry II's Assize of Arms of 1181 shows how far this had gone. It was found necessary to insist that, on the one hand, every tenant-in-chief who had not enfeoffed his necessary quota of knights must at least make sure that he had the horses and equipment to arm all the knights he owed, and on the other, that all those holding knights' fees must ensure that they possessed the requisite arms and armour. All these

Early examples of the elaborate and ponderous protection developed for the medieval knight: (*above*) twelfth-century mail armour; (*below*) twelfth-century helmets; (*right*) a Crusader of the twelfth century.

latter were also to ensure that they had been duly sworn as knights, showing how even at the lowest end of the hierarchy the possession of a fief was losing its original *raison d'être*. Yet another development was the increasing commutation of military obligations with a simple cash payment. This was known as scutage. At first it was a device by which fractional grants of land could be made though these could not truly be deemed enough to support a knight. The land was assessed financially in terms of that proportion of a knight that it would support and the money paid to the crown. Later, however, the practice of replacing military service with a cash sum became much more common and was applied to much bigger fiefs whose tenant had lost interest in military service.

This reduction of traditional feudal commitments to simple cash transactions is also evident in the way the English crown began to recruit its armies. Even when the feudal summons still had sufficient force to bring the vassals to war it was soon established that

they should be paid, not least for the 40 days free service they supposedly owed. Later the traditional summons was given up completely. In 1277, only 6 per cent of those who should have attended did so. In 1327 the turn-out was equally disastrous and after 1385 it was never invoked again. But these fourteenth-century summons were mere lip-service to ancient traditions and no one expected that they would produce sufficient mounted men. Long before this it had been realized that the only way to produce an adequate cavalry force was to pay the horsemen. Financial incentives must replace what was no more than a memory of the original obligations. The first record we have of a contract for knight service, for a particular campaign, was drawn up in 1213, but developments in the previous century had already shown the way things were going. In England, and elsewhere, there emerged what was known as the *fiefrente*. The composite word tells its own story. 'Fief' acknowledges the old feudal forms in that the holder of such a grant was regarded as being a vassal of the

57

The humble and pious knight. Although such was the chivalric ideal, knightly practice usually fell far short. Except for the great lords, many of whom refused to honour their feudal obligations, most knights were preoccupied with questions of money – through pay, booty and ransom.

crown. But his duties were of a very practical nature. He was granted an annuity in cash in exchange for equipping a certain number of troops, cavalry and infantry, when required. These soldiers were also to be paid by the grantee whilst on service. This was only a transitional device and by the following century troops were raised by means of indentures. These contracts with the crown had no feudal overtones at all. The contractor simply undertook to provide the king with a mixed force of horsemen, archers and others for one specific campaign and to pay them during that time. An agreement of 1360 between the king and the Earl of Kent is typical. He agrees to serve himself 'at the usual wages of war' and to provide 60 men-at-arms and 100 mounted bowmen.

This contract is significant on two counts. Not only were the vassal's feudal obligations reduced to the 'usual wages' but the majority of the men he was to supply were to be recruited outside the feudal framework. Only ten of the mounted men-at-arms were to be knights. Just as the more powerful fief-holders were shrugging off their military duties so was there growing up a whole group of lowlier men – landless sons of knights, dissatisfied members of the middle class, even peasants and criminals – who would fight for anyone prepared to pay and equip them. Such soldiers tended to be less lavishly equipped than the nobles still prepared to go to war but they formed an increasingly important part of the army as a whole. They were often referred to as sergeants to distinguish them from the authentic feudal retinue. But by the fifteenth century such distinctions had disappeared from the vocabulary. All horsemen were referred to alike as 'helms', a further indication of the way in which questions of wealth and status by birth have given way to a shared sense of military professionalism, in which being a paid soldier was the crucial common denominator.

Social and military developments in France were very similar. In some ways the French crown did succeed in asserting the feudal authority that seemed to have passed away with the death of Charlemagne. Because of successive foreign invasions, notably by the Emperor Otto IV, defeated at Bouvines in 1214, and the English during the reign of King John and the Hundred Years War (1337–1453), French lords were in constant fear of outright disappropriation or of rebellion by their minor vassals and peasantry. This forced them to rally behind the throne in a relatively united body. Nevertheless, they were rarely willing to concede that their military obligations were as absolute as feudal theory attested. The Capetians were forced to pay those who turned out and many exacted the right to commute their military service with cash payments. Under Philip Augustus (1180–1223) an elite force of 800 cavalry and 2000 infantry was established which was completely independent of all feudal ties and was paid by the crown. Charles V (1364–80) expanded this royal force and the Great Ordinance of 1374 established mounted companies of men-at-arms and mounted crossbowmen, all of whom were in the king's pay and were commanded by lieutenants appointed by the crown. This force began to disintegrate in the following years but was reconstituted and revivified by Charles VII (1422–61). His Ordinance of 1445 set up a standing cavalry force divided into *compagnies d'ordonnance*. Each horseman was armoured, leading two spare horses with him and two mounted crossbowmen. Each of these three-men groups was known as a 'lance', there being 100 lances in each company. These men were the backbone of the great French army that invaded Italy in 1494, and their successes there will be examined in the next chapter. What is important to note at this stage is that by the end of the fifteenth century the French military forces, like the English, had lost their genuinely feudal characteristics. The cavalry in both countries still maintained close links with the aristocracy. The subsequent history of Europe, right up to World War I, reveals the stranglehold kept by the dead hand of aristocratic romanticism upon military institutions, in particular the cavalry. But the relationship was only 'feudal' in a popular pejorative sense. The actual mechanics of military service revolved around money, either state salaries or, curiously enough, aristocratic payments *to* the crown to give younger sons a hobby. The links were traditional rather than functional. Cavalry service was a nobleman's right rather than being a basic reason for his tenure of extensive feudal privileges.

Elsewhere in Europe feudal forms developed in different ways and at a quite different pace. In Spain and Germany, for example, though the land was eventually divided up into typically feudal estates, these came too late to involve the military obligations that had originally been so important in France and England. Other military institutions had evolved in the meantime. In both countries the fighting knights came from a relatively humble social milieu. In Germany they were not even free men. After the collapse of the Carolingian Empire the German provinces were characterized by a mixture of great dukes, an ancient tribal aristocracy and a mass of free peasants. Successive emperors found it impossible to form reliable armed forces from such elements and they turned instead to servile groups from which they recruited the *ministeriales*. Though they fought as armoured cavalry and were paid by being granted a fief, they remained unfree and their relationship was not based upon that voluntary reciprocity of obligation that characterized the normal feudal relationship between king and vassal.

The greater part of Spain was occupied by the Moors, and in the few independent areas in the north feudal landholding had not yet emerged. Most estates were allodial, held independently of any landlord. Nor did the constant warfare against the Arabs involve the same sort of military demands that had faced the Franks. The *Reconquista* was not a war along far-flung frontiers, involving the creation of a mobile and independent armoured elite, but a

A fifteenth-century knight, when chain mail had been generally superseded by plate armour.

localized border war based upon continual petty raids and skirmishes. The bases for such raids were small walled towns, with surrounding pastures, on the frontiers themselves. Obviously mounted men were essential for such hit-and-run tactics, but not anything comparable to the Carolingian *panzers*. Because the object was only to intercept a raiding party, recapture stolen horses, sheep or booty, or make incursions of their own, rather than smash the enemy in pitched battle, the horsemen were lightly equipped, mounted on sturdy but nimble steeds. Such men did not need extravagant resources to maintain themselves in readiness for war, though they did require the freedom to practise their skills and to be available to ride out at a moment's notice. Thus again we see the emergence of a group of low-born professionals on whose shoulders fell the real burden of fighting. They were known as *caballeros villanos*, or non-noble knights, and often lived in the towns, owning no land of their own. Whatever prestige they had was only that accorded to the military expert and they were granted no economic base from which to extend their power. For most of them the mere loss of a horse or the need to sell it could instantly reduce them to the ranks of the ordinary tax-paying townspeople.

As the *Reconquista* gathered momentum, and large tracts of land became vacant, a powerful aristocratic elite did emerge, the land being divided among them in return for cavalry service, in the traditional manner. For by now the aim was to engage the

A German *Ministerialis*. Unlike the knights of France and England, most of those in Germany were recruited from among servile groups, though many of them later acquired great estates and influence.

Saracens closing in for the kill during the chronic wars against the Christians in Spain. Until the advancing Spaniards had reached the great plains of the Douro and the Ebro they relied largely upon light cavalrymen fighting in the Muslim manner.

Moors in large-scale pitched battles and to drive them out of Spain, rather than simply to contain them through guerrilla warfare on the frontiers. But this nobility was just as averse as its counterparts elsewhere to fulfilling its military obligations. In Castile, Sancho IV (1289–95) had to spend a whole peripatetic winter riding from lord to lord to try to persuade them to appear when summoned. After him, Fernando IV (1295–1312) gave up the unequal struggle. He simply handed over most of the revenues of Andalucia to two of his nobles on condition that each of them would supply him with one thousand heavy cavalry. In Aragon, in the late fourteenth and fifteenth centuries, the crown found it equally difficult to muster men. Little more than a thousand knights ever answered the royal summons and these soon demanded that they be paid for the duration of a campaign.

In Italy one first discerns the results of a key development during the medieval period. There the rise of urban communities completely upset the more traditional relationships based upon the ownership of land. Cavalry was still important, but the ability to appear on horseback was merely a sign of social status rather than a necessary function of an agreement with superior authority. Although, during the eleventh and twelfth centuries, there was a real distinction between the civic nobility who served as armoured cavalry and the ordinary mass of urban freemen who appeared on foot, this distinction did not hinge upon anything like the absolute difference between a fief-holder and a mere peasant. It was rather a mere gradation in terms of money income and denoted a very flexible hierarchy. The nobility was an open caste, always ready to absorb those with the necessary resources. Nor did they reserve to themselves the monopoly of mounted service. Commoners, be they rich merchants or manufacturers, were allowed to serve as armoured cavalry. The preeminence of money revealed itself in other ways that foreshadowed developments elsewhere in Europe. The Italian cities were among the first to employ mercenaries on a large scale, and from the early fifteenth century these began to give way to permanent standing armies in the pay of the state. These were usually cavalry forces. The 2000 *famiglia ducale* of Milan were an early example, as was the Neopolitan desmenial cavalry raised entirely from the royal estates. By the middle of the century almost every state had its contingent of *lanze spezzate*, usually recruited from disbanded *condottieri* groups, but now directly dependent upon the state rather than the intermediary mercenary paymaster.

These various mutations in the nature of feudal military obligations represent a crucial watershed in the evolution of European warfare. For hundreds of years the integral relationship between landholding and military service on horseback continued to figure largely in feudal theory. In practice, however, there had been far-reaching changes. The economic benefits of the possession of a fief became the holder's prime concern, the military obligations merely an irksome corollary. It is in this context that one should explain the later medieval stress upon the links between knighthood and nobility. The great lords were not trying to revitalize the feudal side of their military role so much as to invoke the memory of their passing dominance on the battlefield as a further proof of the exclusivity of their caste. They were not concerned with their duties to the crown but with their status within society. Chivalry and the notion of the moral superiority of the knight, like the new awareness of lineage and the growth of heraldry, were part of the ideology of an exclusive elite, trying to protect themselves against the growing power of the crown and the rise of new classes within the towns. As far as the actual terms of service went the knights were concerned only to strike the most advantageous financial arrangement. Fighting was only a trade, one, it was hoped, of which they should have the monopoly. Unfortunately for them, by encouraging this transition from duty to contract, the knights were helping to bring about their own demise. If the new availability of money was to be the touchstone of military service, they had to be prepared for the rigours of cost-benefit analysis. Not surprisingly, when the crown came actually to hire its armies the relative cheapness of substantial infantry forces was not to be gainsaid. By the end of the fifteenth century, not only had cavalry service ceased to be one of the mainsprings of economic and political power, it was fast becoming less and less important on the battlefield.

The Knight in War

The traditional conception of the armoured knight on the battlefield is one of the irresistible rush of close-packed horsemen, lances couched, smashing through the enemy line. But the more one examines the campaigns of the pre-Renaissance period the more it becomes evident that this tactic was rarely applicable on the battlefield, let alone successful. Only in a few instances does one find examples of both sides abiding by the 'rules of the game' and putting themselves in a position where such a headlong charge could be effectively employed. Much of medieval warfare consisted either of petty, localized wars, where very few knights could be

Italian men-at-arms of the
fourteenth century. The Italian
city-states were among the first to
replace feudal obligations with
simple cash payments, either to
mercenaries or to native
professionals.

gathered together and the basic aim was to avoid
battle by holing up in a castle, or of campaigns on the
frontiers of Christendom, where the enemy were at
pains to deny the horsemen any opportunity for their
hammer-blows.

Even in larger campaigns within western Europe

it was not often that success could be attributed to
the decisive charge of the knights in armour. At
Hastings, in 1066, it might be thought that the
Normans had clearly vindicated the superiority of
feudal cavalry. However, the decisive actions of the
day were the gradual erosion of the Anglo-Saxon

shield-wall by William's archers and the ill-judged sally by a part of Harold's infantry line. On their own the cavalry had been unable to make much of an impression, charge after charge being repelled by the doughty axemen. Unfortunately, the knights themselves were the last people to admit their less than vital role. An account of the battle by Guy of Amiens, written two years afterwards, offers an early example of the horseman's aristocratic contempt for mere infantry. Thus the Anglo-Saxons are 'a race ignorant of war' and 'they scorn the solace of horses and trusting in their strength they stand fast on foot'. A little later the author recounts an incident involving the Duke of Normandy himself and the words he puts into William's mouth are eloquent testimony to the mounted warrior's feeling of innate superiority:

Harold's brother . . . poising a javelin . . . hurled it from afar . . . The flying weapon wounded the body of [William's] horse and forced the Duke to fight on foot; but reduced to a foot-soldier, he fought yet better, for he rushed upon the young man like a snarling lion. Hewing him limb from limb, he shouted to him: 'Take the crown you have earned from us! If my horse is dead, thus I requite you – as a common soldier.'

The subsequent history of the Normans does not, in fact, encourage much faith in their own propaganda. It has already been seen how the more powerful beneficiaries of the post-Conquest settlement tried to foist the military burden on very lowly elements. But no matter who actually fulfilled the duty to provide knight service, they were usually inadequate for the military demands of British warfare. In Wales, for example, the Normans faced poorly armed infantry but the combination of difficult terrain and the ponderousness of the slow-moving armoured columns made it impossible for the latter ever to bring the Welsh guerrillas to battle. After the abortive campaigns of William Rufus in 1097 and Henry I in 1114, both against Gruffydd ap Cynan, the Normans fell back on a purely positional strategy, trying to hem the enemy in with a network of castles. The knights were to issue forth only in the event a band of Welshmen was discovered *returning* from a raid. Only then, because their opponents were so burdened down with plunder, could the Normans hope to pin them down for the decisive onslaught. Elsewhere in Europe, the Normans did not even attempt to rely on armoured knights. Early in the eleventh century they had invaded southern Italy and were very successful in carving out kingdoms for themselves in Capua, Apulia and Sicily. Once they were given land, however, these freebooters proved themselves very unreliable feudatories. From an early date the Norman rulers, notably Frederick II (1197–1250), relied on Moslem mercenaries deported *en masse* to the mainland to serve as infantry and mounted archers.

English history in the later Middle Ages offers further proof of the increasing ineffectiveness of the mounted knight. Three major points emerge, all equally important in other parts of Europe. One is the tendency to use more lightly armed horsemen. As has been seen, this was partly attributable to the rise of the sergeants and non-knightly men-at-arms but there were also straightforward military reasons. This was particularly the case in the wars against the Scots. After the débâcle of Bannockburn, when the pride of English chivalry refused to take any account of the unfavourable terrain and blindly charged straight into a thick morass, later rulers were obliged to content themselves with trying to prevent Scottish incursions across the border. The Scots relied upon horsemen mounted on small, sturdy ponies, who wore little armour and lived rough, surviving on oaten bannocks cooked on iron plates which they carried with them. They were able to fight on foot or on horseback and moved far too quickly for the heavy English horse ever to have much hope of catching them. Their horses were called hobins, from which came the word 'hobelars' that was attached to the raiders. Eventually, the English began to raise hobelars of their own in the Border counties, and such mounted spearmen, who often fought on foot, were an important part of the English forces at Dupplin, in 1332, and at Halidon Hill, in the following year. Paradoxically, then, though the armour of the high-born knight was becoming ever more elaborate and heavy (see the technical note at the end of this chapter), the rise of the more lowly professionals and the actual demands of frontier warfare were leading to a quite different style of cavalry combat. Indeed, it might well be argued that the nobles' attempts to close ranks encouraged the development of military equipment quite inappropriate to the actual demands of warfare. Plate armour served a purpose in that it highlighted the few men of substance that could afford it. Militarily it was of dubious value. Already, in the twelfth century, one German emperor had noted scathingly that 'armour protects the wearer, and prevents him from injuring others'.

A second point thrown up by the English experience was the tendency for the men-at-arms to fight on foot. From the very beginning of the twelfth century, at least a proportion of the English knights would dismount as soon as the battle lines were

A knight of the early fourteenth century.

longbow. It was first used by the men of south Wales and came to the attention of the English during Edward I's wars against these people. The Assize of Arms of 1252 ordered that all English foot levies should equip themselves with this weapon and it was first used in a major battle at Falkirk, in 1298. It was some time, however, before the military leaders hit upon the proper combination of foot-archers and dismounted knights. Probably the first example was an engagement at Boroughbridge in 1322 between Andrew Harcla and certain Lancastrian rebels. This was little more than a skirmish and it was not until the great set-piece battles of the Hundred Years War that the full impact of the new tactic was felt. At Crécy (1346), Poitiers (1356) and Agincourt (1415) well-directed archery and the central reserve of what were effectively heavily armoured infantry reduced the French cavalry attacks to a shambles. Protected by the knights behind and a thick palasade of pointed stakes in front, the bowmen had nothing to do but let the French come forward into a continuous hail of arrows. Their armour offered some protection and the greatest casualties were amongst the horses. After having been thrown from their mounts in full armour, even those Frenchmen who were able to stagger to their feet were in no condition to fight off the English knights who moved amongst them, hewing limbs off with great swords or deftly removing helmets and slitting the owners' throats.

Of all individual battles, Crecy should have occasioned a revolution in warfare. Froissart has described the thoughtless chaos of the French advance as the proud horsemen jostled to be the first to get to grips with the infantry 'rabble'. The French king had ordered them to hold still but 'each wished to be the first in the field. The van . . . halted. But those behind them kept riding forward, and would not stop, saying that they would get as far to the front as their fellows, and that from mere pride and jealousy. And when the vanguard saw the others pushing on, they would not be left behind, and without order or array they pressed forward, till they came in sight of the English.' Yet even after their crushing defeat the French knights continued to demand that theirs should be the right to lead the assault and that there was no need for any pre-paratory softening-up by their own bowmen. At Poitiers the only concession they made to the new tactics was of limited value. It is often claimed that the men-at-arms advanced towards the English lines on foot because that is how they had seen the English fight. This seems unlikely unless one is prepared to write their leaders off as complete idiots. The latter hypothesis is tempting but it seems more probable

drawn. The military reasons for this are unclear. Perhaps the tradition of the infantry shield-wall was still strong. Certainly the Anglo-Saxon Chronicle and that of Florence of Worcester tell us that the English suffered one severe reverse at the hands of the Welsh because a Norman earl made the English fight on horseback and many of them simply fell off again. Anglo-Saxon attitudes are also made clear in a rune poem which states: 'Riding seems easy to every warrior while he is indoors, and very courageous to him who traverses the highways on the back of a stout horse.' Whatever the reason, the battles of Tinchebrai (1106), Bremule (1119) and the Standard (1138) all offer examples of many of the knights dismounting for the combat itself.

This technique really came into its own when used in conjunction with other arms, and here one comes to the third and most important aspect of the English experience. For it was their armies that initiated the resurgence of infantry firepower that was so to limit and finally negate the cavalry's role on the battlefield. Their weapon, of course, was the that the French were trying to avoid the shattering effect of tumbling off their horses encased in a hundredweight or so of metal. But the gesture was not enough. For one thing it meant that the knights took longer to cover the distance between them and the enemy and thus allowed the English to pour even more arrows into their ranks. Such was the density of their fire that hundreds of knights were felled as the arrows struck home through the various vulnerable points in their armour. At Agincourt the French plumbed the depths of military incompetence. Jostling for position, just as Froissart had described years earlier, 'all the lords wished to be in the first battalion. For each was so jealous of the others that they could not in any other way be reconciled.' So wrote Jean Juvenal des Ursins, and so animated did this absurd bickering become that the French rode down their own crossbowmen, squeezing the survivors far out on to the flanks. Again the main assault was on foot and again the English archers laid down a devastating barrage such that 'the air was darkened by an intolerable number of piercing arrows flying across the sky to pour upon the enemy like a cloud laden with rain.' The fortunes of the battle were grotesquely disproportionate. French casualties were at least 7000 men, most of them knights, whilst the English lost little more than a hundred.

These English victories were not just exceptional examples of the infantry finding the measure of heavy cavalry. Elsewhere in Europe the balance was beginning to swing back to the footman. The reasons for the change are various. One was that the transition to money contracts with the crown made infantry an attractive economic proposition. The infantry was available in substantial numbers because of the growth of the towns, where even fairly prosperous citizens found it difficult to maintain horses and practise mounted skills. But the peculiarities of local terrain and national custom were also of importance. This was particularly the case in Switzerland where the mountainous nature of the country made the use of cavalry almost impossible. There the essence of warfare was the defence of the various passes through which an invader might try to pass. In the early fourteenth century this was the Austrians, against whom three of the Swiss forest cantons formed an alliance. The Swiss infantry did not rely upon missile weapons but on halberds, and later much longer pikes. Nor was the cohesion of the Swiss infantry dependent upon a stiffening of dismounted men-at-arms. There was no cavalry force of any description and the pikemen relied entirely upon their own phalanx-like formation to keep the enemy horsemen at bay. The first

major battles were Morgarten (1315) and Laupen (1339) when they were still armed with 8ft halberds. At Morgarten the terrain was decisive in that the Austrians were lured into a narrow defile, assailed with stones and boulders from above, and then the panic-stricken mass of men-at-arms were cut to pieces at leisure. At Laupen, and Sempach some fifty years later, the infantry actually took the offensive and showed themselves strong enough to remorselessly drive through the enemy horse. This remained the classic Swiss tactic, particularly during the heyday of the 18ft pike in the next century. They advanced in three deep columns arrayed diagonally, at an angle to the enemy line, though only the first four ranks actually projected their pikes to the front, keeping the spearheads pointing downwards.

Right through the fifteenth century no European army found an adequate response to this simple formation, and certainly not the cavalry. For them it

Crossbowman and dismounted man-at-arms of the Agincourt period. The combination of these two types of soldiers gave the English temporary dominance during the albeit rare pitched battles of the Hundred Years War. Whether mounted or on foot the French knights found it impossible ever to get to grips with their enemy.

Missile weapons spelt the end of
the armoured knight, as they
forced him to adopt heavier and
heavier, and proportionately
more expensive, armour.
Artillery was one of the most
important nails in the coffin, in
this case a sixteenth-century
cannon.

was another nail in the coffin, a further indication that the mere fact of being mounted on horseback was not an automatic guarantee of victory. For the foot were no longer just an irrelevant rabble. New weapons had appeared and, more importantly, the self-respect of the independent cantonal peasantry or the English yeoman archers had encouraged an awareness of the advantages of discipline. Longbow and pike were potentially adequate counters to cavalry but that potential could only be realized when the men who wielded them gained the self-confidence to act together as a disciplined whole. In this respect, the cavalry, as usual, missed the point. All they saw was that the new weapons prevented them from getting to grips with the enemy. The whole knightly ideal in combat was to fight hand-to-hand and lay into one's opponent with the necessary zeal. Any soldiers who managed to avoid this kind of cacophanous brawl were not credited with tactical

acumen but with the arrant cowardice of upstart knaves. In 1139 knightly propaganda forced the Lateran Council of Pope Innocent II to rule that: 'The deadly art, hated of God, of crossbowmen and archers, should not be used by Christians and Catholics on pain of anathema.' Somewhat later a *chanson de geste* of Girart de Viane succinctly expressed the knights' bigoted point of view: 'Cursed be the man who first became an archer: he was afraid and did not dare approach.' Byzantine theoreticians might have drawn rational military conclusions from this dramatic change in the balance of power on the field of battle and devised new tactics to restore their superiority. The European horsemen, on the other hand, had recourse only to abuse and helped initiate the pernicious western tradition, particularly amongst the cavalry, of anathematizing whatever they could not understand.

Yet another example of cavalry ineffectiveness

against infantry was the campaigns of the Czech and German knights against the Taborite, or Hussite heretics, under the command of John Žižka. The main features of the Taborite army were worked out by Žižka in 1420 when he began organizing his peasant levies. Horses were unknown and the whole force fought on foot, one part being armed with flails whose swipples were specially studded with iron spikes, a second with long pikes and lances, and a third with crossbows. But Žižka realized that such a force, in which religious fervour was not an adequate compensation for the lack of training or discipline, would not be able to stand up against armoured cavalry. So he devised a means of providing his men with a solid defensive perimeter that could yet be moved from place to place, whether on the march or on the battlefield itself. This was the war wagon, at first just the original four-wheeled peasant cart, and later specially manufactured with protective boards

hanging down one side, to protect those in the wagon, and other movable boards to cover the wheels and the gaps between the wagons. The whole defensive position was known as a *wagenburg*, a cross between the Romans' fortified camp and the American pioneers' circle of covered wagons.

In this defensive form, the *wagenburg* was not just a localized aberration. It was typical of a whole east European and central Asian mode of fighting. Bela of Hungary and Hajek of Hodjetin, in Bohemia, had used baggage wagons as defensive cover for their crossbowmen. The Petcheneg Turks preferred this kind of defence to the more usual mounted archery of the steppe nomad, and the Lithuanians used it, in the fourteenth century, in their wars against the Knights of the Teutonic Order. The Russians provided their columns with numbers of specially constructed wagons which could be formed into a defensive ring, or *gulaigorod*, to protect the infantry

67

against Mongol light horsemen or German knights.

Where Žižka do go beyond previous practice, however, was in the armaments he employed and in his conception of the tactical role of the defence. He was one of the first commanders to make extensive use of hand-guns. Though these first portable guns had a lamentably slow rate of fire, they were able to penetrate the thickest plate armour and, more importantly, had an immense psychological impact upon the attacking horsemen. This is something very difficult for us to understand today. Nevertheless, though it seems reasonable to criticize medieval men-at-arms for not evolving any tactical counter to traditional missile weapons like the bow, it is difficult to escape the conclusion that the cavalry response to gunpowder was determined by a more fundamental trauma, akin to the terror of a two-year-old child in whose face a loud firework explodes. But Žižka did not simply rely upon defensive strength. Once the initial enemy charge had been brought to a halt, openings were made in the *laager* and spearmen and the deadly threshers poured out to grapple with the demoralized horsemen. Such was the extent of their panic that the very sight of the Taborite infantry usually signalled a precipitate retreat. Sometimes Žižka used the whole formation in an offensive role. Certain descriptions of how this was done, all based upon the writings of Aeneas Sylvius, have now been exposed as being physically impossible. Even so, one remark of the Hussites' faithful chronicler, Brezová, does command attention. According to his account, at the battle of Kutna Hora (1421) the Taborites took the offensive and 'they marched forward and by shooting at the enemy with their guns they drove the King and his whole army from the positions that they had held.' Had this combination of mobility and defensive firepower been developed elsewhere, this book might well have ended at this point.

Even though this was not the case, the cavalry had been dealt a decisive blow. All across Europe infantrymen had shown that it was quite possible to devise methods to prevent horsemen ever coming to grips. The knights relied completely upon the impetus of their charge. The English and the Taborites had broken this up with their missile weapons, though each recognized that firepower alone was not necessarily enough. Thus the English bowmen protected their front with a thick wooden fence and were backed up by substantial numbers of dismounted knights. The Hussites fired from behind wooden ramparts. The Swiss relied entirely on the protective screen created by the great pikes they carried with them, as did Maximilian's carbon-copy

landsknechts, first formed in Germany in 1497. Nor was this an exclusively European response to armoured cavalry. It has already been shown that the Chinese were aware, even in 99 BC, that protected infantry could hold off the best horsemen. The Arabs, too, learnt the lesson. A historian of the Arab rule in Spain, Abu Bakr at-Turtūsī, described their tactics against the mail-clad Spanish knights in the eleventh century:

> The infantry with their antelope shields, lances and iron-tipped javelins are placed kneeling, in ranks. Their lances rest obliquely on their shoulders, the shaft touching the ground behind them, the point directed towards the enemy. Each one kneels on his left knee with his shield in the air. Behind the infantry are the picked archers who, with their arrows can pierce coats of mail. Behind the archers are the cavalry. When the Christians charge, the infantry remains in position, kneeling as before. As soon as the enemy comes into range, the archers let loose a hail of arrows, while the infantry throw their javelins and receive the charge on the points of their lances.

In fact, the hell-for-leather charge of the armoured lancers was not a typical Spanish tactic. The bulk of their horsemen were the much more lightly armed *caballeros villanos*, more akin to the English hobilars than to the chivalry of Crécy. Also referred to as genetours, these horsemen relied upon skirmishing tactics, wheeling away in front of the enemy and throwing light javelins with considerable force, rather than getting involved in hand-to-hand combat or trying to smash their way through the enemy. They learnt these tactics from their Arab and Berber adversaries and there is a clear link with the methods of Hannibal's Numidian cavalry. This mode of combat was still predominant in the late fourteenth century. Froissart gave a brief description of it, and his remarks are all the more revealing in that he was unable to resist looking down on warriors who tried to avoid 'honourable' hand-to-hand combat:

> The manner in which the Spaniards generally act in war [is this]. It is true that they make handsome figures on horseback, spur off to advantage, and fight well at the first onset; but as soon as they have thrown two or three darts, and given a stroke with their spears, without disconcerting the enemy, they take alarm, turn their horses' heads, and save themselves by flight as well as they can.

A light horseman depicted on a Persian miniature of the late fourteenth century.

Light cavalry were also used in Italy, but these were not native troops. Most came from Albania, introduced by the Venetians for their war against the Turks between 1463 and 1479. They were known as stradiots and fought very much as the Spanish genetours, with several javelins and a light lance or crossbow. Some wore a breastplate and helmet though many were completely unarmoured. Their duties in battle were to disrupt the enemy's rear and attack his baggage. At other times they were a simple weapon of terror. Even in wars between Italians their masters paid them one ducat for every enemy head.

The final trend in cavalry tactics in this period, already noted among the English horse, was the habit of fighting on foot. This spread in particular to Italy, in the wake of the successes of certain English mercenary bands. The most famous of these was Hawkwood's White Company. His men were divided into 'lances', each comprising two men-at-arms and a squire. All three rode to the battlefield, but dismounted for combat, the two knights advancing towards the enemy with one lance held between them. If they themselves were attacked they relied on their swords, often fighting back-to-back. One of their most famous victories was at Castagnaro, in 1387, though even here a quarter of the force remained on horseback, awaiting the chance to charge into the enemy flank.

Another example of knights fighting on foot offers an extreme example of medieval warriors clinging to traditional methods even in the most inappropriate circumstances. During the mid-fourteenth century the Knights of the Teutonic Order were involved in chronic border warfare with the Lithuanians, a savage, pagan people locked away in marshy primeval forest. Horses were quite irrelevant. Warfare consisted of year-long treks through the pathless woods, with the constant danger of ambush or getting hopelessly lost. Even if the enemy were found there was no conventional battle, but a short bloody assault upon some wooden stockade. Yet the knights always took their armour with them, carried by packhorses or porters. This load must have slowed the column down even more, yet it was deemed essential for how else could the 'noble' knight distinguish himself from his despised foe?

Technical Note: The Development of Armour

The basis of early European armour, from the ninth century, was the hauberk. The earliest mail shirts only reached the hips, but from around 950 they slowly got longer until they covered all the leg to the knees. The way in which the garment was reinforced varied enormously. Some were made of leather with hundreds of brass or iron rings sewn on. Others were made up of overlapping metal scales, usually pointed, arranged to overlap alternately like roof tiles. Another alternative was jesserant work. Here plates of some defensive material were placed between two layers of cloth and the layers sewn together in the gaps between the plates, giving a quilted appearance. Such a garment was usually further strengthened with iron studs fastened to the plates, but protruding outside the material. The other essentials were the helmet and shield. The crested Frankish helmet has already been mentioned, though by the middle of the tenth century this had generally been replaced by the famous conical Norman head-piece, with a strip of metal to protect the nose. At this time face and neck were protected with a veil of leather or mail hanging from the helmet, but by the end of the eleventh century this was attached to the hauberk itself as a kind of hood. At the same time, the helmet was becoming flatter on top and the nasal was becoming broader. Shields were kite-shaped as a compromise between the maximum protection whilst on horseback and the minumum inconvenience.

Between 1150 and 1280 the dominant type of armour was chain-mail made from strips of wrought wire. The links were made by wrapping the wire spirally around a stick, cutting off individual circles, flattening them, and piercing two rivet holes at each end of the circle. The rings were then linked together, each being attached to four others above and below, and the rivets inserted. The hauberk was now also supplemented by chain-mail 'tights'. The conical helmet was extended to become the *heaume* – basically a metal cylinder with apertures for breathing and vision which covered the whole head. One of its great advantages was that only the flat top was actually touching the head, thus greatly diminishing the chances of a fractured skull.

Chain-mail remained the basis of the knight's protection until the first half of the fourteenth century. The main refinement was the appearance of banded mail in which complete circles of metal were threaded on to leather strips and these were sewn on to the tunic. A further strip of metal was sewn between each row of rings to make the garment more pliable, thus giving the banded appearance. This was probably a reaction against archers as the overlapping flattened rings offered a much more substantial protection than the earlier 'string vest' of

Fourteenth-century French
knights.

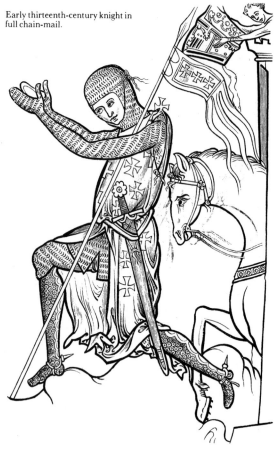

Early thirteenth-century knight in full chain-mail.

marvellously flexible breast and back plates. By the second half of the fourteenth century this flexibility had been given up in favour of more solid protection and one-piece breastplates were now the rule. A mail hauberk with a high collar was still worn beneath the breastplate, though by the end of the century it was usual to only attach metal rings to those parts of the linen backing that actually protruded above or below, or were likely to be uncovered in movement. Protection for the limbs and major joints was retained, and by the early fifteenth century the well-equipped heavy cavalryman was almost entirely encased in plate armour. At no stage, incidentally, were knights winched up on to their horses. The weight of the armour did cause some problems, however. The worst of these was that the special war horses, *destriers*, developed to carry the armoured knight, were only capable of moving at a trot. To use this gait in full armour was torture and special lighter horses, palfreys, were ridden until it was time to 'get on one's high horse' for the charge. The Knights of the Teutonic Order made trotting on a destrier in full armour their Field Punishment No. 1.

The face was invisible, being protected either by a cylindrical helm or what was known as the 'pig-faced' bassinet, the bassinet proper with a pointed, snout-like visor.

Up to the end of the sixteenth century plate armour was the usual equipment of the heavy cavalryman and involved the full gamut of protection for head, torso and limbs. From around 1430 it is customary to refer to the Gothic style, in which functionalism was blended as far as possible with aesthetic appeal. True Gothic armour, though a marvellous example of medieval craftmanship, was also an excellent defence, in which cunningly contrived grooves, channels and glancing surfaces deflected the arrow- or lance-point of an adversary. However, this level of craftsmanship, and the quality of the tempered steel used in the best suits, made them both extremely heavy and prohibitively expensive. And even though such armour was an adequate protection against most missile weapons, it had still proved virtually impossible to solve the problem of the vulnerability of the horse. The combination of these factors led to the gradual abandonment of all-encasing armour. Certain horsemen began to realize that the function of cavalry now should be to get among the shot as quickly as possible, in the intervals between their volley and the sheer bulk of modern armour made this very difficult. Various writers commented on the slow transition, as it occurred in England. As early as 1530, Sir James Smith noted: 'But that which is more strange, these

interlocking circles of wire. The mail was also increasingly supplemented by various coverings for the more vulnerable parts of the body. These included *genouillières*, over the knees, at first of stiffened leather, later of metal; the mail covering for the legs now terminated beneath the knee and started again at the top of the *genouillière*, thus minimizing the intolerable drag on the knees from the sheer weight of the metal. Other additions were the *coudière* for the elbow, *demi-brassarts* – curved pieces of plate metal attached to the outside of the upper arm – and *demi-jambarts*, which were simply metal greaves worn over the mail. During this period the stifling pot-helm disappeared and was replaced by the lighter *bassinet*. These were often little more than the old Norman helmet, though visors were sometimes attached and the mail hood was now attached to the bottom of the helmet rather than covering the whole head.

A transitional development after banded mail was splinted armour, in which narrow splints of steel were attached to a leather backing to give

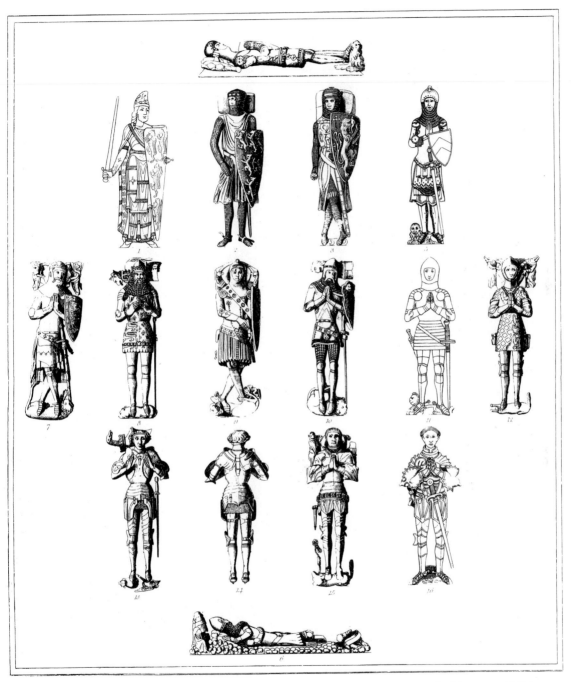

English monumental effigies
showing the development of
armour from the chain-mail of the
twelfth century to fourteenth-
century Gothic armour.

two new-fashioned men of war doo despise and scorne our auncient arming of ourselves, both on horseback and on foot, saying that wee armed ourselves in past times with too much armour.' Sir Richard Hawkins at one stage made elaborate preparations for the equipping of his men: 'I had great preparation of armours as well as of proof as of light corseletts, yet not a man would use them but esteemed a pott of wine better defence than any armour of proofe.'

Eventually, except for a few residual bodies of lancers in the old style, the cavalry abandoned all the traditional protection except for the cuirass and, in some cases, the metal helmet. James I was an influential figure in this respect and his judgement on the efficacy of armour is a suitable epitaph for the armoured knight: 'Armour was an admirable invention, for while it protected the wearer from being hurt, it effectually prevented, by its weight, his causing injury to others.'

Very elaborate Gothic armour in a sixteenth-century jousting scene. The exorbitant cost of such equipment meant that only a few wealthy nobles could afford it, and none of them would be so rash as to wear it in battle.

5 War and the State 1494 to 1797

'I am not of the opinion . . . that we ought to depend
any more on the cavalry, in general, than they did in
former times, for we have often seen them shamefully
beaten of late by infantry.'
Machiavelli

'The King hereby forbids all cavalry officers, under
penalty of being cashiered, ever to allow themselves
to be attacked by the enemy in any action. Prussians
must always attack the enemy.'
Frederick the Great

In 1494, Charles VIII of France invaded Italy and so unleashed a whole series of dynastic struggles that were to dominate European history until the middle of the following century. For certain observers, even the first of these wars seemed to show that methods of waging war were now quite different. The Italian historian, Guicciardini, was quite clear as to what constituted the new element:

> To join up with [Charles VIII's] army there had been brought to Genoa by sea a great quantity of both siege and field artillery of a kind which had never been seen in Italy ... The French made manageable pieces and only out of bronze, which they called cannons, and used iron balls where they used to be of stone and incomparably larger and heavier; and they were drawn not by oxen as was the custom in Italy, but by horses. The men and equipment assigned to this work were so skilful that they could almost always keep up with the rest of the army; and when brought up to the walls they were set up with unbelievable rapidity ... And they employed this diabolical rather than human instrument no less in the field than at sieges, using the same cannon and other smaller pieces ... This artillery made Charles' army most formidable to the whole of Italy.

It has already been seen, in the previous chapter, how various infantry forces had begun to get the measure of armoured cavalry. It might be thought that the addition of powerful field artillery would have swept them from the field once and for all. The proportion of cavalry in most armies did fall – a rough average for the major European powers shows that the cavalry represented 40 per cent of the total force in 1500, 33 per cent during the Thirty Years War, 30 per cent between 1648 and 1715, and 25 per cent for the rest of the century – but this does not mean that cavalry had ceased to be an important force on the battlefield. The reasons for its survival are two-fold. On the one hand, one can discern the inertia of tradition, all the more powerful because the cavalry were still a stronghold of aristocratic vested interests. Yet there were also genuine military reasons. The Hussites had shown the effectiveness of handguns on the battlefield and in the next century the arquebus became a very important infantry weapon. Charles VIII showed what could be done with massed artillery and this lesson was swiftly learnt. Yet all these missile weapons were at a very early stage of development. They were unreliable and they were above all extremely slow. Concerted fire from arquebusiers or gunners could be absolutely devastating, but once the volley or can-

The development of gunpowder weapons that could be carried by one man was a further threat to the dominance of the horsemen. Though the process took hundreds of years, it was handguns, and above all machine guns, that eventually drove them from the battlefield. Here is depicted a match-lock man of the sixteenth century.

nonade had been fired there was an agonizingly long wait before it could be repeated. During such a lull there was often ample time for effective cavalry action. Such action could usually be even more effective if it could be coordinated with the fire of one's own side. If the enemy's arquebusiers were sensible, once they had loosed off their shots they would retire behind the protection of their pikemen. As the Swiss had shown, this forest of long spears was a perfectly adequate defence against a cavalry charge, but if the pike square was first disrupted by artillery fire, enough gaps could be created to allow the horse to get to close quarters. Once that had happened the pikes were merely encumbrances. Thus, there was still plenty of opportunity for effective shock action by massed horsemen. At the very beginning of this period and later, from the middle of the seventeenth century, the point was well taken. Yet in the intervening period, for a hundred years or so, the cavalry allowed themselves to be drawn up a tactical blind alley. As has always been the wont of this arm, though they managed to perceive that gunpowder was a dramatic innovation on the battlefield, they failed to see how it affected their own role. The French, for example, at Poitiers and Agincourt had copied the English dismounted knights yet failed to see that the tactical context was quite different. Just so did the European horsemen of the sixteenth century respond to firearms by adopting them themselves and thus completely nullifying their own primary value as shock troops.

The Cavalry Debilitated

During the early years of the fifteenth century most cavalry, particularly the French, coped reasonably well with the widespread appearance of firearms and even utilized them themselves to overcome an old adversary. Though the arquebus had a longer effective range than the crossbow, approximately 400yd, it was a very difficult weapon to manage and one shot per minute was probably the best that infantry in battle would be able to manage. (A modern historian, J. W. Wijn, has experimented and found that he could manage two shots per minute, though obviously without any of the stress and confusion of battle.) Nor were these firearms deployed in anything like the most effective manner. The Swiss, the Spanish *tercios* and the German *landsknechts* all relied chiefly upon the pike and used the arquebusiers to form a protective girdle right round the square. Though this gave protection on all sides, it severely reduced the number of shots that could be fired at any one time. But, if the shot deployed themselves in front of the pike square, in a solid body, they left themselves very vulnerable to attack once they had fired a volley. It was not for nothing that early experiments in detached units of arquebusiers, thrown ahead of the main body, were known as 'forlorn hopes'. At this stage, then, once the initial psychological shock had worn off, firepower was not sufficient to force the cavalry to abandon the traditional charge at full speed. As long as they did not charge straight at troops who had not yet discharged their pieces, it was a relatively easy task to ride the shot down. Even if the latter retreated behind the pikeman, or into the square itself, the advantage was no longer all with the infantry. If the attacker used his own artillery to break up the square there was bound to come a moment when a cavalry charge could be used to advantage. This is what happened at Marignano, in 1515, when the Swiss pikemen suffered one of their bloodiest defeats. Writing to his mother, the French king described how after the prolonged artillery barrage 'more than thirty-five

charges were delivered, and no one in future will be able to say that cavalry are of no more use than hares in armour'. Here the discipline of the French horsemen seems to have been exemplary, and they came on in successive waves of about 500 riders, dealing hammer blows to the crumbling squares.

Cavalry tactics against other horsemen relied also upon the charge and hand-to-hand combat. Guicciardini has left a description of the battle of Fornovo, in 1495:

> The . . . attack was very fierce and furious, and was met with like ferocity and courage. The squadrons entered the battle from all sides in a mêlée and not according to the custom of the wars in Italy, which was to fight, one squadron against another, and to replace this with another when the first was worsted or began to fall back . . . When the lances were broken, many men-at-arms and horse fell to the ground in the encounter, and they all began to wield with like ferocity maces, short swords and other small arms, the horses fighting with kicks, bites and blows no less than the men.

However, this revival of cavalry shock action was a very brief interlude. The new emphasis upon gunpowder had given the cavalry a brief breathing space in which the sheer novelty of the thing and the inexperience of the foot gunners had created opportunities for bold offensive action. By the 1520s there was evidence of a new expertise amongst the infantry and their commanders. The shot was deployed more effectively and greater recourse was had to entrenchments and field fortifications, denying the cavalry the chance to come to grips. Blaise de Monluc expressed the lancers' disgust with this development:

> Would to heaven that this accursed engine [the arquebus] had never been invented . . . [and had not] so many valiant men been slain for the most part by the most pitiful fellows and the greatest cowards; poltroons that had not dared to look those men in the face at hand, which at distance they laid dead with their confounded bullets.

How were the cavalry to respond to this renewed predominance of missile weapons? Certainly, as the embodiment of honour and chivalry, they were not going to allow themselves to be driven from the battlefield altogether. Eventually, they turned to gunpowder themselves. Handguns had been used by horsemen as early as the middle of the fifteenth century. These were known as petronels, or *arquebus à croc*, which were nothing more than miniature cannon, the recoil being absorbed by resting them

Mounted arquebusiers of the
sixteenth century executing
patently impossible feats of mark-
smanship.

against the breastplate, and the aim steadied with a
fork placed on the pommel of the saddle. Not surprisingly, such weapons were not common and it was not
until the introduction of the wheel-lock, probably
invented in Nuremburg at about the time of Marignano, that the cavalry had access to a feasible
gunpowder weapon. The great advantage of the
wheel-lock was that it did away with the need for a
match, which had to be held in the other hand. The
lock was a toothed wheel which was wound up by a
spring. When the trigger was pulled the spring was
released and the sharp teeth grated against a lump of

pyrites fixed near the pan. Sparks were struck and
these fell into the touch-powder in the pan and this
transmitted a flash to the charge in the barrel of the
weapon. Thus might a rider hope to discharge his
piece, always providing, as Michael Roberts has
pointed out 'the spring did not break, or the wheel
get bent, or the pyrites fall out, or the pistol go off
prematurely in the rider's jackboot.' (Most pistoleers
carried three handguns – two in the belt and one in
the jackboot). The weapons soon spread and were
available in England in 1521 and in France some ten
years later.

Fanciful sixteenth-century cavalry tactics. The adoption of the arquebus and the wheel-lock led to tactics that completely robbed the cavalry of any potential as shock troops. In this particular example it can only be assumed that most of the mounted arquebusiers would dispatch each other.

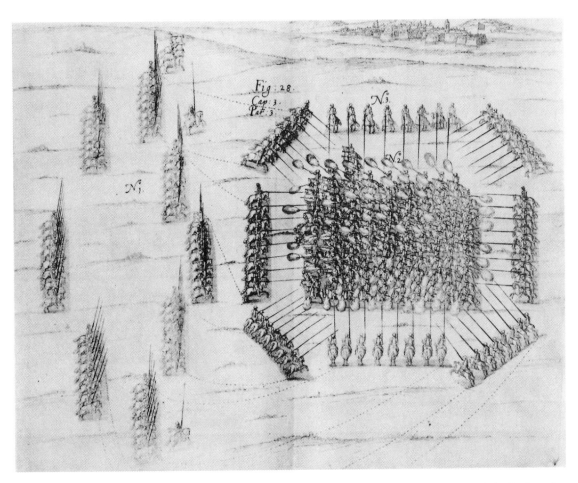

Appropriately it was the Germans who first adopted such weapons for the cavalry, although not until the mid-1540s. These horsemen, generally known as *reiters*, completely abandoned the lance and based their tactics upon pistol-firing, the sword to be used only in direst emergencies. Their classic stratagem was the *caracole*, which was executed in two basic ways. In both cases the horsemen were formed up in a deep column. They rode up to the enemy and pistols were discharged either by ranks or by files. In the former case each rank fired in turn, moving off to the rear once it had done so. In the latter case the column presented its right flank to the enemy and all who could fired off their right-hand pistols, after which they wheeled about and let fly with the left-hand. The first major battle in which this manoeuvre was used was Dreux, in 1562, although cavalry had been recorded as attacking in deep order at St Quentin, in 1557. The tactic spread through much of Europe. The lance was generally abandoned – for example in France in 1594 and in the United Provinces in 1596. Even before this, most cavalry had given up shock action in favour of the ponderous *caracole*. The French met many German

A late sixteenth-century *reiter*. The Germans were the first to develop cavalry forces that relied mainly upon the wheel-lock. Most troopers carried three, one for each hand and one tucked in the boot. The sword was reserved for dire emergencies.

Dram your Pistoll

Order your Pistoll

Draw your Rammer

Lade with Bullet and Ramhome

Guard your Cock

Order your Hammer

reiters during the Wars of Religion (1562–98) and both the Huguenot and Catholic armies gave up the old charge in line for the slow-moving column.

This transition has generally been condemned by modern historians. Indeed, there is very little to be said for the *caracole* itself. It completely deprived cavalry of any capacity for shock action and made them little more than infantry on horseback. Very feeble infantry at that. For the wheel-lock was a poor substitute for the arquebus or the matchlock. It is reckoned that its maximum effective range was not more than five paces. A French contemporary, Tavennes, wrote that 'it is essential that the muzzle is actually touching [the target]'. Thus, as the cavalry were riding up to execute a *caracole* against enemy infantry they could expect to receive at least one volley before they were able to reply. Moreover, the fact that they were forced to come to close quarters and then remain stationary whilst firing meant that it was impossible to charge home in the event one's volleys actually did have any noticeable effect. Clearly, late sixteenth- and early seventeenth-century cavalry was a very debilitated arm. Yet it would not do to condemn the horsemen entirely. At least they showed some awareness of the new importance of gunpowder. An English writer, in 1598, noted:

> It is rarely seen in our days that men come often to hand-blowes, as in old times they did: for now in this age the shot so employeth and busieth the field ... that the most valientest and skilfullest therein do commonly impart the victorie, or the best, at the least wise, before men come to many hand-blowes.

The cavalry realized this and at least desisted from the suicidal tactics of many armoured knights before them had employed.

Moreover, gunpowder *was* the answer to their problem. Cavalry charges could still be effective if the enemy was first softened up by one's own infantry or artillery. But such tactics demanded that the various arms act in combination. Great commanders were to realize this. As will be seen, Gustavus Adolphus used musketeers to give each cavalry unit its own integral firepower whilst, on a grander scale, Napoleon used massed artillery to soften up those parts of the enemy line into which the cavalry was to charge. The great mistake of the sixteenth-century horse was to believe that they by themselves could make effective use of missile weapons and retain a useful offensive role. But the mistake was probably inevitable. They were so convinced of their centrality upon the battlefield, so sure

that infantry and artillery were no more than base poltroons, that it would have been inconceivable for them to accept that their continued success depended upon combined action. Reliance upon others demanded respect for others and this the horsemen had yet to concede.

The Return of Shock Action

By the time of the Thirty Years War (1618–48) cavalry was in the doldrums. By the end of the eighteenth century it had once again found a valuable battlefield role, thanks mainly to the efforts of several great commanders. The first of these was Gustavus Adolphus (1611–32) whose extensive military reforms created the most efficient army in Europe. The crucial element in his thinking was to make much fuller use of the attributes of the various arms, and properly to coordinate their action. Firepower was increased by extending the infantry frontage and increasing the number of artillery pieces, many of the latter being allotted to the individual infantry brigades. But this did not simply mean a strengthening of the defensive. Rather it was a springboard for more effective offensive tactics. Fire power was to be used to break up enemy formations as a prelude to attacks either by the infantry (pikemen – Gustavus actually increased the proportion of pikes in each brigade) or the cavalry. For the latter, the *caracole* was completely abandoned and with it the old formations in depth. The horsemen were drawn up in a line of only three ranks. Pistols were retained, but now only the first rank was allowed to fire, and then with one gun only, when they could see the whites of the enemy's eyes. The second and third ranks kept their pistols charged but were only to use them in an emergency. The key weapon was the sabre, to be used as all three ranks charged home at the gallop. However, such a minimal use of gunpowder was rarely sufficient to break up enemy infantry. To overcome this problem, Gustavus allotted groups of musketeers to his horsemen, either placing them between the squadrons on the battlefield or attaching them to units sent out to skirmish. They were to disorganize the enemy infantry by pouring in a volley just before the charge and, if necessary, provide some sort of protection if the cavalry were repulsed. One of the king's Scottish mercenary officers has left a clear description of such a combination, at the battle of Breitenfeld (1631):

> The Horsemen on both wings charged furiously one another, our Horsemen with a resolution, abiding unloosing a Pistoll, till the enemy had

Pikemen and musketeers were still very important during the Thirty Years War. However, thanks to Gustavus Adolphus, the Swedish king, cavalry began to regain a significant role on the battlefield. Gustavus's most important innovation was to reinstate the sword at the expense of pistols.

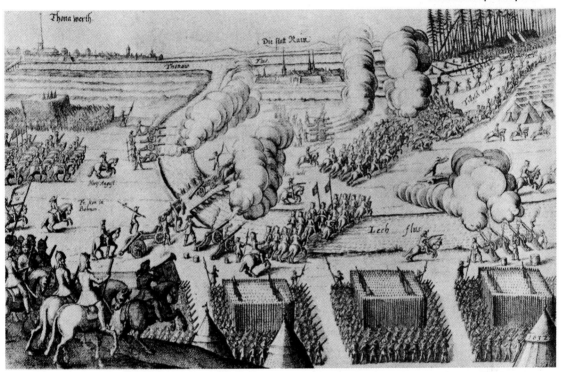

discharged first, and then at a near distance our Musketiers meeting them with a Salve; then our horsemen discharged their Pistolls, and then charged through them with swords; and at their returne the Musketiers were ready again to give second salve of Muskets amongst them.

Such a close tactical combination of horse and shot did have certain tactical disadvantages, however. Though the cavalry were supposed to ride in at the enemy at the gallop, it seems unlikely that they ever achieved much more than a fast trot. Even if acting alone, there would be no time to build up any real speed after discharging their pistols at the obligatory very short range. Also, when they were acting in concert with musketeers, both units would soon lose contact if the cavalry were allowed to charge for more than a hundred yards or so. Thus, though Gustavus had restored the attacking role of the horsemen, the closeness of his tactical combinations meant that they were still hampered by their gunpowder support and were never able to charge home in the true sense of the word.

Other armies were not slow to learn the basic lesson. The *caracole* was swiftly abandoned and the heavy horsemen concentrated again on getting to grips with their opponents. Cavalry-*versus*-cavalry encounters became particularly common as such captains as Tilly, Wallenstein and Piccolomini all tried to infuse their troopers with the offensive spirit. Often enough one side would not even stand to receive a charge. When they did, or if they themselves broke into a counter-charge, the ensuing mêlée was a confused affair, a whole series of hand-to-hand encounters rather than one united blow. Swords did not figure in the reality of the battle as much as theory tried to suggest:

A cuirassier would rush past his opposite number, and veering, shoot him in the back as being the

Prince Rupert of the Rhine in full
seventeenth-century armour.
During the English Civil War,
most troopers wore only a breastplate or a stout buff leather coat.
Rupert and the Cavaliers relied on
charging at the gallop, which
made it difficult to regroup
afterwards; Cromwell's Ironsides
advanced at the trot, knee-to-
knee.

The quality of horses and standard of horsemanship
had deteriorated very badly. Elizabeth I's muster at
Tilbury, in 1588, produced only 3000 poorly
mounted riders. By 1625 a military commentator
restated ancient Anglo-Saxon prejudices about the
mysteries of riding. In *The Soldier's Accidence*, Stuart
Markham wrote:

> Infinite great (and not without much difficultie)
> are the Considerations which dependeth on him
> that taketh upon him to Teach, Command and
> Governe a Troope of Horse . . . to bring ignorant
> man and more ignorant horse, wilde man and
> mad horse, to those Rules of Obedience, which
> may crowne every Motion and Action with
> comely, orderly and profitable proceedings; *Hic
> Labor Hoc Opus*.

Yet only twenty years after this was written, both
Royalists and Parliamentarians were organizing
their own regiments of cavalry and, on the Puritan
side at least, were having much success in instilling
these very 'Rules of Obedience'. At first, the Royalist
cavalry, under the dashing leadership of Prince
Rupert, had the advantage. They were better
mounted and had more men accustomed to riding,
both in the hunt and in wars abroad. Rupert had
learnt two of Gustavus's most important lessons in
that he always tried to attack first and obliged most
of his men to reserve their fire until they actually
closed with the enemy. The early Parliamentary
army seems to have been most unsure about what
should be their tactics. In the event, at both Edgehill
(1642) and Worcester (1642), they simply waited for
the Royalists to charge into them and fired their own
pistols much too early. On both occasions their horse
was decisively routed. They were not slow, however,
in learning their lesson. The cavalry of the Eastern
Association, under Cromwell, began to copy their
opponents' tactics and when the Association was
absorbed in to the New Model Army, in 1644, the
horse on both sides was very evenly matched. The
Ironsides no longer sat still and waited for the enemy
to charge, but always tried to take the initiative
themselves, or at least meet the Royalists half way.
They also began to reserve their fire until the last
possible moment. Nor were the pistols quite done
with when they had been discharged. Major-
General Morgan's instructions to his troopers
during an expedition to Scotland, in 1654, stated
that 'no man should fire till he came within a horse's

part of the body regarded as being more vulnerable. Or he would try to ram his foe's steed, thus –
with luck – jolting his rival out of the saddle to slay
him on the ground. Or he would endeavour to pull
him off by his bandoleer. Alternatively, two
cavalrymen coming sufficiently close together
would enclose each other in their arms and both
be torn from their mounts, after which they
crashed their heavy pistols against one another's
skulls. This is not to mention skilled manoeuvres
like training a horse to lash out its heels behind,
and so hold off a pursuer, or having such control
over it that it would spring and bite its
counterpart, furnishing a good opportunity to
thrust a sword into an opponent's visor-opening or
the unprotected area between cuisse and greave.

But the real heir of the Swedish king was Oliver
Cromwell whose New Model horsemen reapplied
his basic teachings in an English context. The previous hundred years had not been favourable to the
development of an adequate English cavalry force.

Mughal warriors of the early
seventeenth century, from a
contemporary book painting.

Cromwell's Ironsides on patrol. By the later stages of the English Civil War the Parliamentarian horse generally had the advantage in battle, because their superior discipline enabled them to execute successive charges upon enemy formations, rather than trusting everything to one mad dash.

The Scots Greys at Waterloo.

length of the enemy, and then (after firing) to throw their pistols in their faces, and so fall on them with the sword.'

Cromwell's horsemen did not charge as such. The pace never got above what he, describing his first encounter with the Royalists, in 1643, called 'a pretty round trot'. This was because the advance was always made in very close order, which was not to be disturbed right up to the moment of contact: One soldier wrote that 'those troops that are to give the first charge are to be at their close order; every left-hand man's right knee must be close locked under his right-hand man's left ham.' Because of

this, the Ironsides rarely broke the enemy lines at the first onset. In a letter telling of a battle near Gainsborough, in 1643, Cromwell gave this account of the cavalry mêlée: 'We came up horse to horse, where we disputed it with our swords and pistols a pretty time, all keeping close order, so that one could not break the other. At last, they a little shrinking, our men perceiving it, pressed in among them, and immediately routed this whole body.' But the greatest strength of the Parliamentarian cavalry was not their close order, and certainly not an innate man for man superiority over the Royalists. It was their discipline, which made it possible for Cromwell to rally his men very quickly and renew the pressure upon the enemy. Nowhere was this more in evidence than at Marston Moor (1644), where the Puritans charged and rallied four times to finally break their

Marlborough's cavalry at the Battle of Oudenarde. Like Cromwell, the Duke insisted upon the necessity of discipline during the charge and his regiments never advanced at more than the trot. The use of firearms was explicitly prohibited during ordinary combat.

opponents. Clarendon, in *History of the Great Rebellion*, was keenly aware of the essential difference between the cavalry of the two sides:

Though the King's troops prevailed in the charge and routed those they charged, they seldom rallied themselves again in order, nor could be brought to make a second charge the same day . . . whereas the other troops, if they prevailed, or though they were beaten and routed, presently rallied again, and stood in good order until they received new orders.

There will be further cause to notice how this lack of discipline could be a fatal flaw to the horsemen's effectiveness. With so many European regiments, as with the Royalists, a cavalry charge was not so much a manoeuvre as a more-or-less controlled riot.

Bringing up the British cavalry for the decisive charge at the Battle of Ramillies. It was a feature of Marlborough's tactics that he always held back a substantial mounted reserve for the *coup de grâce*.

After the Civil War the Cromwellian tradition remained dominant in the British army. The next great English commander, Marlborough, emphasized discipline at the expense of maximum impetus, and he never allowed his cavalry to advance at any more than a fast trot. The charge was a twin-squadron affair, each squadron drawn up in two lines, and Marlborough always took great pains to ensure that he kept a substantial force in reserve that could be used for the *coup de grâce* at the decisive point of the battle. The value of such a reserve was successively proved as the battles of Blenheim (1704), Ramillies (1706) and Malplaquet (1709). At Ramillies, moreover, he was able to extricate his horsemen after the first charge, reform the squadrons, and send them crashing again into the French lines. In one respect, however, he did not follow earlier example. He was totally unconvinced of the value of firearms for cavalry and forbade their use in ordinary combat. One of his commanders, General Kane, recalled: 'The Duke of Marlborough would allow the horse but three charges of powder and ball to each man for a campaign, and that only for guarding their horses when at grass, and not to be made use in action.'

In this respect Marlborough was anticipating a dominant eighteenth-century tradition. In Sweden, Charles XII, though he subscribed to Gustavus Adolphus's views on the offensive role of horsemen, was adamantly opposed to their using firearms on the battlefield. In fact, he was only emphasizing tactical precepts that had been worked out by earlier

Vasa kings. The Swedish regulations of 1685 had abandoned the charge at the trot and stipulated that the horse should advance in three lines, by squadrons, and break into a full gallop once they were within 150yd of the enemy. These regulations did see some place for firearms, however, and pistols were to be fired when the troopers were within 40 and 25yd away. Charles realized that this was an unsatisfactory compromise. Few soldiers would be able to hit even a solid wall of the enemy when they were charging at full tilt and any attempt to steady the aim could only reduce the momentum of the assault. Thus they were expressly forbidden to use their pistols during the charge. In one order to the cavalry, Charles wrote: 'My friends, get to grips with the enemy, on no account fire, that is how poltroons behave, and strike them at sword-point; you will soon see how correct this is.'

Perhaps the greatest advocate of the *arme blanche* was Frederick the Great. Guibert wrote of him: 'In all his camps, at all his reviews, wherever Frederick sees his cavalry, it is to these important charges in large numbers that he gives the most attention, these that he values the most highly.' The cavalry force he inherited was a very inadequate body – huge men on huge horses, who had little idea of how to handle themselves and were quite incapable of launching a serious charge. Frederick went to work to improve this state of affairs almost immediately. His main pre-occupation was that his horsemen should be accustomed to all-out offensive action. This was a logical tactical corollary of his major strategic problem. Surrounded as Prussia was by states that could muster much larger armies, Frederick had to gamble everything on swift, decisive victories, gained before an enemy could unite all its own forces or effectively act in concert with those of other powers. A well-timed cavalry charge could contribute enormously to this end, either to fall upon already disorganized infantry units or to clear away the cavalry from that flank towards which Frederick was concentrating his famous oblique attack.

His orders and strategic writings constantly hammer home the necessary attributes of cavalry in such a role. The cavalry must not use firearms as these would only interfere with the momentum of the charge. One of his cavalry commanders, Major-General Warnery, echoed his master's sentiments on this point: 'Experience has convinced me in more than a hundred occasions, for I have never seen a squadron depend on its fire that it has not been over-thrown by that which came upon it at speed without firing.' The king himself made the point crystal clear in his instructions to his officers: 'The squadron commanders must be responsible for seeing to it that no cavalryman or dragoon uses either carbine or pistol during battle, but that they act only with sword in hand.'

In this respect Frederick was only following his father's example,* but in other ways he improved the Prussian cavalry out of all recognition. Their speed was to be of the essence. Thus 'with the cavalry attack it is not the size of the horse but the impetuosity of the charge that turns the scales.' On another occasion he insisted that 'all movements of cavalry are swift. It can decide the fate of a battle in one instant.' But it was not enough that the cavalry always charged at full tilt; they must also ensure that they attacked first, to give them the maximum possible advantage over the enemy: 'In the open field the cavalry must charge the enemy instantly and attack him; this is a fundamental rule and my most serious order.' In the Order of Battle before Leuthen (1757) he made the point brutally clear: 'The King hereby forbids all cavalry officers, under penalty of being cashiered, ever to allow themselves to be attacked by the enemy in any action. Prussians must always attack the enemy.' Throughout his wars Frederick tried constantly to increase the effectiveness of this basic tactic. The number of cuirassier regiments, wearing armour front and back, was increased to give maximum weight to the front line. Riding schools were established in each regiment to ensure that the men were physically capable of all-out action. The regulation distance of the charge was increased to permit the maximum possible impetus. In 1748 it consisted only of an advance at the trot for 300yd followed by 400yd at the gallop. Two years later this was climaxed by a further 500yd at full speed, and in 1755 the preparatory trot and gallop was increased to 1200yd. For Frederick the impetus of the cavalry was everything and under ideal circumstances no mêlée was expected. As he explained to a French observer:

I make the squadrons charge at a fast gallop because then fear carries the cowards along with the rest – they know that if they so much as hesitate in the middle of the onrush they will be crushed by the remainder of the squadron. My intention is to force the enemy to break by the speed of charges before it ever comes to hand-to-hand fighting.

In this he seems to have been very successful. The sheer impetus of the charge usually forced the enemy

*A regulation of 1727 read: 'Every commander is held bound, on his honour and reputation, to allow no shooting, but always to ride home with the sword.'

to turn and flee even before the Prussian troopers had come to grips. Writing on the Prussian 'system', in 1788, Mirabeau recorded: 'Veteran and intelligent cavalry officers have told us that when two bodies of cavalry charge one another, it almost always happens that one party flees before the other can meet it. Sword blows are dealt only during the pursuit.'

The word 'veteran' is important here, however. By the end of Frederick's reign the heyday of the Prussian cavalry was passed and its glories were limited to old soldiers' memories. A speech given by Frederick at Potsdam, in his last years, shows the way things were going: 'Gentlemen, I am entirely dissatisfied with the cavalry; the regiments are completely out of hand; there is no accuracy, no order. The men ride like tailors; I beg that this may not occur again, and that each of you will pay more attention to his duty, more particularly to the horsemanship.' By 1770, in fact, Frederick was beginning to completely rethink the cavalry's role. His writings give as the main reason the new reliance upon massed artillery and field fortifications that were then the hallmark of Austrian tactics. 'It is therefore necessary to impress firmly on the mind that henceforth we shall have only a war of artillery to wage, and fortified positions to assault.' Under such conditions the role of cavalry was necessarily limited, with no possibility of the old hell-for-leather charge in line. The king's instructions of that year offered the cavalry a highly qualified opportunity, far removed from the pre-eminence of Seydlitz's cuirassiers at Rossbach or Leuthen. 'The right moment [to attack] is when the enemy artillery begins to slacken its fire and the enemy infantry has already fired. Then, if your infantry has not already decided the affair, and providing the slope leading to the enemy is not too rugged, have your cavalry charge the enemy infantry in column.' Perhaps the new role of firepower was Frederick's main reason for these new instructions but the emphasis upon attacking in column almost certainly shows that he was fast losing confidence in the horsemanship and innate discipline of his troopers and was forced to take refuge in the mob-like protection of this dense but unwieldy formation.

Elsewhere in Europe, the lessons of Gustavus, Cromwell and their successors were not without effect. In France, however, there was never a full acceptance of the overriding importance of the sword and the full-blooded charge. At the end of the seventeenth century all types of cavalry attacked at the trot and, even in 1766, when the standard formation had been reduced to a line of two ranks, the normal attack was conducted *en muraille*, that is in close order but at a very restricted pace. Provision was made for another deployment, *en fourageurs*, in which the horsemen were dispersed and went forward at the gallop but it is not clear how often this was used. The French also clung on to firearms for their cavalry. In the seventeenth century, the charge at the trot was usually preceded by an attenuated *caracole* as the troops, one by one in parade-ground style, came to the front, halted, and discharged their pistols or carbines. They remained of importance in the next century, though by now the horsemen, because of their shallower formation, all fired simultaneously before spurring in to the enemy. Certain commanders did reject these tactics. Both Condé and Turenne had some success in forcing their horsemen to behave more aggressively. Marshall de Saxe also tried to get the cavalry to abandon firearms and he even advocated a return to the lance. A passage of his writings outlines very Fredrickian precepts for the management of the shock arm: 'The movements should be simple and solid; it should be taught nothing but speed and lightness; the chief point is to show the cavalry how to fight together, and not to split up . . . It is above all necessary to teach cavalry to gallop long distances. A squadron that cannot charge at full stretch for 2,000 paces without breaking order is only fit to be placed in the rear.'

In the Austro-Hungarian Empire several factors militated against the wholesale adoption of more orthodox European tactics. The presence of Hungarian and Balkan peoples within the empire meant that many of their horsemen were brought up in quite different, eastward-looking traditions where the emphasis was upon speed, dispersal and harassment (to be dealt with in the next section). The threat from the East, the Ottoman Empire, also meant that Austrian horsemen had to cope with such tactics being used against them. By the eighteenth century an explicit distinction was made between the measures orthodox horse should adopt against Christians and Turks. Firearms figured largely in both and Hapsburg cavalry never relied exclusively upon the charge. Indeed, one of their most important cavalry theorists, Khevenhüller, maintained that between 1726 and 1734 he never saw a fast charge by his cavalry. Against the Turks, firearms were relied upon almost exclusively. The horse were to form up in three ranks and move against the enemy at a very slow pace. As soon as they had closed up they were to sit tight and deliver as many volleys as possible into the Turkish ranks, with the intention of breaking them by firepower alone, rather than having to enter

Muscovite cavalry in the early sixteenth century. Despite their prolonged contact with the Mongols, the Russian horse had by this time become a very debilitated arm. Though forming the bulk of the army, their performance was generally abysmal.

into hand-to-hand combat. Firearms were almost as important in the prescribed tactics against Europeans. This time the horse were to be deployed in two ranks, each man having a pistol in both hands and a sword hanging from one wrist. They were to gallop to within 20 paces, discharge their pistols without slowing down any more than was necessary, and then come to close quarters. Nor were their guns yet redundant, for it was recommended that the troopers endeavour to brain the enemy horses with the butts of the empty pistols. This tactic is not without precedent. Spanish men-at-arms, during the sixteenth century, were universally despised because they deliberately aimed their blows at the opposing steed, rather than the rider. A saying of theirs summed up the admirable logic of this: '*Muerte el caballo perdide el hombre.*

Further east, in Russia and Poland, cavalry were proportionately more important than in other European countries. In the early Middle Ages, in both countries, knights in armour had formed the core of the armies, supplied by the great landowners and their retainers. Russia, after the Mongol invasions, slowly expanded its power and large landowners continued to supply the bulk of the fighting men. These latter displayed the usual reluctance actually to come to war when summoned and Ivan III (1462–1505) tried to create a more loyal army by giving land grants, dependent upon unquestioning military service, to the members of his own retinue. Here too the army was made up almost exclusively of horsemen, though by now Asiatic styles and tactics had become dominant. In 1553, Richard Chancellor wrote an excellent account of contemporary Russian military manners:

All his men are horsemen . . . The Horse-men are all Archers, with such Bowes as the Turkes have, and they ride short as do the Turkes. Their Armour is a Coate of Plate, with a skull on their heads. Some of their Coates are covered with Velvet or Cloth of Gold: their desire is to be sumptuous in the field, and especially the Nobles and Gentlemen ... They are men without all order in the field. For they run hurling on heaps, and for the most part they never give battayle to their Enemies: But that which they do, they do it all by stealth.

Another traveller, Giles Fletcher, in 1588, emphasized this typical link between the cavalry and the powerful land-owning groups: 'The soldiers of Russia are called ... [*deti boiarskie*] or the sons of gentlemen ... For every soldier in Russia is a gentleman, and none are gentlemen but only the soldiers, that take it by descent from their ancestors.'

However, this type of army, with its complete lack of discipline and tactical coordination was simply not adequate to the task of protecting the western frontiers or expanding in this direction. Peter the Great (1689–1725) realized this quite clearly and he set about reforming the army along western lines whilst reinforcing the nobles' and gentry's obligation to provide military service. One of his advisors, Ivan Pososhkov, in a memorandum of 1701, described the parlous condition of the unreformed cavalry:

We ourselves would feel ashamed even to look at the cavalry; they would show up on poor nags, with blunt sabres, ill-equipped, ill-clad, not

A sixteenth-century noble Russian horseman. A contemporary wrote that they were 'men without all order in the field, for they run hurling on heaps, and for the most part they never give battayle to their enemies'.

A seventeenth-century Polish
hussar. By this time the hussars in
Poland had become heavy shock
troops. This rider has feathers
attached to his shield. Others
wore them on their backs,
mounted on wooden 'wings'
strapped to the shoulders.

knowing how to use any firearms ... I can only
compare them to cattle. Sometimes, when they
would kill two or three Tatars, they would gaze
upon them in amazement and account it a great
achievement ... [even] if they had lost a hundred
men of ours.

In fact, the shortage of adequate mounts continued
to bedevil the Russian cavalry. Peter was obliged to
concentrate upon creating regiments of dragoons
rather than heavier shock troops, though the old
emphasis upon the mounted arm remained. In 1720,
for example, out of an army of just over 90,000 men,
there was a cavalry force of 33,363. But it was not
until the second half of the eighteenth century that a
substantial number of these horsemen began to be
trained in all-out offensive tactics. In 1766, the

Instruction to a Cavalry Colonel was circulated, in which
the values individual horsemanship were stressed
and which demanded the introduction of riding
masters for each regiment. In 1770 it was laid down
that firearms were only to be used in battle upon the
express instruction of the colonel of the regiment.

The pattern in Poland was broadly similar. At
first western traditions were dominant and the
armoured knight occupied the centre of the stage.
Such troops formed the main striking-force at the
battle of Grunwald, in 1410, when the Knights of the
Teutonic Order were vanquished. By this date,
however, the Poles had already formed a union with
the Kingdom of Lithuania (1385) and this state
provided a contingent of much more lightly armed,
mobile horsemen. They were armed with spears and
wore leather boots as well as the famous fur pelisse,

John Sobieski, one of the most
famous kings of Poland, who used
large numbers of horsemen to
inflict several decisive defeats
upon the Ottoman Turks.

dangling from one shoulder. By the beginning of the sixteenth century such horsemen were becoming more and more numerous, and at the battle of Orsza (1514), against the Muscovites, the first regular squadrons of hussars appeared. By the beginning of the seventeenth century, however, the hussars had become heavy shock troops. They rode powerful horses, wore a cuirass front and back, and were the first to protect their heads with the well-known 'lobster pot' helmet. They also wore the pelisse, often of leopard-skin, but their most striking equipment was a pair of 'wings' – curved pieces of gilded wood attached to each shoulder and decorated with eagles' feathers. Their weapons were the sword, a pair of pistols and a 24ft lance. Such troops were battle-winners at Klusyn (1610) against the Russians and Kircholm (1605) and Trziana (1629) against the Swedes. 3000 of them composed the elite force of the army of John Sobieski (1614–76) and executed the decisive charges against the Turks at Chocim (1671) and Leopol (1676).

The Rise of Light Cavalry

The Italian Wars, as has been mentioned already, represent a watershed in the history of warfare. A further reason for this being so was the increased role given to the light cavalry. Hitherto they had hardly been acknowledged as a distinct type of horseman, but rather seen as rapacious cowards or as the mere servants of the authentic men-at-arms. In the first years of the sixteenth century, however, though the armoured lancers still regarded themselves as the elite force, the more lightly armed troopers were increasingly regarded as having their own part to play. As the Italian Wars proceeded, three developments can be discerned. Firstly, the mounted bowmen and those that made up the bulk of the French and other 'lances' were arrayed in special formations with their own special duties. One Italian commander defined a four-fold role for them: to protect the remainder of the army, both on the march and on the battlefield; to assure the food supply; to watch the enemy's movements and bring back regular intelligence; to hover round the enemy's route of march and keep him in suspense. Secondly, special formations of light cavalry were used to a greater and greater extent. There has already been cause to mention the Albanian stradiots employed by the Venetians against the Turks. Their use spread to all European armies and the word 'stradiot' ceased to necessarily mean that the horsemen were Albanians, nor even from the Balkans as a whole. Their equipment changed slightly and they abandoned the shield in favour of

An early seventeenth-century dragoon. Even after the rejection of the pistol as the central cavalry weapon, continual attempts were made to combine infantry firepower and mounted mobility.

helmet and cuirass whilst many of them adopted the mace instead of the lance as their principal weapon. Their tactics, however, hardly changed at all and clearly show the Turkish influence. At Fornovo, for example, they conducted ceaseless charges and retirements and tempted the enemy to pursue them. Once these men-at-arms had become sufficiently disorganized and strung-out, they suddenly turned on them and cut the isolated groups to pieces. The third major development was the appearance of mounted arquebusiers. The most notable innovators in this respect were the Marquis of Pescara and Giovanni di Medici, both of whom put a substantial number of their shot on horseback so that they could keep up with the cavalry on the march and manoeuvre much more freely on the battlefield itself. Medici's men were decisive in this role at the battle of Sesia (1523) between the French and Imperialist armies. Even before this, there had been several

98

notable attempts to combine infantry and cavalry by mounting the former on the horsemen's cruppers. This was done in 1509 by raiders trying to capture Pitigliano in 1512, during a Venetian sortie against Brescia, and by the Spanish and German forces defending Brescia in 1516. Yet another variation was seen at the battle of Pavia, in 1525, when Guido Baglioni employed what was known as the 'Italian lance', consisting of a rider and two knifemen hanging on to his stirrups. The latter were responsible for dispatching or capturing those soldiers that the lancer was able to knock to the ground.

All these three developments continued throughout the following centuries. The French, in particular, made great use of light mounted men with firearms, referred to variously as *dragons* and *carabins*. Pierre Strozzi, in 1543, and Marshal de Brissac, in 1550, are variously credited with introducing the dragoon into the French army, though as has been seen the actual device of putting shot on horseback was far from new. For the dragoons the horse was purely and simply a means of avoiding fatigue on the march. As Montecuccoli put it in the mid-seventeenth century: 'Dragoons are still infantry to whom horses have been given to enable them to move more rapidly.' The *carabins* seem to have been somewhat different in that they actually fought on horseback. However, as this English description of 1587 shows, they were never expected to be able to withstand a charge. They were 'light-horsed without armour, serving either with pistol or petronell; and as the shot on foote beeinge charged doo retire for succours to theyr pikes, so these carbines may skirmidge loosely, and delivering their volleies are not able to stand any charge, but must retire to the launce for his safety.' A similar split between mounted infantry and light cavalry proper operated in the Spanish army, in the second half of the sixteenth century. Though the number of heavy cavalry remained small, sometimes as little as 8 per cent, increasing numbers of mounted arquebusiers were used, supplemented by *herreruelos*, who adopted identical tactics to the French *carabins*.

In the seventeenth and eighteenth centuries the growth of dragoons went on. The Dutch introduced them in 1609. In England, in the 1670s, certain cavalry squadrons were discouraged from shock action and taught to fire muskets from the saddle. But the experiment was fairly soon abandoned as the muskets, slung across the shoulder, with a swivel attached to help the men in bringing the firearms to bear, bumped against the men's backs when they were moving, whilst the bayonets with which they

A British dragoon of the late eighteenth century. By this time the dragoons in Britain, France and Prussia had been virtually absorbed into the regular cavalry, with whom they were expected to charge when the occasion demanded.

were also supplied proved utterly useless. With the reign of King William, English dragoons ceased to be mounted infantrymen and joined the ranks of the heavy cavalry – in tactical terms at least, for it was a long time before they received equal pay. Elsewhere the merging of dragoons and regular cavalry was not so swift. Louis XIV had many regiments raised according to the old principle. In 1658 there was only one unit of dragoons in the whole French army, but by 1690 there were forty-three regiments. Peter the Great also relied heavily on dragoons, largely, as has been indicated, because of the poor quality of Russian horses at this time. The two regiments available in 1700 were increased to thirty during the next ten years.

Frederick the Great, however, preferred the English example. At one stage he wrote: 'In many instances the dragoons must dismount and fight on foot if the infantry is not in position. Therefore they

Various seventeenth-century Hungarian cavalrymen. It was such horsemen that gave the impetus to the formation of western European hussar regiments in the eighteenth century. Their main functions reconnaissance and ambush rather than charges on the battlefield.

learn to attack on foot just like the infantry. Since this is only required of them in an emergency, however, one must not insist upon great perfection ... Their main service is always on horseback.' A similar process became evident in France. By 1770 there were thirty dragoon regiments out of a total of fifty-two for the whole cavalry. They were all expected to fight in the line, however, though it was not until 1784 that the status-conscious 'genuine' horsemen permitted the dragoons to call themselves 'cavalry'.

The other great light-cavalry innovation was the introduction of hussar regiments. The inspiration was east European, notably from Poland and Hungary, where Asiatic traditions of highly mobile, skirmishing horsemen had long been dominant. Though some of the Polish hussars evolved into heavy shock-troops, the bulk of their cavalry still clung to eastern habits. Under Stephen Batory and John Sobieski the brunt of the action was borne by clouds of Polish Cossacks, *pancerni* and Wallachians. The *pancerni* were so called because of the main item of equipment, the *pancerze*, an Old Polish word meaning coat of mail, as opposed to plate armour. The mail shirt usually had a hood attached and the riders also wore baggy trousers and boots, and were armed with bows and pistols. Under Sobieski, at the battle before Vienna, in 1683, the *pancerni* were virtually indistinguishable from the Turkish horse and had to wear twists of straw around their arms and shoulders. The Wallachians wore no armour at all and were mainly distinguished by their fur hats and thigh-length coats. They too used the bow as their principal weapon.

Hungarian light horsemen had been used as early as the mid-fifteenth century by Matthias Corvinus (1458–90). He ordered that every ten *jobbágy* (minor gentry) households should contribute one mounted soldier for service at home or abroad. But these could be called up only in time of war and were not to serve

A trooper of the 15th King's Light Dragoons in 1815. The light dragoon was the British version of the hussar. In fact, by this date, the role of the hussars was not significantly different to that of heavier cavalry regiments.

for more than three months. The bulk of Matthias's army was made up of Hussite mercenaries. In the early 17th century the emperor began to raise semi-permanent regiments of light Magyar cavalry, and in 1688 some of these were put on a permanent footing. The French were not slow in following the imperial example. In 1635, Richelieu raised a small unit of so-called 'Hungarian Horse', and in 1692 the first Hungarian officer to be seconded to European service, Colonel George Ráttky, joined the French army and, after the battle of Höchstadt (1703), took command of 300 hussars formerly fighting for the Elector of Bavaria. By 1704 there were four regiments, and another three had been added by the middle of the century. In Prussia the first regularly paid hussars appeared in 1721 and they were greatly increased by Frederick the Great. By 1786 there were something like 15,000 hussars, perhaps 10 per cent of the whole army.

Opinions as to their merits differed widely. One French soldier of fortune, de la Colonie, at the beginning of the eighteenth century, described them as 'properly speaking, nothing but bandits on horseback'. But at almost the same time Marshal Villars felt 'obliged to state that there are no troops who will serve with greater courage in the face of greater danger or will stand heavier fire or more severe losses in men and horses. There never were

A seventeenth-century Polish
light cavalryman. He carries two
swords, one for spitting his
opponent, the other, the sabre, for
hacking downwards or sideways.

soldiers better than these. I would to God our own cavalry had such spirit.' In most armies they adopted a classic light-cavalry role. De la Colonie wrote of the Austrian hussars: 'It is impossible to fight them formally, for although they may, when attacking, present a solid front, the next moment they scatter themselves at full gallop, and at the very time when they might be thought to be entirely routed and dispersed, they will reappear, formed up as before.' Thirty years later, Père Daniel gave an excellent description of their equipment and capabilities:

> The arms of the hussar are a large curved sabre, or straight-bladed and even larger variety . . . [which are] for sabering right and left and for striking downward. Some, in addition to the sabre, carry a long thin sword which they . . . place . . . along the sides of the horses from breast to crupper . . . to use to spit the enemy . . . When they employ them they rest the butt against the knee . . . Good use is made of this militia in small parties for carrying out reconnaissances, for forming the advance and rear guards, for covering forage parties or for raiding, because they are very light and mobile. However they cannot stand up against squadrons in full order of battle.

This was not always the case, in fact. Frederick the Great, always anxious to maximize the shock value of his cavalry, bluntly ordered that 'in battle we require our hussars to render the same services as the cuirassiers and the dragoons.' In fact, it was in their original role that true hussars had the greatest impact on Frederick's campaigns, though this time fighting against him. During the War of Austrian

Succession (1740–8) Maria Theresa managed, in an emotional appeal, to persuade the Hungarians to fight wholeheartedly with her. Soon there were at least 20,000 horsemen ranged against the Prussians, many of them operating in small independent bands roaming far behind Frederick's lines. He himself has given ample testimony to their disruptive activities. Referring to the operations in Bohemia, in 1742, he wrote:

> The enemy's light troops operated with such activity and success, that all food supplies were cut off, and for weeks the Prussian army was without news from Prague . . . The Hungarian troops . . . cut off all communications . . . The Prussians . . . dare not venture out of the camp, and when one attempted to make reconnaissance, one almost always had to suffer certain losses. Eventually, the royal army, trapped in camp, unable to obtain forage, and without any supplies at all, was obliged to retreat by the same road which it had taken when entering Bohemia.

Cavalry and Nobility

It should already be clear that the decline of feudal obligations, even though it necessitated the growth of professional attitudes among the medieval soldiery, did not necessarily mean that nobles ceased to serve in the royal armies. As long as they were assured that the ownership of their estates was not legally contingent upon their going to war when summoned, many of them were happy to pander to their self-esteem and flaunt their luxurious arms and equipment before one another. And for the lesser nobles war was more than mere exhibitionism. The consolidation of private estates and the growth of primogeniture produced a whole host of younger sons desperately seeking a way to make their fortune. The aristocratic ethic barred such vile pursuits as trade and manufacture, and military service remained almost the only outlet. At the worst they would be paid, and if things went well they might expect rich plunder or to so distinguish themselves in battle that they would be brought to the king's attention and rewarded with one of the offices or estates within his gift. The following biography of a knight that Froissart met, in the 1350s, shows just how important were financial considerations to such wandering soldiers:

> The first time I bore arms was under the captal de Buch at the Battle of Poitiers; by good luck I made that day three prisoners, a knight and two squires, who paid me, one with the other, 4000 francs. The following year I was in Prussia with the count de Foix . . . [then I joined] the king of Navarre in his pay . . . In Picardy . . . we took many towns and castles . . . [and] were masters of the country and rivers, and gained very large sums of money. [Later] we joined the king of England and his children . . . [but] the treaty of peace being concluded it was necessary for all men-at-arms and free companies . . . to evacuate the fortresses or castles they held. Great numbers were gathered together, with many poor companions who had learnt the art of war under different commanders . . . and they said among themselves that though the kings had made peace together it was necessary for them to live . . . [We joined the king of Burgundy and] the Battle [of Brignais] was of great advantage to the companions for they were poor, and they enriched themselves by good prisoners, and by the towns and castles which they took.

Nevertheless, though armies became more centralized and increasingly dependent upon the royal paymaster, this professionalization, particularly among the cavalry, did not necessarily involve recourse to new social groups. Referring to the Valois army of 1521, Blaise de Monluc told how he first joined one of the *compagnies d'ordonnance*: 'I was presently put into an archer's place in [de Lescun's] company, a place of great repute in those days, there being in those times several lords and great persons who rode in troops, and two or three men who were archers in this . . .' Even though the mounted archers were regarded as having a very subsidiary role to that of the actual lancer, or man-at-arms, it was in no way *infra dig* for a nobleman to serve as such.

An earlier incident, at the siege of Pavia, in 1509,

reinforces this indentification of cavalry and nobility, and also gives yet another example of how the horsemen felt that their status defined the way in which they should fight. At one stage during the battle it was suggested, not unreasonably, that the French cavalry should dismount to help storm a breach. The Chevalier de Bayard was appalled: 'Considers the Emperor it to be a just and reasonable matter to peril so much nobleness together with his infantry . . . who had not their honour as do we gentlemen?' Maximilian's German men-at-arms were equally outraged. One of their spokesmen pleaded that 'they were not such as went on foot, nor to go into a breach, their true estate being to fight like gentlemen on horseback.' The German cavalry, in fact, retained a particularly feudal appearance. The transition from sword and lance to pistol had meant that the man-at-arms' squire or batman could also be incorporated into the main body of horsemen, it being generally admitted that any fool could loose off a wheel-lock. Nevertheless, the German horse still appeared as noblemen and retainers, the former being paid according to the size of his retinue. Further east this feudal aspect persisted even longer. In Poland, in 1794, during Kosciuszko's revolt, regiments of National Cavalry were organized. They fought in two ranks; in front were the nobles and gentry carrying lances and wearing the distinctive czapka; in the second line were the ordinary troopers, usually the tenants of the lancers, and these served as squires, equipped with a carbine and wearing an inferior floppy hussar's hat.

By this time, other countries in Europe could not boast such a large contingent of genuine noblemen amongst their ranks. The sheer size of armies in the seventeenth and eighteenth centuries meant the bulk of the soldiery had to be found amongst lower social groups. No longer was a military commentator likely to point out, as did de la Noue, in 1585, that 'it is curious that the French . . . still continue to attack in a single rank. This is because no knight or nobleman can suffer another to ride in front of him.' Nor was he likely to doubt the advisability of arming cavalry with pistols on the same writer's grounds that gentlemen could hardly be expected to load and clear their own whilst one's servants were so unreliable. However, though the composition of the

(above) The Cuirassiers' last fling at Waterloo.

(below) The 17th Lancers leading the Charge of the Light Brigade.

cavalry rank-and-file changed radically, the aristocratic traditions remained. Though the catchment areas for the lower ranks were extended, the officers were still recruited from the nobility. In Prussia, Spain, Austria-Hungary, France and England the officer corps remained the preserve of the lesser nobility and gentry. In Prussia, for example, Frederick the Great carried on his father's policies and 'the officer corps in each regiment was purged of those men whose behaviour or birth was not compatible with the vocation of men of honour, and since then the officers' sense of decency obliged them to accept only gentlemen above reproach as their companions.' In France, in 1764, the marquis de Crénolles expressed identical sentiments: 'The nobility has its privileges . . . which cannot be violated without disturbing the social order. The most real one remaining is military service; the one is made for the other. When subjects destined for another type of service take up the place of gentlemen, it is a contravention of the rule.'

The centuries before the French Revolution were not a period of significant military innovation. Despite Guicciardini's reactions to the appearance of more efficient artillery, once the original shock had been overcome it became clear that there was still a role for cavalry on the battlefield as long as it desisted from charging headlong into fully manned artillery or unbroken infantry. Colin was absolutely correct when he observed that 'nearly one thousand years were needed before the invention of gunpowder really transformed war.' To this extent, the continued aristocratic domination of the army, and their insistence upon the pre-eminence of the horse in war was not absolutely at odds with tactical common sense. Yet the point is worth stressing because these years saw the formation of a fatal contradiction within European societies. Because the art of war was relatively stagnant for such a long

period, the aristocracy were able to bury themselves within the military and continue to shape their doctrines according to the precepts of their chivalrous past when, it was believed, the man on horseback, the pell-mell charge and hand-to-hand encounters had been decisive. Yet the world outside was changing. New classes were coming to the forefront and the first steps were being taken that would revolutionize human productivity. By the end of the eighteenth century the beginnings had been made in the techniques of mass production and metallurgy that were to make possible the production of precision weapons in huge quantities. Yet the officer corps was aloof from these developments, increasingly so, in fact, as real economic power passed into other hands. Whilst scientific experiment, methods of production of industrial investment all hastened the development of devastatingly powerful weapons, the military elites shut themselves off entirely and an atrophying aristocracy pored over glorious memories and the seemingly immutable rules of war. For hundreds of years they just about managed to give the impression that they knew what they were doing. The nineteenth century made many people wonder, whilst World War I belied the possibility of even amateur competence. This story will be told later, but it is important to realize at this stage the extent to which later attitudes were rooted in the survival of traditional links between the military and the aristocracy. The British High Command did not send in the cavalry at the battle of the Somme because anyone had logically proved that they had any chance. They sent them in as an act of blind faith, because centuries of stultifying tradition told that the horsemen were the masters of the battlefield, the physical embodiment of such noble attributes as panache, courage and honour. The machine gunners knew nothing of this . . .

(above) Hodson's Horse charging Sikh cavalry during the Indian Mutiny.

(below) Cavalry in action at the Battle of Nashville during the American Civil War.

6 Beyond Europe 1096 to 1800

'I am not a man for luxury and wine-cups. These shoulders and these long fingers did not win their strength for a career of ease. If the battlefield is cruel and the fighting harsh, God will be my associate, and my fortunes will triumph. You will see how I acquit myself in the fray, how on my rose-coloured charger I plunge into bloodshed . . . When I cover my breast with armour the world will have reason to fear my quiverful. No fortress that has once suffered the onslaught of my mace . . . will again call for engines of war to guard it. When my lance goes into battle, even a stone will have its heart drenched in blood.'
The Shāh-nāma *by Firdausī*

The dew comes down, the banners drizzle,
Cold bronze rings the watches of the night.
The nomads' armour meshes serpents' scales.
Horses neigh, Evergreen Mound's champed white.

In the still of autumn see the Pleiades.
Far out on the sands, danger in the furze.
North of their tents is surely the sky's end
Where the sounds of the river streams beyond the border.
Li Ho (AD 791–817)

Arabs and Turks

In 622, under the Prophet Mohammed, the Arabs burst out of the Arabian peninsula, driven to seek fresh pastures by the increasing aridity of their original homeland. For reasons that are far from clear, small Arab forces were able to inflict decisive defeats on much larger Persian and other armies. In the first battles, such as Badr, 624, they had no cavalry at all. Their mobility derived from camels, which they dismounted actually to fight – a tactic used by the Nabateans at the siege of Jerusalem in AD 67 – and their success on the field from religious fervour and a solid battle line. Within ten years, however, they had come to appreciate the importance of a genuine mounted arm and used captured horses to build up a substantial force of cavalry. Horsemen were central in such battles as Yarmūk (636), Siffīn (636) and Quādissiya (637). Camels, however, continued to be important. For many years they were the standard mount whilst on the march, serving just the same function as the European knight's palfreys.

The horsemen also occupied the same privileged political and social position as the European knight. As the Arabs pushed on into Egypt, Syria and Persia they seized large estates for themselves. The very extent of the empire forced them to allow non-Arab recruits into their armies. Such warriors had to adopt the true faith and, more importantly, were not allowed to ride horses. This was a great source of grievance to the *mawālī*, as they were called. It is interesting to note that one of the Arabs' most vehement accusations against the rebel al-Mukhtar, defeated in 687, was that he gave his *mawālī* followers horses to ride. Under the Ummayads (659–750) and the Abassids (750–1258),* however, increasing use was made of non-Arab mercenary cavalry.

Muslim tactics and equipment did not change much over the centuries. A typical Ummayad battle formation was drawn up in three lines. In the first ranks were the infantry armed with swords, in the second the mounted lancers and in the rear the horse-archers. This formation was also divided into three distinct blocks, comprising a centre and two powerful wings. There was also a vanguard of skirmishers and a rearguard to protect the baggage and supplies. The whole five-fold formation was known as the *ta'bīya*. The same basic organization was retained by the Abassids, with two important modifications. The infantry component disappeared almost completely and the cavalry lines were made

*Though the Seljuk Turks seized secular control of the Caliphate in 1055.

An Arab light cavalryman. In the seventh and eighth centuries AD such riders extended the sway of Mohammed and his successors through most of the Middle East and North Africa.

more flexible. During the time of the Prophet and the Ummayad caliphs the horsemen had formed three solid blocks but from the reign of Marwān II these were split into numerous smaller units, known as *kārādis*.

Their weapons were the sword, lance and bow. The Arabs themselves were indifferent archers, but from the beginning of the nineth century they made increasing use of Turkish mercenaries whose tactics were based around headlong charges and retreats in which three or four arrows were loosed off in quick succession. Speaking of the Saracen armies, those from Egypt and Syria, the Byzantine Emperor Leo noted that 'their sole hope of victory is based upon arrows'. But under the influence of their Arab pay-masters the Turks gained proficiency in shock tactics as well and were quite capable, at the right moment, of closing with their enemy with lance or sword. Most wore some kind of armour, either the original

Turkish leather or metal breast-plates and helmets. Most also carried a round shield and all the Turks rode with stirrups. Sometimes the lancers and archers were drawn up in separate units and on other occasions the main distinction was between different kinds of lancers. In most battles commanders and other officers of high rank wore very elaborate armour, consisting sometimes of two breast-plates and full protection for the back and limbs. Interestingly enough this equipment was known as the *tannūr*, a word which literally meant 'oven' (see the derivation of the *clibinarius* below p. 38). Certain sources seem to indicate that whole squadrons were sometimes equipped in this way. Leo wrote that the Saracens 'have copied the Romans in most of the military practices both in arms and in strategy. Like the Imperial generals they placed their confidence in their mailed lancers . . . [But], horse for horse and man for man, the Byzantines were heavier and could ride the Orientals down when the final shock came.' Describing a Muslim invasion of India, in 1192, the historian Minhaj-i-Siraj observed that there were substantial numbers of heavy cavalry present. On this occasion, however, it was the mounted archers who took most of the credit for the victory. At the battle of Tarain 'the light unarmoured horsemen were made into four divisions of 10,000, and were directed to advance and harass the enemy on all sides . . . with their arrows. When the enemy collected his forces to attack, they were to support each other and to charge at full speed. By these tactics were the infidels worsted.'

The Turkish influence is also evident in the armies of Mahmud of Ghazni, a ruler who threw off the suzerainty of the caliph in 999. In three great battles against the Abassids, Merv (999), the Transoxianan Turks, Baikh (1007), and a Hindu confederation, Peshawar (1009), as well as numerous large-scale plundering raids, he carved out a substantial empire for himself. At one battle against the Hindus, Mohammed al'Utbi wrote of 'line advancing against line, shooting their arrows against one another like boys escaped from school, who at eventime shoot at a target for practice'. But Mahmud was equally aware of the necessity for the decisive charge. Many of his horsemen were also armed with heavy maces and after they had softened up the enemy lines, by riding forward in rotation in squadrons of 500 and firing their arrows, the whole cavalry body would charge forward.

The Muslim military system was shown to considerable advantage during the Crusades (1096–1270), when the European knights proved

During the first years of the Arab conquests the camel was the most common mount and it maintained some sort of role during the following centuries. Here are depicted Saracen standard bearers of the twelfth century.

themselves consistently unable to match their elusive tactics. The Crusaders fought both Turkish and Arab armies and were soundly defeated by both. Notable defeats included the battles of Dorylaeum (1097), Carrhae (1104), Hattin (1187), Acre (1190) and Mansourah (1250). The first contact between Crusader and Muslim in open country was in June 1097. The experience was traumatic. William of Tyre left an account based on interviews with many of the survivors:

The Turkish squadrons immediately attacked our army, shooting off a great cloud of arrows that fell from the sky like hail. The first shower . . . had barely fallen when a second, just as heavy, followed it . . . Our soldiers had . . . to watch their horses fall all the time without being able to do anything to protect them . . . They tried to repulse their enemies by charging them with glaives and lances. The enemy . . . could not stand up to this kind of attack and withdrew immediately to avoid it. So our men found no one to oppose them and, failing in what they had tried to do, were obliged to fall back into the main body of our army. While they were thus retreating . . . the Turks were quickly rallying their forces and beginning to send another shower of arrows raining down . . .

Carrhae was virtually a repetition of the defeat of Crassus over eleven hundred years ago. The Crusaders, still arrogantly confident of their innate superiority over the 'heathen', left their infantry, notably the archers, behind and thus had no means of keeping the Turkish horse-archers at a distance. At one stage of the battle they were surrounded on all sides. As Fulcher of Chartres, who was present, wrote; 'Crushed one against the other, like sheep penned up in a fold, we were shut in by the Turks on every side.' The force was only saved from complete annihilation by the timely arrival of reinforcements who were able to take the Turks in the flank and drive them from the field. Carrhae was again a classic example of Muslim tactics. This time they tempted the Crusaders to charge and kept just out of range of their lances until they saw that knights and horses were utterly exhausted. Then they turned to face their pursuers and with the help of fresh reinforcements cut them to pieces.

At the battle of Hattīn, the Crusaders were again caught whilst on the march, their troubles being compounded by a desperate lack of water. Muslim tactics had changed not at all. A contemporary Christian source gives an excellent picture, hardly different from the account of William of Tyre though almost a hundred years had passed. 'The Infidels . . . were a constant trouble. When charged they are wont to fly and their horses are more nimble than any others in the world . . . When they see that you have ceased to pursue them, they no longer fly but

return upon you . . . The Turk, when you wheel about after driving him off, follows you home without a second's delay, but will fly again if you turn on him.' Once again Saladin's forces succeeded in surrounding the desperate Christians and once again they were gradually cut to pieces in the grinding series of volleys and swift charges and retreats. An Arab historian, 'Imad ād-Din, stumbled over elaborate metaphors as he endeavoured to give due credit to the victors: 'The bows hummed and the bowstrings sang, the warriors' pliant lances danced, unveiling the brides of battle, the white blades appeared naked out the sheath among the throng, and the brown lances were pastured on entrails . . . Not even an ant could have escaped and [the Crusaders] could not defend themselves by charging. They burned and glowed in a frenzied ferment. As the arrows struck them down those who had seemed like lions now seemed like hedgehogs.'

Even during the penultimate Seventh Crusade (1248–54) the basic tactics of both sides remained unchanged. A passing remark of Simon, Lord of Joinville, is a revealing encapsulation of European attitudes in that they still felt that the all-out charge alone was the 'honourable' method of warfare. Speaking of one minor incident at the battle of Mansourah, in which Joinville and his companions prevailed, he insisted: 'You must understand that this was a great feat of arms, for no one drew a bow or crossbow. It was a hand-to-hand combat with maces and swords between the Turks and ourselves, with

An unsubstantiated example of knightly technology during the Crusades. This picture is taken from an Arab manuscript.

both sides inextricably entangled.' Such was the psychological basis of Crusader warfare. Missile weapons were the devices of coward and the true *chevalier* could only seek honourable combat sitting face-to-face with his foe. Given this it is hardly surprising that the Crusaders were forced to succumb to Muslim pressure. It is arguable that their whole situation in Syria and Palestine was strategically untenable. Probably the most open-minded flexibility and a willingness to modify their tactics to match those of the enemy could not have long deferred the final outcome. What is certain is that the armoured knight's conviction of his own omnipotence, even in the face of an enemy who concentrated wholly upon keeping out of his way, was a sure guarantee of military impotence.

The picture is not completely one-sided, however. Certain occidental commanders did succeed, sometimes more by luck than judgement, in gaining temporary victories on the battlefield. Three main lessons were involved, though all were forgotten time and again. The first was the use of missile weapons. King Baldwin, in 1119, gained a clear-cut victory at the battle of Hab when he supported his knights with three strong bodies of infantry, mainly armed with crossbows, who were able to keep the Muslims at a distance and create such confusion that his own cavalry were able to effect a successful charge. At the battle of Jaffa, in 1192, Richard I of England used infantry as the core of his force. His lines were composed of spearmen, kneeling in front, with their lances pointing towards the enemy, supported by a second line of crossbowmen. Each of the latter had a second man by his side to keep his bows constantly loaded. Behind them were a mere fifty mounted men-at-arms though these, once again, were able to launch an effective charge into the disorganized enemy. The line was also bolstered by a low fence of tent-pegs in front of the spearmen, whilst the latter's shields offered further protection. None of this is new to us, of course. It has already been seen how the combination of missile weapons and physical barriers is one of the most effective counters to cavalry. Nevertheless, Richard should be given due credit for being one of the first west European commanders to realize its potential, though one is entitled to wonder whether 'chivalric' instincts might not have proved too strong had he had a strong force of knights to hand. For even if his own tactical acumen had remained unimpaired he might have been unable to back his judgement in the face of the men-at-arms' blustering bravado.

The second lesson takes us back more than a thousand years. Mark Antony had managed to extricate his forces from another Carrhae only by maintaining the strictest discipline, not allowing stragglers and refusing permission for reckless sorties against the hovering enemy. The more perspicacious amongst the Crusaders also realized the necessity for such precautions. The statutes of the Knights Templar included a strict ordinance that no rider should ever leave the ranks, except to look to his horse, or to go to the aid of a Christian in immediate danger. Any knight who broke formation for any other reason was to be expelled from the Order. Richard the Lionheart showed a similar concern for maintaining the strictest order whilst on the move. An Arab historian, Boha-ed-din, described the march from Acre to Arsouf, in 1191:

> The enemy moved in order of battle: their infantry marched between us and their cavalry, keeping as level and firm as a wall ... The infantry were divided into two halves: one marched so as to cover the cavalry, the other moved along the beach and took no part in the fighting, but rested itself. When the first half got wearied, it changed places with the second and got its turn of repose ... The Moslems sent in volleys of arrows from all sides, endeavouring to irritate the knights and worry them into leaving their rampart of infantry. But it was all in vain: they kept their temper admirably and went on their way without hurrying themselves in the least.

When Richard got near to Arsouf this discipline broke down for a time, but in the ensuing battle evidence was given that some of the knights at least had learnt a third important lesson about cavalry shock tactics. Though they broke from the column into a precipitate pursuit of the Turks hanging around their flank, on this occasion they did not carry on until men and steeds were exhausted. As soon as they had scattered the enemy they halted to regroup and subsequently delivered two more compact charges.

One way in which Muslim and Christian military systems did show great similarities was the existence of feudal landholding to permit the fielding of large cavalry forces. The first Arab forces had been based around the groupings of all free tribesmen and were known as the *muqātila*. Within a hundred years or so many of these warriors began to acquire local attachments in the conquered regions and started to reside permanently on estates granted by the government. Under the Abassids this early military aristocracy lost its original function and there emerged an essentially peace economy based upon agriculture and trade. Landholding ceased to be a military arrangement and the armies were increasingly made up of Turkish mercenaries, residing in garrisons and paid out of state revenues. By 850, however, these mercenaries had virtually taken control of the Caliphate and were powerful enough to make or break individual rulers. Their influence was profoundly disruptive and in the second half of the ninth century the administration and economy gradually fell to pieces. The state no longer had the necessary revenues to pay its soldiers in cash and the old system of supporting officers by land grants, known as *iqtā's* came back into prominence. They differed from the early Arab estates, and from European practice, in that they were handed over only for a limited period of time. Also, *iqtā'* holders were moved frequently from estate to estate to try to prevent the growth of hereditary aspirations. Such military fiefs were also very important in Egypt and Syria during the Ayyubid period, initiated by Saladin. The core of the latter's armies were Turkish and Kurdish knights and their retainers. These were divided into a few great landholders with their own slave armies and a much greater number of minor noblemen, known as the *al-halka al-khassa*. Finally, some of the sultan's personal slaves, or *mamlūks*, had fiefs of their own, a situation somewhat analagous to that of the German *ministeriales*. Again, attempts were made to limit the knight's rights to these estates and usually they were only granted the revenues therefrom, rather than the land itself, and often they were only entitled to a portion of that revenue.

The *mamlūk* system offers a further fascinating parallel to later European experience. By 1250 these so-called slaves had followed the example of the Caliph's mercenaries and were powerful enough to nominate puppet sultans, as well as having obtained rights in all the major estates. Both the Bahrite dynasty, until 1382, and that of the Circassians, until 1517, were completely under the sway of *mamlūk* knights. Yet the very power of these knights completely undermined the resilience of the Egyptian military system. Isolated from the rest of society, and from the world outside, the *mamlūks* became an ossified military elite with their own aristocratic ethic that upheld the virtues of traditional modes of combat at the expense of modern developments. They were indeed first-class light cavalrymen, using the time-honoured oriental combination of bow, sword and lance. But when such soldiers came up against the Ottoman armies, one of the few outside Europe to rely heavily upon gunpowder weapons, they found themselves at a grave disadvantage. Yet, just like the western officer corps of the nineteenth and early twentieth centuries, the *mamlūks* refused to acknowledge that firearms had altered the old balance on the battlefield. To the bitter end they continued to insist that the old methods, *furūsīya* (training in horsemanship and exercises with the lance and bow) and the self-confidence and innate superiority that come from the mastery of such exercises, must suffice. A *mamlūk* historian gave a definition of *furūsīya* that might well have been written by a nineteenth century European cavalry officer:

It is something different from bravery and intrepidity, for the brave man would throw down his adversary by force of courage, while the

A *mamluk*. Such warriors, originally Turkish mercenaries fighting for the Caliphate, became the ruling class in Egypt. Their power, and their reactionary reliance upon horsemanship and cold steel, was shattered by Ottoman gunpowder in the early sixteenth century.

horseman is one who handles his horse well in his charge and in his retreat, and who knows what he needs in matters pertaining to his horse and his arms and the arrangement of all this in a manner that he may follow the rules known and established among the peoples of this art.

But there was the rub. The 'rules known and established' had changed. The *mamlūks'* traditional art, excellent as it was, was of little value in the face of massed Ottoman batteries or disciplined volleys from the Jannissary arquebusiers. But they dare not admit this lest it undermine their supremacy within society as a whole, based as that society was upon their role as the military elite. They continued to look down on firearms as dishonourable weapons, fit only for cowards, and of no relevance to 'real' warfare or a 'fair' fight. In 1495, one young Sultan, an-Nāsir Abū as-Sa'ādāt, did try to introduce his own corps of black-slave arquebusiers. The *mamluk* aristocracy was appalled. One of their number, Ibn Iyās, wrote of an early demonstration: 'The black slaves were firing in front of him [and the whole demonstration looked] like that of a governor of a sub-district. He has disgraced the honour of the kingdom.' So the *mamlūks* were defeated again and again until the final débâcle at Marj Dabiq, in 1516, which heralded the final collapse of the empire. To the very end they protested that the whole thing was unfair and that they had never had a chance to show what real cavalry could do because of the accursed guns. After one defeat an *amir* wrote: '[If we had been able to indulge] in lance-piercing and sword-beating we should have taken them to the last man, for the Ottomans have no determination and no power except that of being able to shoot with firearms and when the shooting stops and nothing is left but sword and lance they are incapable of doing anything.'

The Ottoman Turks, whose empire was founded by Osman, in 1299, were also a redoubtable enemy for the Europeans. In this contest, however, they did not have a monopoly of gunpowder weapons and their overall role was nowhere as important as in Egypt and Syria. Their most effective weapon against the Christians were the great masses of light cavalry that made up the bulk of their forces. All their major adversaries commented on this. According to Montecuculi: 'It is not the Turkish infantry which the German infantry must fear, it is the cavalry.' Valentini wrote that 'their infantry is only an accessory to the cavalry, for which it serves as a refuge.' Prince Eugene of Savoy described their riders as 'at one and the same time the truly national and the most important weapon of the Ottomans'.

From the early sixteenth century to the eighteenth the basic Ottoman line was always the same. In the centre was the sultan with his Jannissaries and the artillery massed before them. In front of them were the foot skirmishers, the *azab*, and in the foremost position the light cavalry, or *akinji*. On the sultan's immediate left and right were the household cavalry, the *alti bölük*, and on the flanks were very large contingents of *sipahis,* the horsemen supplied by the fief-holders and their retainers. The usual Ottoman ploy was for the *akinji* to lure the enemy forward to be pounded by the artillery and musketeers and then enveloped by the *sipahi* wings, which endeavoured to close round the flanks and rear until the original crescent formation had become a noose. It was this envelopment by the cavalry that was the main pre-occupation of European commanders, rather than the effects of their firearms.

It is to be noted once again that the need to raise large forces of cavalry led to a feudal type of arrangement. Ottoman fiefs were very similar to the *iqtā's* already mentioned and were divided into two main types, according to size. The smaller estates were called *timar*s, the larger *zi'amet*s. In most of the former and all of the latter the fief-holder had to bring a mounted retinue with him when called to war. The retainers proper were known as *jebeli, sipahi* being a collective name for both lord and follower. They are often also referred to as *timariot*s. As was often the case among the Arabs, the *timar* was not a grant of land as such, but the right to enjoy the tax revenues of a particular estate or area. They were, however, usually hereditary.

The weapons of the Ottoman cavalry were the bow, sword and lance. The wealthy *timar* holders were also obliged to provide themselves with armour, usually breast- and backplates. A Venetian diplomat of 1585 observed: 'As for the cavalry, some are lightly armed with fairly weak lances, huge shields and scimitars; they look more like mummers than warriors ... Others carry nothing at all to protect their bodies, and rely chiefly on bows and arrows, with which they can do a lot of harm.' The latter type were most likely the *akinji*, as well as the *deli*s, Croatian, Wallachian, Serbian and Tatar contingents of ferocious irregular light horseman. Ironically, like their *mamlūk* counterparts, the Ottoman cavalry showed themselves most reluctant to make use of firearms that were obviously of such importance for the infantry. Referring to a sixteenth-century experiment, a French visitor recorded: 'The Turks were also against this armature because it was slovenly (the Turks, you must know, are much for cleanliness in war), for the troopers' hands were

115

Ottoman light cavalry of the late eighteenth century. Despite their early adoption of gunpowder, the Ottoman Turks continued to use horsemen to supply the bulk of their armies. Their main role was to lure the enemy on to the guns in the centre.

black and sooty, their clothes much full of spots and their case-boxes, that hung by their sides, made them ridiculous to their fellow soldiers, who therefore jeered at them.' Even though many of the sultan's bodyguard were issued with short-barrelled arquebuses in 1600, a European, sixty years later, noted a great disinclination to use them. The parallel with *mamlūk* attitudes is made even more apparent in a passage from the memoirs of Baron de Tott, who had visited Turkey in the 1780s. At one point he had become involved in a discussion about the impact of the Russian artillery during recent campaigns with the Ottomans:

> [The Russians] prevailed said [the Turks] because of the superiority of their fire, which made it impossible to come near: but when they stop this abominable fire, when they come forward like brave men fighting with cold steel, then we will see how these infidels stand up to the slashing sabres of the true believers.

For the most part the Ottomans preferred to rely on the classic eastern tactics of swift rushes and withdrawals, firing off arrows from a distance or closing suddenly to stab and slice with lance and sword. Even in the wars of 1768–74 this was the essence of their battlefield practice. A participant in this conflict, Guinement de Kéralio, wrote:

These are light troops of the best kind. They attack in lively fashion, without order, without coordination . . . They surround [the enemy] and fall upon him from all sides . . . An attack so confused is of little danger to a veteran and disciplined army; but that which allowed its lines to be broken by these troops would be lost; no one would escape because of the speed of their horses, managed by riders who rarely deal out blows without effect. One must avoid the skirmishes that they ceaselessly endeavour to provoke, small detachments, open ground and affairs of outposts. In these above all, when they are on the defensive, their courage, patience and stubbornness are extreme.

In such encounters, when they were actually allowed to come to grips, their 'slashing sabres' were probably the most effective of all their arms. In the eighteenth century yet another European observer, Valentini, had this to say about their proficiency with cold steel:

The superiority of the Turks in the use of this arm rests as much on the quality of the material as on the national manner . . . of wielding it. In the fist of a sturdy European peasant, a Turkish blade, built up of fine steel wire, would perhaps shatter like a glass at the first blow. In the hands of a Turk . . .

who slices rather than hacks ... this sabre splits helmets, cuirasses and all the rest of the enemy's armour, and separates the head from the body in an instant ... There is rarely a question of light wounds in an engagement between cavalry and the Ottomans.

The Mongols

The Mongol armies of Genghis Khan and his successors* represented the most perfect example of the eastern nomadic archer at war. Under the former's outstanding leadership, all the innate tactical expertise of these steppe horsemen was harnessed into an invincible military system. It would be impossible to over-emphasize the very magnitude of the Mongols' successes. In AD 50 they were just another agglomeration of wandering tribes and clans who gradually pushed the Huns out of their homelands in Mongolia. Under Genghis the tribes were for the first time united. In 1220 they overthrew the Kwaresmian Empire. In 1237 they overran Russia. In 1241 they plunged into Europe and smashed two armies at the battles of Mohi and Liegnitz, only stopping short of further conquests to the west because of the death of Ogodai Khan. In 1258 they captured Baghdad and took over control of the Eastern Caliphate. In 1279 they conquered China and established their own (Yuan) dynasty of emperors. In 1274 they even attempted to invade Japan, having organized massive battle-fleets, but for once the novelty of the enterprise and, more importantly, the appalling storms they encountered thwarted their attempts.

Horsemanship was the basis of their successes. Like all nomadic peoples, Mongols began to learn to ride at the earliest possible moment, largely because hunting was such an important component of their economy. Hunting, moreover, was excellent training for war. The Great Yasa, the body of laws that regulated all aspects of Mongol life, contained a reference to hunting that shows just how easily these horsemen could redirect their energies from peace to war, and how almost all their everyday pursuits were also ways to refine their military skills:

Whoever has to fight shall be trained in arms. He should be familiar with the chase to know how the hunters must approach the game, how they must keep order, and how they have to encircle the game, depending on the number of hunters. When they start on a chase let them first send scouts who shall obtain information. When they are occupied

*Notably Genghis (1167–1227), Ogodai (1229–1241), Batu (1226–1255) and Kublai (1259–1294).

Mongols in battle. Under Genghis Khan and his successors the Mongols formed the greatest cavalry army in the history of warfare. They moved faster, more unexpectedly, and destroyed their enemies more utterly than any other force before or since.

with war, they shall devote themselves to the chase and accustom their army to that. The object is not so much the chase itself as the training of warriors who should acquire strength and become familiar with drawing the bow and exercise.

The lessons of the hunt were important both for the individual, as an archer, and for practice in the coordinated action of the whole battle array. As archers, the Mongols first began to practice when they were a mere three years old. By the time they had reached early manhood all were capable of handling their compound bows with consummate skill. The bows required a pull of almost 170lb, more than that of an English longbow, and had an effective range of between 200 and 300yd. On campaign the archers carried two or three bows and two quivers of arrows, with perhaps sixty shafts in each. There were also two types of arrow, one light to fire from a distance to rain down on the enemy, and one heavy, with the points soaked in brine for piercing enemy armour at close quarters.

As regards tactics and strategy, the hunts taught the warriors the value of intelligence and swift movements *en masse*, as well as the quickest way to execute the favourite sweeping or encircling movement, the *tulughama*. The essence of the strategic ability was intelligence and mobility. In a Mongol campaign their army was divided into five or six separate columns who kept in touch by means of signals and mounted messengers. They moved far faster than any of their opponents. During September 1221, Genghis Khan, hoping to overtake the Kwaresmian Jalal ad-Din, went from Bamian to Ghazna *via* Kabul in two days without allowing his men a single halt to prepare food. The distance covered was about 130 miles, even more remarkable in that it was across some of the most rugged terrain in Afghanistan. In 1241, an army under his grandson Batu invaded Hungary and, in crossing the pass of Ruska in the Carpathians, the vanguard is reported to have marched 180 miles between 12 and 15 March. But the aim of this phenomenal mobility was not to elude the enemy but to suddenly bring the various columns together, when his own main army was least expecting it, and to utterly destroy it. Merely causing the enemy to flee was not enough. After any battle numerous detachments were sent forth to hunt down as many of the defeated remnants as possible. The sturdy horses of the steppe were the crucial factor in all these operations. Each warrior had several remounts tagging along behind so that they could continually change horses. A Hungarian bishop interviewed Mongolian prisoners and discovered that 'They are followed by many riderless horses, one man riding in front and twenty or thirty riderless horses after him.' The *Secret History of the Mongols* underlines how important it was not to overtax individual mounts:

Take care of the led horses in your troop, before they lose condition. For once they have lost it you may spare them as much as you will, they will never recover it on campaign ... You will encounter much game on the march. Do not let the men go after it ... Do not let the men tie anything to the back of the saddle. Bridles will not be worn on the march – the horses are to have their mouths free. If this is done the men cannot march at a gallop ... As for those who have disobeyed my personal orders ... the unimportant ones are to be beheaded on the spot.

The strings of horses were not simply to serve as rotas of remounts. They could also be slaughtered for food, which obviated the need for a supply column or expeditions in search of supplies.

Mongol armies were not all simple bowmen. There were two fairly distinct types of troops. One was the ordinary mounted archer, the other the more heavily armoured lancer. It seems possible that this distinction arose from the same kind of social differentiation that has been noted amongst earlier steppe peoples. Even before Genghis Khan the Mongol clans had split up into smaller groups, each with its own ruling elite based around a few noble families. Class distinctions had emerged between the horse-rearing aristocracy, the common sheep-herders, and the captured serfs at the bottom of the scale. Though Genghis united these clans together in a vast confederation, he did nothing to try to break down local social divisions. These, therefore, may well be the basis of the distinction between light and heavy cavalry. The former made up the bulk of the armies and wore little or no armour. The lancers were the members of a khan's retinue, or *nököd*, and relied upon the lance and extensive armour for themselves and their horses. Genghis Khan himself had a large imperial guard, each squadron mounted on different-coloured horses, and taken from the best of the *nökörs*. A papal ambassador of 1246, Giovanni de Plan Carpin, has left a detailed description of these heavy cavalrymen:

Many have helms and cuirasses of leather. The latter are made of strips about a palm broad, sewn together in threes and stiffened with bitumen; the sewing is so managed so that the strips overlap ... They have bardings of leather for their horses, made in five pieces, which protect them as far as their knees, and iron frontlets are fixed on their foreheads. Their own body armour ... is in four parts, a long front piece and back piece reaching from the neck to the thigh, and joined together by two iron plates fastened by buckles, and two long armpieces reaching from the shoulder to the waist. And on each leg they have cuissarts, which, like the armpieces, are joined to the body armour by straps and buckles ... Some of them carry lances, with a hook where the lance head joins the shaft, with which hooks they try to drag an adversary out of the saddle in close combat.

The lancers were the shock troops, used to deliver the decisive blow once the archers had softened up the enemy formations. The archers made up the whole of the skirmishing vanguard and usually of the centre. The flank divisions were invariably composed of both archers and lancers. A typical array here was a chequerboard of 100-man squadrons, in each of which the first two ranks were composed of lancers, the last three of archers. At the beginning of the battle the bowmen would pass through the gaps between the squadrons and deluge their opponents with arrows. Once they were considered to be sufficiently off-balance the lancers were ordered forward, to act either on their own or as the spearhead of a general charge.

Ironically, despite their shattering victories, the Mongols' military system did not leave much of a mark upon the conquered peoples. Once they had divided the conquests between the members of the imperial retinue, the Mongols were fairly easily absorbed into local cultures. Their predatory conception of statecraft and landholding set the great civilizations of the East back hundreds of years, but they occasioned no particular revolution in warfare. After the close of the thirteenth century, nomadic warfare became once again a very disparate threat – the depredations of localized bands, tribes and hordes, rather than a single concerted assault. The most famous heirs of the Mongol tradition were to be found in Russia, first the Tatars and later the Cossacks, the former authentic steppe horsemen, the latter an admixture of nomadic stock and wandering frontiersmen and freebooters.

The Tatars of the fifteenth, sixteenth and seventeenth centuries were a great menace to the newly expanding power of Muscovy. In the 1570s they inflicted two severe reverses on Ivan the Terrible at Kazan and Astrakhan. Between 1607 and 1617, and 1632 and 1634, they conducted large-scale raids into the heart of Muscovy and carried off vast amounts of booty and prisoners. The Mongol legacy is clear. The basic military unit, like that of Genghis's followers, was a group of ten men, known as the *kos*. Each man took at least three horses with him when setting forth on a raid and changed mounts as much as five times a day. The best soldiers came from the tribal aristocracy, the *mirza*, who served in the khan's retinue. There were some differences, however. The Tatars do not seem to have had the distinction between light and heavy cavalry, though some of their bands included contingents of foot arquebusiers. They operated in much smaller groups than the Mongols and tried to avoid battle whenever possible. A marauding band would set up camp in some inaccessible area and send out numerous small raiding parties, each going in a different direction every time. Also, whilst on the march, they moved slowly, to avoid tiring their horses, and relied on the nature of the terrain rather than their speed to conceal their movements.

An early nineteenth-century Cossack. The Cossacks were made up of a nucleus of descendants of the Mongols and Tatars plus a large number of frontiersmen and runaways attracted by their free way of life.

Nevertheless, when forced to fight, their tactics were very much those of the steppe nomad. A seventeenth-century source summed them up as 'monkeys on greyhounds'. Marco Polo wrote: 'When these Tatars come to engage in battle, they never mix with the enemy, but keep hovering about him, discharging their arrows first from one side and then from the other, occasionally pretending to fly . . .' The Ottomans, too, suffered from their ceaseless raiding. The Sultan Selim I observed: 'I fear the Tatars most of all. They are as fast as the wind upon their enemies, for when they march they cover five or six days' road in one day, and when they run away, they disappear as quickly. Especially important is the fact that their horses do not require shoes, nails or fodder . . . their own food, like their bodies, is nothing much.' Their main diet on the march was cheese made of mare's milk. Montecuculi was envious of the simplicity of this arrangement: 'When required for use the Tatars scrape a little into a pannikin of water, stir it up with their finger, and swallow the mixture . . . If we could all exist on such food, what a deal of trouble would be spared the world in general!'

The Cossacks, too, traced their origins to Tatar groups but they had a quite different role within the Russian state. Though they formed the backbone of many rebellions against the Tsar, their main function was to man the frontiers and hold the Tatars at bay. In 1650, the government first began to found military colonies of men deemed 'Cossacks' and eventually some of these were converted into regiments of regular hussars. From this time state subsidies were an increasingly important source of revenue and the election of Cossack leaders had to be approved in Moscow. Economy and administration became dependent on the central government, and the Cossacks never achieved the same sort of self-sufficient mobility that characterized true nomadic groups. Many of them worked on settled farms and their wages were not enough even to pay for a horse. Paid military service to the state was the only outlet for martial aspirations. Numerous Cossack regiments were formed in the eighteenth century and by 1826 there were 70,000 of these horsemen on active service. In 1881 they provided 45 per cent of a total cavalry complement of 92,000 men. They proved excellent troops. In 1775, Marshal Rumyantsev was convinced that their exploits against the Turks 'were an outstanding factor in hastening all the glorious successes of Russian arms . . . They were daunted neither by want nor by disadvantage . . . In both small and large-scale encounters they were the first into the fire, distinguishing themselves with outstanding bravery.' Unlike the Tatars, the Cossacks were not archers but relied upon muskets or rifles and long, slender lances. The former they used defensively, sometimes in the old-style wagon laagers, sometimes from behind their horses, which they made to lie on their sides as a breastwork. But their favourite cavalry formation was the *lava*, a long line, preferably overlapping the enemy's flanks, that curved in at each end. Two or three of these lines would charge at the enemy in swift succession, veering back from any strongpoints and looking all the time for gaps through which they could dash.

China

During the whole period up to the beginning of the nineteenth century, Chinese military activity was devoted to repelling nomadic threats on the northern frontiers. Except for the débâcle of 1279, when the Mongols overran the whole country, they were largely successful. Their tactics varied from period to period, sometimes aiming to beat the nomads at their own game and employing large numbers of horsemen, sometimes relying on positional defences to keep them at bay. During the Tang Dynasty (618–907), Chinese forces usually included a large cavalry component. At the beginning of this period there were at least 300,000 Bactrian horses available on state ranches, and under the most famous general of the epoch, T'ai Tsung (also known as Li Shih-min), large numbers of native cavalry and Turkish mercenaries, notably the Uighurs, were recruited. Many of the native horsemen wore metal armour, some being armed with very powerful crossbows, others with lances.

The state had at an early date assumed responsibility for the recruitment and equipping of the armies and their leaders never had to fall back on the normal expedient of buying cavalry service with grants of land or the revenues therefrom. At the beginning of the Tang period, however, there was an attempt to create a semi-professional militia based on small free landowners in the frontier districts, analogous in some ways to the Byzantine thematic system. The idea was not new. It had been introduced in western Wei in AD 542, and the Sui emperors had made use of it in the late sixth century, as they attempted to reunite the empire. Speaking of the first years of the following century, the historian Tu Mu gave a brief description of how it worked: 'For three out of every four seasons [the landholders] worked at farming . . . For one season they perfected themselves in the military skills of riding, swordsmanship and archery, being examined by the lieutenant-colonels. Fathers and elder brothers gave instruction, and were allowed to have no other profession.' However, the very success of these soldier-farmers worked against them; just as in the Byzantine Empire, when the frontier areas were pacified they were bought up by powerful nobles who now saw them as attractive investments. By the end of the seventeenth century there were insufficient militia men to protect the borders adequately and the emperors had to rely more and more on paid professionals living in barracks. Towards the end of the Tang period the native cavalry had almost entirely disappeared, though large forces of mercenaries were still called upon occasionally, as in 883, when Sha-t'o Turks were used to expel the invading armies of Huang T'ao. At the beginning of the Sung period (960–1279) a contemporary commentator, Sung Ch'i, was bemoaning yet another of those military lapses when the Chinese showed little evidence of being able to master the equestrian skills of their enemies: 'The reason why our enemies to the north and west are able to withstand China is precisely because they have many horses and their men are adept at riding; that is their strength. China has few horses, and its men are not accustomed to riding; this is China's weakness.'

During the Sung period the cavalry remained at a very low ebb. A further reason for this was that large areas of northern China had been overrun by Khitan nomads who established their own independent

A Cossack.

dynasty which lasted from 916 to 1119, and this deprived the emperors of almost all the traditional breeding areas for their horses. But it did not mean that the Chinese were militarily weak. A prodigiously efficient production machine was created that enabled the generals to put huge, well-armed infantry armies into the field and these were quite capable of warding off all but the largest cavalry offensives. At one time the Sung had one and a quarter million men under arms, with their manufactures turning out three and a quarter million weapons annually as well as several thousand sets of armour, in three standardized types. The infantrymen thus equipped were armed with crossbows or halberds, the basis of their tactics being a laager of iron-sheathed carts, chained together, behind which the halberdiers presented a protective barrier to the archers. As Han Ch'i, a Sung official, wrote: 'Because they could be used on the level lands of Hopei, it was possible to stem the headlong rush of the enemy on the battlefield, and by forming them into an array, to form a strongpoint.' Only against the Khitans did this method prove inadequate. These latter realized that the crossbows could easily outrange their own archery and they were astute enough to make the necessary tactical adjustments. Firstly they copied the ponderous Sung iron armour, turning it out in large quantities from their own production points. Then the mounted archers were divided into three types, according to skill. The best, who fought in the front ranks, were given full armour, as were their horses. The second category wore half-armour and the worst had none at all. Later the Khitan cataphracts exchanged their bows for halberds and were used to come to close quarters with the Chinese, forming a protective screen for the bowmen. As Li Kang, one of the most forceful advocates of the armoured carts noted: 'The men of China rely above all on armoured horsemen to obtain the victory.' The power of their empire was overcome, in the devastating campaign of 1114, only because the Chinese recruited large numbers of nomadic Jurchet horsemen. Like the later Mongols, these latter divided horsemen into two categories, archers and armoured lancers, and they were able to fight the Khitans on their own terms.

As regards mounted warfare, the remaining history of Imperial China is of scant interest. Nomadic groups were always the chief enemy, except for the brief and disastrous encounters with European firearms in the nineteenth century, but the Chinese were never again able to field effective cavalry forces of their own. The Ming emperors (1368–1644) had a very large army but almost all

were infantrymen. Most were musketeers or halberdiers and extensive fortifications were employed to break up the enemy's charges. Under the Manchus (1644–1911) cavalry vanished almost entirely. The few that remained formed an elite group in the central army, and were armed with crossbows almost to the very end. Typically, these proud horsemen remained very contemptuous of firearms, perhaps not without justification. Engravings of the battle of Altshur, in 1759, purport to show the horse-archers of General Fu-te defeating Hodja mounted musketeers during a war in the north west.

Japan

As picturesque as it is, the military history of Japan has only a few basic lessons to offer in the field of mounted warfare. The whole period up to the nineteenth century can be divided into three broad areas: the pre-Samurai era, until the tenth century; the pre-gunpowder era, until the mid-sixteenth century; the era of Samurai ritualism.

Until the seventh or eighth century AD warfare was the province of a tribal warrior elite. Then, during the Nara period, all peasants became state serfs who owed taxes and military service to their overlord. By the tenth century, however, this land system was beginning to break down and large private estates expanded rapidly. As the peasant army declined in numbers, individual landowners came to rely more and more upon bands of private retainers. At first these warriors lived with their lord on his estate, but increasingly they were granted their own fiefs in return for the promise of military service when called upon. Under the Kamakura Shogunate (1185–1334) a network of military vassals grew up which had much in common with the feudal system of medieval Europe. Just as was the case in Europe, the vassals provided military service as heavily armoured horsemen, known generally as *samurai*. There were, however, important differences from European practice, even on the purely military level. The main Japanese weapon was the bow, more akin to the English longbow than to the compound weapon of the Hunnic and Mongolian steppes. Their mode of warfare was known as the *Kyûba-no-Michi*, the Way of the Horse and the Bow, and the ceaseless training to become expert in these aspects of the military art

(above) Indians bringing back stolen horses after a raid – a painting by C. M. Russel.

(below) A United States cavalry officer in campaign dress, painted by Frederic Remington.

(*opposite*) British Hussars charging Zulus in 1879. The popular image of the cavalry, depicted here, ignored the fact that machine guns did most of the damage.

A seventeenth-century *Samurai* warrior, depicted by a contemporary Dutch artist. Until the introduction of gunpowder in the sixteenth century, the mounted *Samurai* dominated Japanese battlefields. Their prime weapon was the bow rather than the sword.

was very similar to the *mamlūk* system of *furūsīya*. As the *Yoshisada-ki* expressed it, in the early fourteenth century: 'For statesmen, the practice of arms is of supreme importance. They consist of archery, horsemanship and strategy.'

Yet strategy, and to a large extent tactics, were noticeably lacking during the Kamakura and the following Ashikaga Shogunate (1338–1573). Battles tended to follow a distinctly Japanese pattern and had little in common either with the close-packed charge of the western knights or with the hit-and-run archery of the Asian mainland. The emphasis was almost exclusively upon individual prowess. Battles were in three stages. After both armies had drawn up, a leading notable from each side would trot forward and give a tediously detailed recital of his own ancestry and of the justness of his army's cause. Sometimes this would lead to a contest of arms between individual champions. Next, two 'humming arrows' were fired into the air to signal a general exchange of arrows. To be sure of hitting their targets with sufficient force the *samurai* had to come within 50yd of each other. After the arrows were expended, or one side had decided that the wind or terrain favoured their opponents too much, the horsemen would charge forward, though little

momentum could have been built up over 50yd or so. The object was not to smash through the enemy line but to seek out a worthy opponent, of at least equivalent rank and merit, with whom to do combat. As a modern historian has justly remarked: 'There must have been considerable confusion as the various warriors milled about shouting their qualifications.' Once a suitable adversary had been found, both warriors began to hack at each other with their swords, not so much to deal a fatal blow – then virtually impossible because of the extensive lacquered steel armour – as to unseat the other prior to leaping down and slitting his throat with a sharp dagger.

Infantry were of negligible value in these battles, though after the Ōnin Wars (1467–76), which temporarily smashed the power of the Shogunate, some importance was attached to the presence of contingents of light spearmen known as *ashigaru*, or 'lightfeet'. Foot-archers seem not to have been used at all, doubtless because the *samurai* were not willing to forego their monopoly of the bow. Nevertheless, as elsewhere, it was missile weapons that ended the primacy of Japanese horsemen. Arquebuses had been introduced by the Portugese, and in the 1570s they spread rapidly. A decisive battle was at Takeda,

An Indian horse-archer of the
Mughal period. For most of her
history Indian armies relied
heavily upon their cavalry arm.
Repeated nomadic invasions led
to the widespread adoption of
mounted archery.

in 1575, when Oda Nobunaga broke up his
opponent's cavalry charges using musketeers behind
barriers of spearmen and pointed stakes. At about
this time Takeda Shingen, the lord of the province of
Kai, is supposed to have announced to his retainers:
'Hereafter guns will be the most important.
Therefore decrease the number of spears and have
your most important men carry guns. Furthermore,
when you assemble your soldiers, test their marks-
manship and order that the selection be in
accordance with the results.' In 1573, his army
included only 30 per cent horsemen, whilst in 1590,
Toyotomi Hideyoshi ordered that one of his armies
need not include more than thirty horsemen.

Hideyoshi, along with Tokugawa Iesaya, was the
founder of the Tokugawa Shogunate (1603–1867).
Their pacification of Japan, at the turn of the
sixteenth century, was based upon the use of
firearms. They were very conscious of the power that
their units of musketeers gave them and were loth for
the monopoly to slip from their hands. Thus there
arose in Japan yet another example of a cavalry elite
setting their faces resolutely against the use of
firearms, though this time because their rulers
deliberately encouraged such an attitude. Samurai
were explicitly forbidden to own firearms and the
dissemination of technical information about them
was banned. The horsemen were encouraged to
believe that the use of guns was demeaning and, from
the seventeenth century, much greater importance

was attached to the artificial code of *bushidō* which stressed personal virtue and courage at the expense of rational military analysis. Just as chivalry came to prominence at the very time when the power of the European knights was on the wane, as a last attempt to restore their pre-eminence through caste exclusivity, so did the formalization of the *samurai* ethic coincide with their military impotence.

India

It has already been seen how dependent Indian rulers were on their cavalry. This continued to be true right into the nineteenth century. In the Gupta Empire, during the fourth century AD, great reliance was placed upon heavy mounted archers rather akin to the later horsemen of Belisarius. An Indian source tells us that 'each horseman was equipped with a coat of mail going down to his knees, a powerful bow and quiver of arrows. The cavalrymen marched in well-ordered lines in close formations. Chariot formations of earlier times were conspicuous by their absence.' The use of the bow was not typical of Hindu warfare, however, and later horsemen tended to rely upon the lance and sabre. Such troopers were the *Rajputs*, a distinct Hindu military caste based upon descendants of the Sakas. They formed a kind of chivalric brotherhood, all members of which were entitled to handle sword, bow and lance and to ride horses. Their tactics were based upon the charge. Their line usually galloped in at full tilt until one section of it suddenly peeled off and attempted to get around the enemy's flank. They were employed by local rajahs and many of them were given grants of land in return for rendering mounted service when summoned. As was common in the East these grants were neither inalienable nor hereditary.

From the beginning of the eighteenth century extensive portions of the Indian subcontinent were dominated by Muslim invaders. There has already been cause to mention one of these, Mahmud of Ghazni. Another important figure, the real founder of the Muslim domain in India, was Mohammed Ghori who defeated a *Rajput* army at the battle of Tarain, in 1192. The Hindu cavalry showed themselves incapable of countering Ghori's classic tactics. His light mounted archers were divided into five divisions, four to lay down a constant harassing fire, and the fifth held in reserve for the final charge. As Muslim rule was imposed, the usual Middle Eastern methods of providing troops were similarly imposed. The bulk of the soldiers were cavalry and these were brought to battle as the retainers of the *iqtā'* holders. In India the *iqtā'* was known as a *jagir* and consisted either of a grant of land or a

percentage of the revenues from that land. A Muslim historian, Sham-i-Siraj Afif, has left a description of the arrangements made by Firoz Shah, who ruled from 1351 to 1388.

> The soldiers of the army received grants of land enough to support them in comfort, and the irregulars received payment from the government treasury. Those soldiers who did not receive their pay in this manner were, according to their necessity, supplied with assignments upon the revenues. When these assignments of the soldiers arrived in the fiefs, the holders used to get about half the total amount from the holders of the fiefs.

Jagir-holders were often known as *mansabdars*, and the retainers they supplied were of two kinds. Some, known as *silladars*, supplied their own horses and equipment whilst others, the *bargirs*, were kitted out by their lord. Many *bargirs* came from important slave tribes such as the Muizzi and the Shamsi.

The same kind of semi-feudal system was retained by the Mughal Emperors after Babur's conquest of India in 1525. The historian 'Abbas Khan wrote of the sixteenth-century Mughal army under Shir Shah and he reveals how the *jagirs* were used as depots for continual reinforcement or renovation of the army in the field: '[He] always kept about him 150,000 horsemen and 25,000 infantry, armed with matchlocks or bows, and on campaigns he had more . . . . After a time he would call in the troops who had enjoyed ease and comfort on their *jagirs*, and send away in turn the men who had toiled and endured in his victorious army.'

The original Mughals were descendants of the Uzbek Turks and during their rule in India they never abandoned their reliance upon horsemanship. Their cavalry trained incessantly, as individuals, and resurrected many of the ludicrously elaborate exercises laid down in the *Arthashastra*. Their equipment consisted of a sword, either curved or straight, a shield, a battle-axe or mace, a short convex bow, occasional pistols and a long steel-tipped lance known as the *neza*. Most wore armour. An account of the battle of the Ganges, in 1540, tells of 40,000 cavalrymen 'all mounted on *tipchak* horses and clad in iron armour'. The latter was sometimes chain-mail alone and sometimes supplemented by breast- and backplates. Man for man the Mughals were easily a match for the later European invaders but they suffered from an almost complete lack of discipline. Mounstart Elphinstone criticized their inability to fight for any sustained period: 'They formed a cavalry admirably fitted to prance in a procession and not ill-adapted to a charge in pitched

Sikh cavalry, in 1849, being charged by the 3rd King's Own Light Dragoons. Until their adoption of European uniforms, drill and tactics the Sikhs were formidable guerrilla horsemen.

African cavalry in northern
Nigeria in 1670. Cavalry formed
the basis of many of the Savannah
kingdoms of Africa right up until
the nineteenth century.

An Abyssinian mounted warrior.

battle, but not capable of any long exertion, and still less of any continuance of fatigue and hardship.' R. O. Cambridge, who fought against them in the mid-eighteenth century, was careful to counter any racialist assumptions: 'Those are greatly mistaken who attribute their dread of firearms and particularly of artillery to a dastardly disposition and an invincible timidity. The true cause lies in the inexperience of their leading men who never understood the advantages of discipline and who have kept their infantry on too low a footing.' Cambridge also noted that for many of the *silladars*, their horse and equipment was everything they owned, and thus caution was not 'so much for their lives as for their fortunes'.

The Mughal armies were not the only Indian cavalry force. Two other states emerged in the seventeenth century, the Marathas and the Sikhs,

both of which placed great reliance on horses. Both also used their cavalry in a different way from the Mughals and owed little to the traditions of nomadic tribesmen. The Marathas made their first gains with foot-soldiers, mainly because of the mountainous nature of their homeland. Later, however, great numbers of horsemen appeared and were used for extended raiding and ambush. All their cavalry was very light. Swords and small shields were the chief weapons and hardly anyone wore armour. Most were clad only in a turban, breech-clout and ample cloak, though some tried to protect themselves with quilted cotton jackets. In the eighteenth century, however, the very success of their mobile guerrilla operations convinced them that they were capable of taking on European armies on equal terms. Regiments of infantry were formed and were given uniforms and drilled by European mercenaries. This

worried many British observers but one at least was astute enough to realize that the Marathas had renounced their most effective tactics in favour of a mode of warfare that would take long years to master. In an argument with his brother, the Governor-General, Arthur Wellesley observed: 'With no infantry the Maratha cavalry would commence those predatory operations for which formerly they were so famous . . . I should still consider those operations to be more formidable to the British Government than any infantry that they can form. On this ground, therefore, I think that they should be encouraged to have infantry rather than otherwise.'

The Sikhs made just the same mistake and were duly defeated in the two Sikh wars, in the first half of the nineteenth century. Prior to that, however, they had relied almost exclusively upon mobile groups of light horsemen. What infantry there were were treated with contempt. 'The infantry soldier was considered altogether inferior to the cavalry and was in time of war left behind to garrison forts, to look after the women or to follow, as best he could, the fighting force, until he in his turn could afford to change his status and buy or steal a horse for his own use.' Unlike the Mughals, all Sikh cavalrymen had to supply their own horses and this fact alone was sufficient to make them very cautious about launching head-on charges. An excellent account of Sikh cavalry tactics in the 1790s, by a contemporary observer, shows that their horsemen were much more like true dragoons than other conventional Indian cavalry:

The predilection of the Siques for the matchlock-musquet and the constant use they make of it,

A Galla tribesman in eighteenth-
century Ethiopia.

causes a difference in their manner of attack from that of any other Indian cavalry; a party from forty to fifty advance in a quick pace to a distance of carbine shot from the enemy and then, that the fire may be given with the greatest certainty, the horses are drawn up and their pieces discharged, when speedily, retiring about one hundred paces, they reload and repeat the same mode of annoying the enemy. Their horses have been so expertly trained to a performance of this operation that on receiving a stroke of the hand they stop from a full career.

Africa

In the last few years serious examination of the history of pre-colonial Africa has begun and scholars are beginning to piece together the essential features of African warfare. One basic point that has so far emerged is that in certain parts of Africa cavalry was of great importance. The main cavalry region was the Sudan, a broad belt of savannah, or sparse scrubland, stretching from the Atlantic to the Nile delta and Ethiopian mountains. To the north there is desert and to the south thick forest, both obviously areas in which it is impossible to rear horses. These animals had been present in the Sudan for many hundreds of years, all of them small, scraggy but very tough beasts. Certain peoples, such as the Bedde and the Angass, had ridden them from the beginning, though their equestrian techniques were exceptionally rudimentary. They had neither stirrups nor saddles and had a unique way of keeping

their seat. An early twentieth-century traveller wrote: 'The natives ride their mountain ponies bare-backed, and as they themselves wear no clothing, with the exception of a . . . loin-cloth of plaited grass, riding the frisky ponies is somewhat difficult. So they scratch the backs of their animals until the blood exudes, and glue themselves to the beasts with their blood.' These tiny ponies were known in various parts of Africa and several peoples had recourse to them as a means of improving their mobility in wars with other groups. East of the Niger, Seku founded the Dyula Empire of Kong, at the beginning of the eighteenth century, using musketeers mounted on such ponies. In south-west Africa, during the eighteenth century, conflict between the Nama and the Herero was chronic and indecisive. But the balance was tipped in the following century when the latter obtained horses and guns from Cape Khoi groups fleeing from the Cape Colony. In what is now Lesotho, in the 1830s, the Sotho tribe under Moshoeshoe transformed themselves into mounted gunmen to fight off Griqua and Korana bandits. It was the Sotho, in fact, that developed the famous 'Basuto pony'.

Amongst such groups, however, the horse was simply a means of getting from place to place, rather than an adjunct to authentic cavalry shock action. Only in the Sudan did the latter type of horsemen emerge. The process began in the fourteenth and fifteenth centuries when much larger steeds were imported from the north, in return for slaves, and some selective breeding was undertaken. In the savannah region several states emerged, whose military power was founded upon large numbers of cavalry. Amongst these were Mali, Songhay, Bornu, Habe, Mossi and Kano. Further south certain of the Yoruba peoples established the Oyo Empire, whose army included important cavalry contingents, at least from the 1670s. The rest of the Yoruba states were infantry powers because beyond the Oyo frontiers the savannah changed into thick rain forest. There were also important cavalry forces in Ethiopia. Some were highly mobile raiders, such as the Galla tribesmen, though there seems to have been an attempt to build up a more regular central strike-force. An Arab historian has described the reign of King Yeshaq (1412–27) whose 'power grew thanks to a Circassian *mamlūk* . . . who came to his court and established there an important arsenal in which were stored . . . sabres, lances, armoured coats, etc . . . An *amīr* named Altunbughā . . . being well versed in the art of arms and in cavalry tactics . . . gained a strong influence over the king, teaching his soldiers archery and fighting with lances and sabres.' A Portugese traveller of the first half of the seventeenth century also mentioned an Ethiopian cavalry force, though he made no reference to mounted archers. The men fought with light javelins and only a limited number were clad in chain-mail. One curious feature he mentioned was that the Galla auxiliaries used stirrups but placed only their big toe in them.

It is difficult to discover exactly how the savannah kingdoms used their cavalry. Pitched battles were rare, most military ventures being raids in search of slaves and plunder. One western account of Yoruba warfare ascribes to the horsemen a fairly conventional battle role, not dissimilar to that of Hannibal's Numidians:

> The duties of the cavalry are to reconnaissance, to hover about the enemy waiting for an opportunity they can take advantage of such as a weak or unguarded point through which they can dash to break the ranks of the enemy, and throw them into confusion. Also to cover retreats on a defeat or to cut off stragglers when pursuing an enemy.

Certainly their actual fighting must have been done hand-to-hand for there is hardly any record of these peoples using mounted bowmen. From time to time, however, they probably put some of the foot-archers on horseback to increase their mobility in intransigent terrain. There is some evidence for a split between light and heavy cavalry, the latter presumably being the ones who were to break through the enemy's lines. In the Oyo Empire, for example,

A warrior from central Africa wearing quilted armour.

there existed a separate body of *bada*s, the personal knights of the principal chieftains, each with his own small retinue. Both types definitely existed in the kingdoms of the Mossi complex, though the heavy horsemen were used in an exclusively defensive role, whilst the lighter went out on the long-distance raids that were the hallmark of Mossi warfare. The state of Macina, in the interior delta of the Niger, is supposed to have maintained a special force of heavy horsemen whose function was to knock down the mud walls of enemy fortresses by hacking at them with huge, shovel-shaped stirrups. The most common weapons were the throwing javelin, for the light horsemen, and the lance. The latter was 6 to 7ft long and was wielded at arm's length rather than couched. Certain Hausa warriors wore two or three pounds of stone bangles on their arms to increase the force of a downward thrust. Some horsemen also wore armour. Chiefs and others wore imported mail hauberks, though more common were quilted cotton jupons stuffed with kapok or paper. A few had metal helmets as well but again the rank and file had to make do with straw or cloth hats reinforced with

Fulani horsemen in 1903. Such riders pitted themselves against European troops and Maxim guns at the Battle of Sokoto, where they were mown down in their hundreds.

leather and surmounted by a turban. Some horses were protected with *lifidi* armour, which dates from the reign of Sarki Kanajeji (1390–1410), the king of Kano. It was not used by the Yoruba cavaliers of the Oyo Kingdom. It took the form of a quilted blanket that went over the chest and shoulders. Sometimes the horse's head was protected by a metal face-plate.

It is not yet clear to what extent this reliance upon substantial cavalry forces brought in its wake typical feudal arrangements. In many states there seems to have been a mixture of the centralization of the Assyrian or Mauryan Empires and necessary concessions to local autonomy. Thus it was usual for the ruler actually to arrange for the importing of horses and to purchase them. But these were then portioned out amongst the individual landowners, who had to bear the cost of their upkeep. This was a considerable burden because horses were not allowed to graze and so all had to be stable fed. This undoubtedly led to the landowners being allowed more control over the revenues of their holdings, and it has been noted by specialists how the cavalry states of the savannah tended to be more decentralized than the autocracies of the coastal forest regions. In the latter, firearms and infantry were the key weapons. The king purchased the firearms, just as his savannah counterpart did the horses, but the former then had few further worries about the cost of upkeep and could store the guns in his own palace, distributing them to his slave regiments when necessary. The role of the infantry in the savannah armies further underlines the point. They were usually the king's slaves, just as in the forest states, whereas the cavalry were free men and often formed a military and political elite. We have already noted the existence of the Yoruba *bada*s. In the Oyo Empire, in fact, the power of the noble horse owners came to be a threat to royal power. One king,

Alafin, tried to counter this by appointing seventy royal slaves to oversee the organization of the cavalry. In the eighteenth century, however, the monarchy lost control of these men too as they forgot their servile origins and merged with the traditional nobility.

As everywhere else, it was firearms that ended the supremacy of cavalry in Africa. The main battles were not fought, as one might expect, between Africans and Europeans, but between the indigenous armies. Firearms became available from a very early date and helped certain groups to overcome their mounted rivals. In 1591, at the battle of Tondibi, the Songhay Empire was overthrown by Moroccan spahis armed with arquebuses. In the early eighteenth century the Asante burst out of the coastal belt into the savannah and their musketeers faced up to several cavalry armies and beat them handsomely. In 1769, the Ethiopian usurper, Mika'el Suhul, finally put an end to the depredations of the Galla when he purchased large numbers of muskets for his army. After the break-up of the Oyo Empire, some of the smaller states that emerged continued to field substantial numbers of cavalry whilst others preferred to improve their infantry. The two policies were put to the test at the battle of Osogbo (1845), when the cavalrymen of Ilorin were utterly defeated by the musketeers of Ibadan. A feature of nineteenth-century Nigerian history was the fierce *jihads* of the Muslim Fulani who soon began to adopt horses, at least for part of their armies. Substantial cavalry forces remained right up until the twentieth century when the Fulani were unfortunate to incur the displeasure of the British. A battle was fought at Sokoto, in 1903, when the horsemen insisted upon repeatedly charging a British square that included five Maxim guns. They were mown down without the slightest difficulty. A Fulani prisoner expressed his bewilderment about this new type of warfare, in which neither side ever got to grips, and his remarks are a fitting epitaph for African cavalry and indeed for all those bold cavaliers for whom the *arme blanche* and face-to-face combat were the essence of warfare: 'War now be no war. I savvy Maxim gun kill Fulani five hundred yards, eight hundred yards far away . . . It be no blackman . . . fight, it be white man one-side war. It no good . . . Black man not get come near kill white man. If he come near he die.'

7 The New Mamlūks 1789 to 1914

'A hussar who is not dead at thirty is a blackguard.'
Comte de Lasalle

'Our cavalry must be officered. We may require from the candidates either money or brains. The supply is most unlikely to meet the demand if we endeavour to exact both.'
Mr Akers-Douglas, 1903

The Napoleonic Wars

The campaigns of Napoleon had a baleful influence upon the subsequent military history of Europe. For those who pondered over them afterwards they seemed to show beyond doubt that the sole aim of war to bring about a short series of massive battles in which vigorous offensive tactics would win the day, and so end the war. Preparatory manoeuvring and the will to close decisively with the enemy against his weakest point seemed to be far more important than any considerations of the sheer material balance of forces. There was truth in this at the time because the firearms of Napoleon's era were still not much different from the muskets of 200 years previously. The well-timed charge could still be a crucial move. Yet the signs were already there that times were changing. Napoleon's field artillery had been vital in softening up the enemy's battalions prior to the assault, whilst the disciplined volleying of Wellington's lines had time and again brought French columns to a halt in the Peninsula. But what remained in the minds of later theorists and practising soldiers were the great set-piece battles, the Marengos, Jenas and Wagrams in which the concerted offensive had won the day. Napoleonic warfare seemed a military ideal. The marches and manoeuvres before the battle were the acme of strategical skill, by which the shrewd could almost defeat the enemy simply by moving his units around on the map and by paying due regard to such a timeless formula as the *manoeuvre sur les derrières* or the 'strategy of the central position'. On the battlefield itself the decisive moment came when the drums rolled, the soldiers cheered and the battalions or squadrons charged forward and physically came to grips with the enemy. Morale, courage and honour were still concepts that counted. Throughout the nineteenth century, European officers continued to believe that this was the reality of war. The Germans were particularly attracted to this paper warfare and spent their time drawing up detailed railway timetables and strategic plans in which victory was to be won by detailed staff work. The French and British tended to stress battlefield capabilities and consistently assumed that the very fact of being a Frenchman or an Englishman, almost independently of weaponry, logistics or technical expertise, was of itself enough to bring victory.

The cavalry, of course, was regarded as the vital battle-winning arm, and here too the lessons of Napoleonic warfare seemed ample justification. The horsemen Napoleon inherited from his revolutionary predecessors made up a very sorry force. Their record had been one of almost unmitigated disaster

Napoleon's cuirassiers. These regiments formed the core of the Emperor's heavy cavalry. Mounted on large horses, and equipped with steel breastplates and helmets, they were similar to Cromwell's Ironsides and like them they usually attacked at the trot. They were largely destroyed during the Russian campaign of 1812.

in which poor mounts and inadequate training led to a whole series of fiascos, relieved only by that one French regiment which, in January 1795, earned the unique distinction of capturing a small fleet of Dutch ships, when they attacked across an ice-bound river. Napoleon's military studies had convinced him that the cavalry were vital in war and he immediately set about building them up. Throughout his campaigns he never lost faith in their capabilities. At one stage he wrote:

Cavalry is useful before, during and after the battle. General Lloyd asks what is the use of large amounts of cavalry? I say that it is impossible to fight anything but a defensive war, based on field fortifications and natural obstacles, unless one has practically achieved parity with the enemy cavalry. For if you lose a battle, your army will be lost.

Even on St Helena his mature judgement was that 'without cavalry, battles are without result'.

The *Grande Armée* included three types of horsemen. The elite, and supposedly decisive force on the battlefield were the heavy regiments, notably the cuirassiers. There were fourteen regiments of the latter, equipped with metal *casques*, plate armour front and back, a heavy sword and two pistols. The other 'heavies' were the two regiments of carabiniers who, after 1809, were equipped in exactly the same way as the cuirassiers. Both were mounted on the largest horses available, French supplies being supplemented by periodic hauls of Prussian and Austrian mounts. They were organized in separate divisions and formed the backbone of Napoleon's reserve cavalry. This force was completely distinct from the seven *corps d'armée* and was made up of two divisions of heavy horse, four of dragoons and one of light cavalry. The force was not only kept administratively separate but was held apart in battle, mainly to deliver the *coup de grâce* against the flank chosen as the *point d'appui*. After 1812, the heavy cavalry never again attained its earlier effectiveness. All the regiments were destroyed during the Russian campaign, in which the whole cavalry force suffered grievously in the snows of Russia. Almost all the horses died and towards the end of the campaign Napoleon was obliged to unite his 500 remaining horsemen into the so-called Sacred Squadron, in which full generals were to be found serving as troop commanders. It was never possible to surmount the dearth of mounts and trained men thereafter. The memoirs of de Gonneville, where they deal with the prelude to the 1813 campaign, are eloquent testimony to the difficulties involved. He was a colonel in charge of training a new cuirassier regiment and the first time he gave the order to draw swords, many scores of horses bolted. A whole squadron stampeded away for a mile or so and all the remaining lines got hopelessly entangled. Many troopers fell off their horses and it was at least two hours before order was restored out of the ensuing chaos and confusion.

The tactics of the French heavy cavalry were based upon shock action. In theory the massed charge was a carefully graduated affair, very similar to that of Frederick the Great's horsemen. The first third of the distance between them and the enemy was to be covered at the trot, when the pace was to quicken to a canter. At 150yd from the target this changed to a gallop and the last 50yd were to be covered at full speed. Contemporary accounts seem to indicate that this was rarely the case in practice. Unlike Frederick's cuirassiers, the French charged in dense column and their pace rarely got beyond the trot. A closer comparison would be with Cromwell's Ironsides. As Count von Bismarck, an eye-witness, wrote: 'The cuirassiers laid special stress upon riding boot to boot, and never moved at a faster pace than the trot.' Hohenlohe's *Conversations upon Cavalry* discussed Murat's handling of the reserve cavalry during the 1812 campaign:

> Murat did not lead his cavalry at all according to the principles of Frederick the Great. He formed deep massive columns, and put them in motion toward the point of attack. Not one of the horsemen in these masses would have been able to give his horse another direction had he wished to do so. Besides, Murat attacked at a trot to preserve the close formation.

Such tactics were the least effective in Russia, where the opposing Cossacks specialized in their ability to change front in a trice.

As in most eighteenth-century armies, the next and most numerous type of French cavalry, the dragoons, had come to be regarded as ordinary horsemen rather than mounted infantry. Under Napoleon, however, there were some ill-fated experiments that severely undermined the dragoons' capacity for shock action. In the training camps of 1801 and 1802 dragoons were taught infantry drill, particularly exercises with the bayonet, and their heavy boots were exchanged for gaiters so that they might move around on foot. During the preparations for the invasion of England, almost all the dragoon regiments at Boulogne were without horses, which they were supposed to seize once they had arrived in Sussex and Kent. Many of these dismounted troopers fought around Ulm in 1805, but their disastrous showing there, with nothing like the steadiness or fire discipline of the line infantry, doomed this experiment to failure. When they were remounted, however, they showed themselves less than adequate cavalry. During the Eylau campaign, in 1807, General Milhaud demanded to be relieved of his command of a division of dragoons on the grounds that their shortcomings could only lead to his continual humiliation. Not until 1808, when 24 of the 30 dragoon regiments were transferred to Spain, though cuirassiers never fought there, did they begin to achieve an adequate standard of horsemanship. After 1814 most of them were pulled out, by which time they had become able to take the place of the lost cuirassiers in the forefront of the cavalry charge.

(*opposite*) British mounted infantry in the Sudan in the 1890s.

A Cossack patrol in 1812. During the campaigns against Napoleon the Cossacks fought for the Tsarist regime rather than against it, and their numerous bands carried out a remorseless guerrilla war against the French.

The third type of cavalry were the light horse, notably hussars and chasseurs. These were mostly attached to the individual *corps d'armée* and their duties were to gain intelligence of enemy movements and to provide a screen for Napoleon's marches and concentrations. The final type were the lancers, reintroduced into regular European armies after more than 200 years. There had been several Polish cavalry units serving with the imperial armies from an early date, but it was only in 1809 that two of the regiments were re-equipped with their native weapon. Prior to that they were known simply as *chevaux légers*. Into 1811 Napoleon converted several dragoon regiments into lancers as well as adding two more such regiments to the cavalry of the Imperial Guard. Their greatest use was as shock troops against enemy infantry squares, when the extra length of their weapon enabled them to outreach the infantrymen armed with musket and bayonet. They proved their worth on many occasions, as at Dresden, in 1813, when the cuirassier regiments were provided with a front rank of lancers, which helped pierce the Austrian squares, though the latter had held off the heavy cavalry alone with little trouble. There were drawbacks, however, and the lancers proved indifferent soldiers in wholly cavalry engagements, for which the lance was more of a hindrance than a help. Speaking of his role in the battle of Carpio (1811), an officer of the 16th Light Dragoons referred to a combat with the Lancers of Berg: 'They looked well, and were formidable till they were broken and closed with by our men, and

then the lances proved an encumbrance; they caught in the appointments of other men and actually pulled them off their horses.'

In many of Napoleon's battles the cavalry played an important part, and did much to justify his claim that large numbers of horse could be used to strike the crucial blow. At Marengo (1800) the turning point was a charge by Kellerman's 400 troopers into the flank of Zach's Austrian column, some 6000 men in all. At Austerlitz (1806) Murat's cuirassiers were used at an early stage to charge the allied horse in the flank and drive them from the field. The cavalry at Jena (1806) really came into their own after the battle, when the whole of Murat's command was used to pursue the Prussians, and they achieved the remarkable feat of covering something like 500 miles in twenty-four days.

Perhaps the most decisive and important of all Napoleonic cavalry actions, indeed one of the greatest cavalry charges in history, was at Eylau (1807) when the 10,700 reserve cavalry moved into the centre and covered 2500yd in an authentic thundering assault on the Russian columns. This action was also remarkable for a classic piece of *chevalier's sang-froid*. At one stage the horsemen of the Imperial Guard were ordered forward to cover the withdrawal of some of those regiments that had been caught up in the mêlée. With shells bursting all around them, the troopers instinctively bowed their heads, until reprimanded by the Colonel of the Horse Grenadiers: 'Heads up, by God! Those are bullets not turds.'

8th Royal Irish Lancers
Wishing you a very happy New Year!
Copyright.
M. H. Nathan & Co.

After this the cavalry was not quite so successful. Friedland (1807) was the occasion of a military mystery when Grouchy and d'Espagne, faced by a mere twenty-five Russian squadrons, failed to move and lost the opportunity for an important break-through. Leipzig (1813) saw many cavalry engagements but the honours of the day were not to go to the French. In the early stages of the battle, near Klein Possna, the cavalry were locked in stalemate. Later, Murat's 10,000 horsemen had some success in an assault against Kleist's corps but they were repulsed by the Austrian reserve cavalry. Later still, Doumerc's cuirassiers, in a famous action, pierced the Duke of Württemburg's flank, but no reserves were on hand to exploit the breach and once again the allied cavalry drove the French back. The cavalry action at Waterloo is too well known to require much elaboration. In essence it was one of those cavalry riots that can so easily occur once the horsemen begin to move off in substantial numbers. The cavalry movement began because Ney thought that Wellington was retreating. As the regiments selected for the final charge moved forward, they picked up more and more horsemen on the way until at least 5000 French cavalry were advancing up the slope towards the allied line. Their pace was no more than a slow trot because of the sodden nature of the ground. They certainly looked impressive enough, and their close-packed lines might well have persuaded some troops to break even before battle was joined. An ensign of the Foot Guards recalled:

Not a man present who survived could have forgotten in after life the awful grandeur of that charge. You perceived in the distance what appeared to be an overwhelming, long moving line, which, ever advancing, glittered like a stormy wave of the sea when it catches the sunlight. On came the mounted host until they got near enough, while the very earth seemed to vibrate beneath their thundering tramp. One might have assumed that nothing could resist the shock of this terrible moving mass.

But the English squares were too sure of their own weapons and discipline to be unduly rattled, and the end of Napoleon's last hopes coincided with a portentous defeat of his cavalry by a combination of firepower and an impenetrable front.

English cavalry in the Napoleonic Wars was never of anything like the same importance. All their battles were won by infantry and musketry, though

it was many a long year before the significance of this penetrated the minds of most senior commanders. When Wellington landed in the Peninsula he had a mere 394 dragoons and 180 horses. More regiments were soon available but even after 1811, when his cavalry complement was doubled, they formed only a relatively insignificant part of his force.* General Mitchell wrote of them: 'It was allowed on all hands that their contribution to the general success bore a small proportion to the quantum of reward bestowed upon them.' There were some successes, though nothing on the scale of Napoleon's great charges. Cavalry versus cavalry encounters were almost unknown but General Maude records eight important clashes with the French infantry, five of which were successful, two failures and one an outright disaster. Notable among the successes was a charge by the dragoons of the King's German Legion, on the morning after Salamanca (1812), when they actually succeeded in breaking two of the squares of Marmont's rearguard. This rare feat was made possible by the thrashings of a dying horse that leapt over the kneeling front rank and struck down over a dozen of those standing behind, creating a gap for the horsemen to penetrate. The general verdict on the horsemen, however, was that they were overly rash and once they had built up to a charge, often ill-conceived, they lost control of themselves and their horses and often ended up miles from the action. The 20th Light Dragoons at Vimeiro (1808), the 23rd at Talavera (1809) or the 13th at Campo Meyer (1811) were all guilty of such headlong recklessness. Slade's Heavy Brigade did no better at Maguilla (1812) when his troopers galloped after a broken brigade and ran into a French cavalry force which enveloped their flanks and rear and did grievous damage. Wellington was not amused. 'I have never been more annoyed ... Our officers of cavalry have acquired a trick of galloping at everything. They never consider the situation, never think of manoeuvering before an enemy, and never keep back or provide for a reserve.' The battle of Waterloo did little to restore his equanimity. The charge of the Union and Household Brigades there is part of English military legend. In fact, this exploit ended as little short of a disaster. Their initial assault upon D'Erlon's infantry columns was an unqualified success but then, as usual, they got out of control and charged against the main French position. Only 20 of the 1200 men of the Union Brigade reached the French lines intact and of the 300 Scots Greys, foremost in the charge, only 21 survived.

The resurgence of the lance – a 5th Royal Irish Lancer in 1880.

*At their peak, in 1812–13, 9000 out of 70,000 men, less than 15 per cent.

After the war Wellington roundly damned the whole British cavalry: 'I considered our cavalry so inferior to the French from want of order, that although I considered one of our squadrons a match for two French, yet I did not care to see four British opposed to four French, and still more so as the numbers increased, and order of course became more necessary. They could gallop, but could not preserve their order.' The French opinion was not much different. Speaking to a British officer, General Excelmann remarked: 'The great deficiency is in your officers who seem to be impressed by the conviction that they can dash or ride over anything, as if the art of war were precisely the same as the art of fox-hunting.'

Theory and Practice

For the rest of the century, however, senior officers in all European armies continued to maintain that the Napoleonic Wars had amply vindicated the retention of large bodies of cavalry. Nothing that happened in the following years caused them to change their minds. Yet even a cursory examination of war in the nineteenth century reveals quite clearly that of all the lessons that contemporary observers should have learnt none was more self-evident than that the day of the mounted attack was over. All the major wars of the period – in the Crimea, in America, in France and in Manchuria – taught the same central point. Firepower was now the dominant feature on the battlefield. This became increasingly true as the century unfolded and improvements in manufacturing techniques – in terms both of precision engineering and mass production – made available vast quantities of accurate, quick-firing weaponry. It became possible to lay down a density of fire upon the battlefield that made it virtually impossible for any dense mass of soldiers to operate in the open. Even the infantry found that the old charge *en masse* was virtually redundant and were forced to spend the greater part of their time huddled in trenches or behind fortifications. For the horsemen the problem was even more acute. It was not feasible to give them adequate protection with entrenchments because of their horses and, when they did try to hurl themselves across no-man's-land, the close-packed ranks of men and horses offered an even more tempting target than assorted battalions of infantry. In short, the cavalry were virtually useless. Every war in the second half of the nineteenth century proved it.

The Crimean War needs little elaboration. The opportunities for cavalry were small and the one occasion on which they did seek to emulate past glories is one of the most famous military blunders of all time. Even before the war broke out, English horsed regiments had been the subject of considerable public outrage. At this stage, however, it was their morals that were in question rather than their military usefulness. In 1840, a radical newspaper, the *Examiner*, bemoaned the fact that the excessive expenses of the cavalry mess had effectively excluded all but the richest officers. Certain types of regiment were singled out: 'We specify Hussars and Lancers, because . . . we find that the greater number of offences against the peace and decency of society have been committed by individuals of those rich and generally aristocratic bodies.' Little was done, of course, and these same aristocratic units went off to Russia convinced that theirs would be the decisive role. They would have done better to follow the example of the French who, in a rare outburst of sanity, sent no cavalry to the Crimea. For when it came to the crunch there were hardly occasions when the horsemen could move forward without being decimated by the enemy's fire. At Alma they did nothing but keep an eye on the equally inactive Russian cavalry. The Light Division was drawn up on a field full of water melons and they whiled away the battle by spearing the fruit with their swords and languidly lifting it to their mouths. It is also reported that a member of the 13th Light Dragoons had managed to get his water bottle filled with rum and this was a further aid in dispelling the ennui of battle.

At Balaclava the cavalry of both sides saw a little more action. But there was hardly anything done that did not serve to underline the fundamental irrelevancy of that arm. A particularly significant event was the attempt by 1500 Russian horse to mêlée with the 93rd Highlanders. The latter, armed with Minié rifles, easily broke up the charge and forced the Russians to withdraw. Later, the cavalry of both sides clashed, when the Heavy Brigade attacked a force of 3000 Russian lancers and dragoons. A vineyard separated the two sides and they met at a leisurely trot. After a short fight the Russians, who greatly outnumbered the British, inexplicably broke and fled the field. It could hardly have been the fury of the fighting that caused this sudden panic, for on both sides the much vaunted *arme blanche* proved of little worth. The press was so dense that the Russians were unable to wield their lances and when they drew their swords it became apparent that very few troopers had bothered to sharpen them. Some British riders survived the engagement with as many as fifteen head wounds, all of which should have been fatal. Nor were their

The charge of the Scots Greys as part of the Heavy Brigade, at the Battle of Balaclava.

weapons much more effective. A sergeant of the Highlanders wrote: 'Their swords were too straight, and so blunt that they would not cut through the thick coats and sheepskin hats of the Russians, so that many of our men struck with their hilts at the faces of the enemy as more effective than attempting to cut with their blunt blades.'

The most famous incident of the day was the charge of the Light Brigade. There are few more apt symbols of the irrelevance of the 'cavalry spirit' upon the post-Napoleonic battlefield. The details of the tragedy are quite straightforward. The Light Brigade was ordered to attack a Russian infantry formation but the vague order was misunderstood and they moved against the enemy artillery. Despite their astonishment the Russian gunners had little difficulty in blowing the regiments out of their saddles. A total of 673 riders set out; after the roll-call at the end of the battle only 195 officers and men could be found. Many stragglers turned up later, but the scale of the casualties amongst the leading regiments was still appalling. The 13th Light Dragoons were under the command of a lieutenant and could only muster 14 men out of 150. Of the 17th Lancers'

145

original 150, only 50 men and 3 officers remained. Yet even in such a fiasco it is impossible not to marvel at the stiff-upper-lipped gallantry of those involved. The 'cavalry spirit' might be irrelevant but it undeniably existed. Whatever the *Examiner* might think of the aristocratic monopoly of the officer corps, it assuredly produced remarkable leaders. Lord George Paget rode against the guns with a still-lighted cigar clenched in his teeth. When describing the battle afterwards, he unconsciously revealed the truth of the Frenchman, Excelmann's, strictures: 'As far as it engendered excitement, the finest run in Leicestershire could hardly bear comparison.' The commander of the Light Brigade, the 7th Earl of Cardigan, showed undue excitement only when it seemed that a subordinate might upset the rigid protocol of regimental hierarchy. As the charge gathered momentum, Captain Morris of the 17th Lancers drew abreast of his commanding officer, only to find the flat of the other's sword against his chest: 'Steady, Steady, Captain Morris!' he yelled, 'Stay, sir! How dare you attempt to ride before your commanding officer!'

Unfortunately it was the memory of such berserk courage that lived on rather than the appalling consequences of pitting the weapons of medieval chivalry against modern technology. Less than ten years later, another war began which again underlined the fundamental point that assaults, particularly by the cavalry, against unbroken infantry were almost certainly doomed to failure. During the course of their civil war, the Americans soon realized this and their horsemen quickly ceased to have much of a role on the battlefield, and were kept instead for long-distance raids behind the enemy lines.* To this end the cavalry largely abandoned the sword and relied upon pistols and carbines, doing most of their actual fighting on foot, using their horses only as a means of getting from one place to another as swiftly as possible. Here was a valuable lesson for European armies. Horsemen could still be used to telling effect as long as it was realized that their prime asset was their mobility off the battlefield and that it was no longer possible physically to pit rider and steed against modern weaponry. The British, French and German armies had numerous observers in the various theatres but hardly any of them appreciated the salient points. On the British side Major Henry Havelock was one who did absorb the significance of this war. In a book called *Three Main Military Questions* he bemoaned

contemporary cavalry tactics with their emphasis upon shock action, which reduced it to 'the jangling, brilliant, costly but almost hopeless reality it is'. A German soldier, who actually fought for the Confederacy, wrote that 'the great improvement in firearms had necessitated a very material change in cavalry tactics'. A 'genuine cavalry fight, with sabre-crossing and single combat . . . [will] very rarely occur in modern warfare.' But these were isolated voices. For most observers the conduct of the American cavalry was more a consequence of military backwardness than a rational response to the material situation. The devastating effect of firepower was ignored and the attachés tut-tutted at the erratic uniforms and shook their heads sadly over the lax discipline. Lieutenant-Colonel J. A. L. Freemantle wrote:

> These cavalry fights are miserable affairs. Neither party has any idea of serious charging with the sabre. They approach one another with considerable boldness, until they get to within about forty yards, and then, at the very moment when a dash is necessary, and the sword alone should be used, they hesitate, halt and commence a desultory fire with carbines and revolvers . . . Stuart's cavalry can hardly be called cavalry in the European sense of the word.

Captain R. Harrison was even more censorious after seeing the Union cavalry in action. As far as he was concerned, they 'would disgrace some of the wildest Irregulars raised in the north of India . . . Their horses were poor and ill-kept, their equipment ragged, and their discipline bad, and they looked more like a disgruntled mob of infantry on horseback, than the cavalry they were intended to represent.'

Just how little had been actually learnt was brought home during the Franco-Prussian War, when the cavalry of both sides clung to its traditional role and involved itself in fiascos every bit as bloody as the slaughter at Balaclava. There had, in fact, been some debate about finding a suitable tactical role for cavalry and considerable emphasis was placed by both sides on their use in reconnaissance and screening the movements of the main armies. In the first weeks of the war the German horsemen were of some use in this respect. The French, on the other hand, never moved in groups of less than a full squadron and were thus tied to the main routes. In their other role, that of exploiting victory or protecting the infantry during a retreat, neither side did particularly well. After the battle of Wissembourg, the German cavalry completely failed to exploit the

---

*For a fuller treatment of the use of cavalry by the Union and Confederate forces see the next chapter. Only European armies and those that slavishly imitated them, e.g. the Japanese, are dealt with here.

demoralization of the French and no pursuit was attempted. It was similarly unadventurous after the battles of Spicheren and Froeschwiller. Steinmetz had two cavalry divisions in his First Army yet, rather than send numerous small patrols ahead to probe the retreating enemy's positions, he kept one division intact on his flank and actually placed the other behind his slow-moving infantry. On the Second Army's front the lack of initiative was directly attributable to the cavalry commander himself who, despite frequent reminders from his corps commander, refused to send his troops forward at all. During Bazaine and Leboeuf's subsequent retreat towards Metz the French cavalry proved itself even more incompetent. The Germans did manage to throw out a handful of reconnaissance patrols and these were enough to provoke panic amongst the French infantry because the cavalry made absolutely no attempt to drive them off. They had been brought up in the traditions of African warfare,* where it was unwise to wander far from the main body, and they continually sought the protection of the infantry columns, slowing down their progress even more.

Doubtless the cavalry were not particularly perturbed by these lamentable displays. For them their very *raison d'être* was the massed charge on the actual battlefield, the act that would decide the fortunes of the day. Reality consistently fell far short of this dream. At Froeschwiller the French cavalry executed two charges. A little after noon, General Lartigue launched Michel's brigade of cuirassiers against the Prussian infantry who seemed likely to overrun his position. They set off furiously down the hill but soon ran into ground cut up by vineyards, hedges and trees. The Prussians, although tired by their earlier advance, took cover here and directed a deadly fire at the horsemen. Some squadrons did break through to the village of Morsbronn but were picked off at leisure from the houses. The main street was so congested with dead men and horses that later attempts to march through had to be abandoned. In all, some nine squadrons of cuirassiers were destroyed. It is not thought that one Prussian was killed. At three in the afternoon another brigade of cuirassiers was thrown against the advancing Prussians. Their infantry were in extended order in just the same kind of terrain that had ensnared Michel's regiments. The French charged repeatedly but were beaten back with heavy losses. Not one cavalryman got within sabre-reach of an adversary.

At Mars-la-Tour both sides launched cavalry

* (see pp. 167–8 in the next chapter)

A German dragoon during the Franco-Prussian War. On both sides the cavalry was singularly ineffective.. The most famous cavalry exploits, Gallifet's charge at Sedan and von Bredow's 'Death Ride' at Mars-la-Tour, resulted in appalling casualties.

charges. Both were equally suicidal. The French moved first when Bazaine answered Frossard's plea for reinforcements by sending up a regiment of the Cuirassiers of the Guard. Their colonel was not enthusiastic about the prospect · of attacking unbroken infantry and said as much to Bazaine. The latter's reply lacked genuine reassurance: 'It is vitally necessary to stop them; we must sacrifice a regiment!' They went forward with a regiment of lancers and both were mown down by a few disciplined volleys. A little later Bazaine himself was surrounded by a few German cavalry, who were then surrounded in turn by French horsemen, and driven off. As Michael Howard, the best historian of this war, has put it: 'On both sides the cavalry forays had been spectacular, invigorating and entirely ineffective.' Even more spectacular things were to come. At one stage von Alvensleben's III Corps was fighting off far superior French numbers whilst desperately awaiting reinforcement by X Corps. By the afternoon his infantry had just about shot their bolt and as a last resort von Alvensleben called upon some of his cavalry, a brigade of cuirassiers and lancers under von Bredow, to create a diversion. For maximum effect he deliberately ordered them to attack the French artillery. The Germans were greatly aided by the fact that they were able to approach within 100yd of the guns without being seen, taking advantage of a depression in the ground. Then they burst forth and thundered down upon the guns, killing many of the gunners and forcing some limbers to ride straight into their own lines. Some of French infantry was driven off and pursued by the German riders until they themselves were caught in the flank by two brigades of French dragoons. Some managed to hack their way out of the ensuing mêlée but of the 800 riders who had started out only a half returned. With good reason was von Bredow's exploit known as der *Todtenritt*, or the 'Death Ride'. Yet, as long as the deliberate sacrifice of men is regarded as valid military practice, it was a success. The French gun-line was thrown into disarray and the danger to German positions in this part of the battlefield was for the moment banished. But there were exceptional reasons for this success, notably the availability of cover right up to the moment of the final gallop, the smoke and dust on the battlefield, and the persistent belief among the French that the cuirassiers were in fact their own troops.

The French were to have their own death ride at Sedan. Again the intentions were virtually suicidal. Above Floing, General Douay's left flank was in grave danger of being turned and his whole force surrounded. In desperation he called upon the cavalry of General Margueritte, ordering them to repulse the advancing Germans *and* batter a passage through their lines to enable the French to break out to the west. Margueritte was horribly disfigured by a bullet even before the charge began and his Chasseurs d'Afrique were shouting for vengeance as they breasted the crest and charged down on the enemy positions. They might have saved their breath. The Germans could see them coming and they gave no sign of panic. A few volleys were sufficient to empty many saddles and send the survivors back to their starting point. An English observer wrote: 'So thorough a destruction by what may be called a single volley probably the oldest soldier now alive never witnessed.' The French commander prevailed upon them to charge twice more and by the time the dust had cleared the squadrons had been all but annihilated.

The final major conflict from which Europeans might have drawn some pertinent conclusions was that fought in Manchuria, in 1904 and 1905, between the Russians and the Japanese. Each side had substantial numbers of horsemen, but in the event they were hardly used at all. There were a few skirmishes in which cavalry met cavalry with drawn sabres but they are hardly worthy of mention. Even the famous Cossacks were sadly under-employed. A German commentator noted: 'Their favourite weapon is no longer the sword and dirk but the rifle.' Certainly it was not the lance. Just before the battle of Liao-Yang some Cossack units were issued with lances, perhaps in an attempt to conjure up past glories. They even charged with them during the battle but no one knew any more how they should be wielded. They rode in grasping them with both hands and using them like quarter-staves. In this way a few enemy riders were unhorsed and then speared like pigs as they lay on the ground. One modern historian has asserted that this was the only occasion in the whole war when wounds were inflicted with the *arme blanche*. This may be compared with the American Civil War, in which a Union surgeon, Major Hart, noted: 'Cavalry men would occasionally get close enough to slash each other with their sabres but these wounds were few and far between.' Again, the German Medical Corps statistics for the Franco-Prussian War showed that out of 65,000 killed or wounded, sabre wounds accounted for 212 wounded and 6 dead.

In other battles the cavalry might as well not have been there – at least not on horseback, for their rifles were always useful in a tight corner. Of the battle of Yalu, Ian Hamilton, a perspicacious British official observer, wrote:

As for the cavalry, Russian and Japanese, they did nothing, which seemed very much to surprise some of my friends . . . Even the warmest advocate of shock tactics and swords must allow, when he follows the course of events on this occasion over the actual ground, that there was no place or opportunity where the horse could have been of any value except to bring a rifleman rapidly up to the right spot.

An even more damning judgement was that given by a Japanese officer with whom Hamilton had a conversation after one particular action: 'Even at a supreme moment such as this there was, however, one group of men who were idle. This was the cavalry. So they were employed to go back and cook food for their companions of the infantry.'

A German cuirassier of the late
nineteenth century. Just such
anachronistic troopers took part
in von Bredow's *Todtenritt* and
were ready to do the same again
right up to World War I.

Japanese cavalry moving up during the Russo-Japanese War. One Japanese commander felt that in battle their only use was to cook rice for the infantry.

(*opposite*) The cavalrymen's version of the Russo-Japanese War. In fact, modern firepower and entrenchments meant that such engagements hardly ever took place.

Yet none of this had much impact upon the military establishments of Europe. Right up to World War I they continued to believe that cavalry must have a central place on any European battlefield. The fact that firepower had proved so devastating on numerous conventional battlefields, not to mention the carnage caused by Maxims and Gatlings during the seizure of Africa, made little difference. There were brief flirtations with the idea of converting cavalry into mounted infantry, particularly in England and France, in the 1880s. But these ideas never took root and more traditional theories about the pre-eminent role of shock action prevailed. In 1907 the English went so far as to close down two out of the three mounted infantry schools that had been set up. In that country, and elsewhere, it was felt that to make allowances for the enemy's

firepower was somehow to admit weakness. It became necessary to believe that any group of sufficiently resolute soldiers could break through the opposing lines. The offensive was regarded as the only real option for an officer and a gentleman, and it was deemed mere poltroonery even to suggest that the balance might have swung to the defensive. The most level-headed military commentators pushed this line. In England Spencer Wilkinson wrote: 'It is true that within certain narrow limits . . . the defender is strengthened by modern improvements in firearms. But . . . there has been no revolution in tactics or strategy, but certain modifications, long since realized, have become more pronounced. The balance of advantage remains where it was.' In Germany, von Bernhadi was equally sure that the advantage still lay with him who attacked most

boldly: 'We must not overrate the importance of practical inventions for war, nor, above all, imagine that mechanical appliances, be they ever so excellent, can make amends for deficiency in military and moral qualities.' Nowhere was this kind of doctrine more eagerly absorbed than in the cavalry. For them, the detritus of an increasingly irrelevant aristocracy, this blinkered evocation of individual courage was an ideal way to shrug off the little understood realities of the new industrial society, and to maintain that there was still a genuine niche in the world for young men with the ability to ride, too much money, and minimal intelligence.

So the cavalry lived on. In Germany the experiences of the Franco-Prussian War made no difference at all. In 1865 Stosch had been full of the 'vehemence and force' of cavalry action, and almost forty years later von Freytag-Loringhoven was adamant that 'the lance is and remains the chief weapon.' An English officer wrote of German practice at this time: 'The idea of shock action is now dominant . . . hence the tendency to discourage all dismounted action, and the introduction of the lance as an offensive weapon.' In France, in the 1899 cavalry regulations, it was laid down that the *arme*

blanche was the 'principal mode of action'. In 1908 an instructor at the *École de Guerre* wrote:

> Certain military writers proclaim the bankruptcy of cavalry and . . . demand the reduction if not the abolition of this costly arm . . . If cavalry is only to be used for fighting foot . . . it can be with advantage be replaced by infantry on ponies. But let those infantrymen on ponies once collide with cavalry that gallops and uses the sword, and they will soon be destroyed.

There were few officers in England prepared to disagree with such views. All senior officers prior to the outbreak of World War I were unanimous that it was impossible to envisage a battlefield upon which the 'cavalry spirit' would not find a place. In 1891 F. Maurice inveighed against the weakening of this spirit by target practice: 'Every hour devoted to shooting by cavalry weakens them . . . Shooting ought to be for them a most subordinate matter.' In 1897 Sir Evelyn Wood saw a horse run amok in the Mall and his subsequent musings perfectly crystallize the horseman's undying faith in the superiority of the resolute rider over any mere material obstacle: 'If it were possible to obtain the same amount of determination from riders, as that

A ludicrous attempt to combine
modern firepower and mounted
tactics, suggested in 1872.

which inspired the unfortunate horse . . . all cavalry charges would succeed, in spite of every sort of missile.'

Later writers followed just the same line of reasoning. In 1906, in his introduction to von Bernhadi's *Cavalry in Future Wars*, Sir John French roundly criticized umpires on military manoeuvres who 'try and inculcate such a respect for Infantry fire that Cavalry is taught to shirk exposure.' For French

such decisions 'disregard altogether the human factor in the problem. We ought the more to be on our guard against false teachings of this nature . . . [and the] inevitable consequences of thus placing the weapon above the man.' French's successor on the Western Front, Haig, gave no more helpful hints as to how he might handle his horsemen in a large-scale conflict. In 1908 he thus characterized the value of the cavalry arm: 'It is not the weapon carried but the

moral factor of an apparently irresistible force, coming on at highest speed in spite of rifle fire, which affects the nerve and aim of the . . . rifleman.' Nor was official cavalry doctrine much removed from such mystical drivellings. The cavalry regulations of 1907 asserted: 'It must be accepted as a principle that the rifle, effective as it is, cannot replace the effect produced by the speed of the horse, the magnetism of the charge and the terror of cold steel.'

A French hussar, needing nothing but the *arme blanche*, waiting for World War I. Even after the war had begun it was many months before the High Commands realized that mounted troops were an irrelevancy.

8 Guerrilla Horsemen the Nineteenth Century

'There are only two arms that cavalry should use in modern warfare – the repeating magazine gun, either rifle or carbine, and the revolver.'
J. H. Wilson, Union cavalry commander

'The Boers are not like the Sudanese who stood up to a fair fight. They are always running away on their little ponies.'
Lord Kitchener

During the nineteenth century many factors combined to render European regular cavalry next to useless. Not only were their tactics entirely inappropriate to the new material relationships on the battlefield, but there was not really any other role that they could have fulfilled. Mounted infantry could have been of only limited value in Europe because communications were too good and the terrain not difficult enough to make possible the large-scale penetrating raids that were such a feature of the American Civil War. Moreover, the fact that most European cavalry horses were entirely dependent on regular care and grain-feeding made it unlikely that they would be able to move far from the main body of the army and the forage dumps. Nor would tactical mobility on the battlefield have been particularly useful as horsemen presented far too vulnerable a target, even when moving over very short distances.

However, there were parts of the world where these constraints hardly applied at all. During the nineteenth century there is discernible a resurgence of the old guerrilla techniques that typified such groups as the Scythians, the Numidians or the Marathas. Peoples who virtually lived on horseback, because it was the only feasible way of getting around over vast distances or difficult terrain, found themselves pitted against regular European armies. They remained on horseback during these wars but they assiduously avoided pitched battles, where superior numbers and firepower must eventually win the day, and used their steeds as a means of swiftly getting from place to place, to set up an ambush or quickly retreat from an unfavourable situation. In mountainous regions their speed was nothing to boast about. What was important was that their horses, used to the difficult terrain and sparse forage, made them relatively much faster than their cumbersome opponents. On the open plains, too, they had the edge over conventional armies, even if the latter were mounted, because the indigenous horses ate less, less frequently, and did not expect their riders to bring special rations with them. For such peoples mobility was the essence of mounted warfare rather than the traditional European reliance upon the close-range impetus of man and horse.

The Americas

It was not only peoples born and bred on horseback that developed such techniques. In America, during the Civil War, numerous cavalry regiments were formed on both sides, many of whose troopers had little experience of riding. But they organized themselves with hardly any reference to European standards and practices, and the tactics they adopted show how formalized were those of the traditional regulars. There were those who wanted to ape European customs. Not surprisingly, these were mostly Confederate leaders, the sons of what passed for the American aristocracy, who left West Point *en masse* to fight for slavery and the plantation system. An English observer, Lieutenant H. C. Fletcher, wrote of J. E. B. Stuart that he had 'admired the *arme blanche* as the true weapon for the horseman, but unfortunately neither time nor means were at hand to organize and discipline a force on the model of European cavalry'. Even those Southerners who were familiar with the horse resisted European methods of discipline, essential though these were to any cavalry that adopted close-formation shock tactics. A Confederate general wrote:

The difficulty of converting raw men into soldiers is enhanced manifold when they are mounted. Both men and horses require training . . . There was but little time, and it may be said less disposition, to establish camps of instruction. Living on horseback, fearless and dashing, the men of the South afforded the best possible material for cavalry. They had every quality but discipline.

Luckily for them, therefore, neither cavalry was expected to play much of a role in battle. It was attempted from time to time when horsemen were placed on the wings in close contact with the main infantry force but they never achieved anything of note, either remaining inactive or suffering a bloody repulse. Instead they were used as highly mobile mounted infantry. Even their weapons owed little to European precedent. One observer noted: 'The cavalry on both sides . . . are merely mounted infantry. They are not taught to use the sword at all, and indeed several regiments can muster but few swords anyway.' A Union cavalry commander, James H. Wilson, explained why this was so:

My division was the first in the Army of the Potomac that had first-class repeating arms. Green regiments, that you couldn't have driven into a fight with old arms, became invincible the very moment that good arms were placed in their hands . . . There are only two arms that cavalry should use in modern warfare – the repeating magazine gun, either rifle or carbine, and the revolver.

Such troops came to form an important element of both armies. In 1860 the United States army could boast a total force of only five cavalry regiments. By

J. E. B. Stuart leading his cavalry near Culpepper Court House. Cavalry came into its own again during the American Civil War, being used for swift, long-distance raids behind the enemy's lines, rather than charges on the actual battlefields.

A Union cavalryman of 1863 as imagined by an artist who had never seen one. The eighteenth century pistol holsters are especially fanciful. Actual uniforms were very *ad hoc* and revolvers were usually stuck in the belt. Sabres were hardly used at all.

the end of the war the North could put 80,000 horsemen in the field, the South half that number.

On both sides the cavalry's main duty was long-distance raiding, either upon the enemy's communications, the newly important railroads, or his supply dumps. It is possible here only to give the briefest sketch of such activity and highlight a few of the more important leaders. Perhaps the most important of all was Nathan Bedford Forrest, whose grey-clad horsemen wreaked havoc in the Union rear. In July 1862, for example, 1400 Confederate cavalry penetrated 90 miles behind the front line and cut the Nashville–Chattanooga railway at Murfreesboro as well as capturing the garrison of 1700 men. Forrest's casualties were a mere 80 men. The line of supply was not repaired for three weeks. When Buell, the Union commander, finally got on the move again the Confederates swept 160 miles into his rear and cut the railway yet again, forcing him to fall back on Murfreesboro. The leader of this expedition, John Morgan of Kentucky, led many similar raids and on one occasion covered at least 1000 miles as he roamed around the Union rear. Forrest struck again in December 1862. As Grant and Sherman, with their vastly superior numbers, were advancing on Vicksburg he was dispatched far northwards where he completely wrecked substantial chunks of the only railway line supplying Grant. The latter was without supplies for over a week and was forced to return to his starting point. Forrest had also inflicted some 1500 casualties and kept 20,000 other men occupied in vain efforts to intercept him. During Sherman's 1864 advance upon Atlanta he was forced to detach 80,000 of his 180,000 men to guard the lines of communication, as well as devote

two fresh divisions, 15,000 men, to the specific task of hunting down Forrest's raiders.

It was not only the Confederates who caused such disruption with their cavalry. In April 1863, a Union commander, B. H. Grierson, rode 400 miles south in 16 days and cut all the supply lines to Vicksburg from the east, as well as completely demoralizing the Confederate, Pemberton, just as Grant was

157

One of the first US regular cavalrymen, during the war against Mexico, in 1847. Even in 1860 there were only five such regiments.

manoeuvring around the city to invest it. Grant claimed: 'It has been one of the most brilliant cavalry exploits of the war.' Grierson's official report gives a measure of the destruction wreaked by his three regiments: 'We killed and wounded over one hundred of the enemy, captured and paroled over five hundred prisoners . . . destroyed between fifty and sixty miles of railroad and telegraph, captured and destroyed over 3000 stands of arms . . . [and] captured 1000 horses and mules.' All for the loss of 3 killed, 12 men sick or wounded and 9 men missing. An even more dramatic raid, and on a much larger scale, was that into Alabama in March 1865, led by James Wilson. Setting off from Tennessee, his 14,000 men rode 600 miles to Selma and in the course of the 28-day campaign captured 5 fortified cities, 23 stands of colours, 288 guns and 6820 prisoners. His own losses were a little over 700 men.

It was numbers above all that explained the eventual superiority of the Union cavalry. From an early date the North took control of the horse-breeding states of Kentucky, West Virginia, Missouri and mid-Tennessee and the Confederates found it increasingly difficult to obtain remounts. An equine infirmary was established at Lynchburg but only 15 per cent of the patients ever returned to active service. By the last year of the war the cavalry were reduced to riding the most inferior nags. The discipline of the troops also declined. As their cause became more and more hopeless, the cavalry began to use their mobility for their own ends and became little more than freebooters. The Confederate humorist, Bill Arp, explained the new situation: 'I have travelled a heap of late, and had occasion to retire into some very sequestered regions, but nary hill or holler, nary mountain gorge or inaccessible ravine, have I found but what the cavalry had been there, and *just left*. And that is the reason they can't be whipped, for they have always *just left*, and took an odd horse or two with 'em.'

But the cavalry tradition, in its somewhat mutant form, lived on in the American army after the Civil War. For the next thirty years their chief enemies were to be the original inhabitants of the country, as various Indian tribes desperately resorted to all-out war in a last effort to retain something of their once boundless hunting grounds. Their struggle was essentially futile, but it nevertheless involved some of the most vicious hit-and-run cavalry warfare that has ever been known.

The reappearance of the horse in America did not alter the Indian's life quite as dramatically as is sometimes supposed.* Many tribes were settled agriculturists and had no particular use for the horse except as a draught animal. Only those Plains Indians whose mode of life had been nomadic anyway took to the horse in a big way. Once they had tamed it, their way of life went on much as before except that now they were able to hunt the buffalo with much greater hope of catching them. They also gained a substantial military advantage over unmounted tribes. As the horse spread over the

*The horse first escaped from white hands in the 1540s, and reached the Indians long before they themselves ever had contact with the Europeans. It slowly spread over the region west of the Missouri and the Mississippi. By the 1680s the Kiowa and Missouri Indians were mounted, by 1714 the Comanche, by 1742 the Snake and the Teton, and by 1784 horses had reached the most northerly mounted people, the Sarsi.

(*opposite above*) Russian cavalry being cut to pieces by Japanese artillery during the Russo-Japanese War.

(*opposite below*) An attempt to resuscitate the cavalry myth during World War I: the Scots Greys at St Quentin, 1914.

ВСТУПАИТЕ ДО ЧЕРВОНОЇ КІННОТИ!

Червона кічнота знищила, Мамонтова, Шкуро, Деникина.
Вона била панів і Петлюру,
        зараз потрібно знищити недобитка Врангеля.

Робітники й селяне—вступайте до лав Червоної Кінноти.

The 5th US Cavalry in the 1880s. Mounted troops were the backbone of the US Army during the Indian Wars, though they used their horses only to get from place to place and usually fought on foot.

Plains to such notable riding masters as the Comanches, the Cheyennes and the Dakotas, continual skirmishing took place between them and other more settled tribes in the mountains and the Missouri Valley. Eventually the latter were destroyed, though it should be emphasized that it is not correct to think in terms of nomadic conquests *à la* Hun or Mongol but of a very long-drawn-out series of minor raids. As some scholars have pointed out, the Plains Indians' war literature contains no record 'of any war party which did not return home again after its first fight'. The very term 'war party' is in fact misleading. Until the desperate fights for survival against the white man, the Indians did not think in terms of organized campaigns and decisive battles, but rather of lightning raids to steal horses and supplies or to blood young warriors. Even their combat revealed ritualistic features that had little in common with western notions of *guerre à l'outrance*.

A recruiting poster of 1919 for the Red Cavalry.

Among the Sioux, for example, much more prestige accrued to the warrior who simply touched his enemy with his coup stick than to the one who knocked him out of the saddle with an arrow.

Yet the Plains Indians, and the Apaches further south, had much in common with those other nomadic peoples discussed above. They prized their horses greatly, and looked upon them as a source of wealth and status. Some tribes kept vast herds, particularly the Comanches. One band of 2000 Indians had 15,000 mounts in tow. All warriors had more than one horse. Like the Mongols they rode them in relays, riding two or three ordinary buffalo ponies until they were in contact with the enemy and the moment came to mount the especially prized war pony. As a white contemporary wrote: 'Every warrior has a war horse, which is the fleetest that can be obtained, and he prizes him more highly than anything else in his possession, and it is seldom that he can be induced to part with him at any price.'

Their weaponry was also typical of the Asian mounted nomad. They relied primarily upon the

'Apache Ambush' by Frederic Remington. Although they were excellent horsemen the Apaches did not attempt to charge their enemies, but relied on mobility to outdistance them and keep up a chronic guerrilla war.

A fanciful version of mounted combat in the 1870s. The cavalryman shooting at the gallop, his sabre, the Indian riding bareback – all are components of later Hollywood mythology.

bow. Amongst the Comanches this was $2\frac{1}{2}$ to 3ft long, made of ash or bone. Different types of arrows were used, depending on whether the need was for velocity or distance. Each warrior would carry about 100 arrows when going off on a raid and these were often barely enough as a warrior, if necessary, could put up to eight arrows in the air at the same time. An unknown cavalryman has left this description of Sioux archery:

The bows were made of the Osage orange . . . strung with twisted deer sinews and strengthened

on the back with strips of raw deer sinew, glued and allowed to shrink on hard until it is almost like steel. The arrows were made of mulberry or ash, tipped with wild turkey feathers . . . On the other end was the spike, two to three inches in length, made of ordinary hoop-iron, sharpened on point and edges and afterwards both hardened and tempered in both fire and water, making them like steel . . . They could throw their arrows with the most deadly accuracy from thirty to fifty yards and at from five to fifteen yards they could send a plain, unspiked arrow shaft entirely through a

Comanche warriors practising one of their favourite tactics. Like the horsemen of the ancient East, most Plains Indians preferred to keep at a distance from their enemy and rarely charged straight at them.

buffalo, and hit a mark as large as a door-knob four times out of five.

Many warriors also carried 14ft lances and among the Comanches, at least, the resemblance to steppe nomads became even closer when they began to protect their horses with 'armour' made from stiffened buffalo hide. This experiment was, however, fairly short-lived. Many Indians got hold of firearms but these were not a particularly significant addition to their armoury as most were indifferent marksmen. A cavalryman wrote: 'Indians fired point-blank, soldiers used the [long-range rear] sight and wind gauge, which the Indians knew nothing about.'

However, there is one crucial qualification to any comparison between the Indians and the warriors of Central Asia. Hollywood notwithstanding, few of the former actually fought on horseback. Those that did were as adept as any Turkic horseman. A pioneer who fought against the Flatheads noted:

They generally fight on horseback and have two bows and two quivers full of arrows with which they defend themselves and greatly annoy their enemies even in flying. They are expert horsemen.

George Catlin painted and wrote about the Comanches. He describes one of their favourite tactics, in which they hung over the side of their horse with one foot hooked over its spine and one arm through a loop around the horse's neck:

In this wonderful position he will hang whilst his horse is at the fullest speed, carrying with him his bow and shield, and also his long lance . . . all or either of which he will wield upon his enemy as he passes; riding and throwing his arrows over the horse's back, or . . . under the horse's neck.

An Indian expecting to fight thus would usually ride bareback. The majority, however, used saddles and stirrups as they had seen the white man do. Most other people, however, did the actual fighting on foot. Such groups as the Crow, the Cheyenne, the Atsina, the Pawnees, the Wichitas and the Dakotas used their horses only to convey them to the area of operations, after which they would dismount and scurry about in search of cover. Even those people that remained mounted hardly ever indulged in frontal cavalry charges. There are only two examples where this was not so: in 1868, at Beecher's Island, when Roman Nose was killed at the head of his charging warriors, and the Second Battle of Adobe Wells, in 1874, when Cheyenne, Comanche and Arapaho bands threw their usual caution to the winds. They suffered the usual fate of horsemen trying to overrun men on foot, in this case buffalo hunters, armed with rifles. A Comanche warrior said of the battle: '[They] were too much for us. They stood behind adobe walls. They had telescopes on their guns . . . One of our men was knocked off his horse by a spent bullet fired at a range of about a mile.'

163

Usually they avoided such frontal assaults, or indeed any kind of pitched battle. They were essentially guerrilla fighters, relying upon mobility and surprise rather than a once-and-for-all combat. One European put his finger on the reason for this and gave a description of Indian martial values that is equally applicable to most of the other horse peoples mentioned in this chapter. He talked of 'a certain order of strategy . . . [whose] great and vital principle . . . is to do the greatest possible amount of damage to the enemy with the least possible loss. There is no pension list with them, and the widows and orphans are thrown upon the charity of their people.' J. Bourke, one of General Crook's adjutants during one of the interminable campaigns against the Apaches, expressed similar views and managed to raise himself above the usual occidental philosophy that regarded any fighter who would not stand and allow himself to be shot to pieces as lacking in courage: 'The Apache was in no sense a coward. He knew his business and played his cards to suit himself. He never lost a shot or lost a warrior when a brisk run across the nearest ridge would save a life or exhaust the heavily-clad soldier who endeavoured to catch him.'

Against this sort of enemy the Americans were forced to try and maximize the mobility of their own forces. It is not surprising, therefore, that the regular army of 1877 contained ten regiments of cavalry, 10,970 men, as opposed to 1900 artillery and a little under 10,000 infantry. Nevertheless, the horsemen were not as mobile as might be supposed and were never a match for such leaders as the Apache, Josanie, whose band, in 1885, covered over 1000 miles in less than four weeks. In fact, in any campaign that lasted more than a few days it was expected that the infantry would be able to cover more ground than the horsemen. This was because the horses were grain-fed and not used to the exertions that Indian ponies took for granted. They were usually overloaded. A cavalryman's equipment weighed over 50lb and each man also carried at least 15lb of grain with him. The sabres alone weighed 5lb and it was soon realized that there was little place for them in Indian warfare. From the early 1870s the *arme blanche* was effectively abolished from the US Cavalry. During the doomed Custer campaign not even the officers carried swords. The most common weapons were the Colt Army ·44 pistol, which was replaced by the single-shot Colt ·45 in 1876, and the Spencer carbine, which was replaced by the Springfield ·45 rifle in 1873.

As far as possible the cavalry tried to adopt Indian tactics. For short campaigns they travelled light.

During Crook's 1876 campaign against Crazy Horse the 800 troopers carried with them only the clothes they wore, a buffalo robe, a tin cup, 100 rounds of carbine ammunition and four days' rations. The horses were to feed upon such grass as they might find by pawing it up from under the snow. One of Crook's officers recorded that he 'did not allow us either knife, fork, spoon or plate. Each member carried . . . a tin cup . . . General Crook had determined to make his column as mobile as a column of Indians, and he knew that example was more potent than a score of general orders.' Other commanders went even further. During the campaign against Geronimo, General Nelson A. Miles finally resorted to dismounting all the heavier troopers and giving the lighter men two horses each, which they were to ride in relay. Another of Crook's subordinates during the Apache wars, Captain Crawford, actually dispensed with all his regular cavalry and set out with four officers and 200 Apache scouts, in the belief that only the latter could hope to keep up with the foe.

But it was not superior tactics that finally put an end to the Indian 'problem'. It was simply a matter of vastly superior numbers and better weaponry. Ultimately the Indians knew that they had no chance of reversing the tide of history, and though they might elude the units sent after them for years on end, and inflict quite disproportionate casualties, they could never hope to regain freedom and peace. Chief Joseph of the Nez Percé ran rings around the US Cavalry in 1877 and was never defeated militarily. Yet at the end of his epic flight he was forced to realize that there was no way of resolving anything by force of arms. In his surrender speech he said: 'Hear me, my chiefs! I am tired; my heart is sick and sad. From where the sun now stands I will fight no more forever.'

It was not only in North America that horsemen were militarily important. Unfortunately there is no space here to deal with the exploits of the *gauchos*, *llaneros* and *montoneros* who played an important part in the liberation struggles of Spanish America in the early nineteenth century. It would be impossible, however, to ignore completely the horsemen of Mexico who appeared so often in times of social and political upheaval. Bands of horsemen, ranging from authentic nationalist guerrillas to cynical plunderers, appeared in the War of Independence between 1810 and 1821. One of their leaders, Vincente Guerrero, eventually became president. They came to the fore again between 1858 and 1861, in the so-called War of Reform, and fought against the imported Emperor Maximilian, lured to Mexico

Left to right: Geronimo, Nachez, Geronimo's son Chapo.

in 1863 by reactionary clerical groups. Prominent leaders were Benito Juárez and Porfirio Díaz. Maximilian's wife was little impressed by their motives: 'No one can foresee whence guerrilla bands may spring up. Theirs is a kind of spontaneous generation. As I understand the matter, a man leaves his village with a horse, a weapon, and a firm determination to prosper by any means except work.' But whatever the relative importance of patriotic and mercenary motives, the guerrillas' tactics were of the classic pattern and the French occupation forces had no adequate response. One of the emperor's retinue wrote: 'By the time one town is freed from the insurgents ... the guerrillas have mastered some other important place, and the troops leave the conquered town to hunt them from their new acquisition. But scarcely are the troops out of sight when one hears the ring of the guerrilla cavalry, which surrounds the deserted town.'

The French were driven out eventually and Díaz took over the presidency, his regime becoming more an more autocratic until yet another political convulsion in 1910. Francisco Madero assumed the provisional presidency and called for limited con-

stitutional reforms. This fairly peaceful change of leadership and even milder programme of social change revealed deep-seated grievances among the whole Mexican population and the situation swiftly degenerated into full-scale civil war. Various local leaders emerged, but perhaps the most famous of all was Pancho Villa (Doroteo Arango). Villa obtained his first few horses in 1913. He made his base in Chihuahua, an area of large ranches, and within a short time had built up a considerable following of cowboys, mule-skinners, bandits, peddlers and refugee peons, known as the Division of the North. Eight men had followed Villa across the Rio Grande in April, yet five months later he was the leader of 10,000 cavalry. In October he attacked Torreón, in November he captured Ciudad Juárez and Tierra Blanca, as well as obliging his opponents to evacuate Mexico City. By the 25th the whole of Chihuahua was in his hands. At about this time Villa formed an elite force of horsemen, known as the *dorados* because of the gold insignia they wore on their olive uniforms and stetsons. There were three squadrons of 100 men each and they were the pick of his cavalry. Each man was superbly mounted, owning two horses, a rifle

Pancho Villa. During the Mexican Revolution Villa's fast-moving mounted columns went from success to success until they were finally brought to a halt by European-style machine guns and barbed wire at the Battle of Celaya, in 1915.

and two pistols. They were the most mobile of his men, being unencumbered with families or camp followers, and were responsible for many of their leader's most daring coups. John Reed, who later reported Lenin's coup d'état, was attached to Villa's army at this time and he explained how the latter managed to make the most of his natural-born cavalrymen:

> Up to this day Mexican armies had always carried with them hundreds of the women and children of the soldiers; Villa was the first to think of the swift forced marches of bodies of cavalry, leaving their women behind. Up to his time no Mexican army had ever abandoned its base; it had always stuck closely to the railroad and the supply trains. But Villa struck terror into the enemy by abandoning his trains and throwing his entire effective army into the field.

It was the mobility of such men that prompted the following message from one of the harassed Federal commanders: 'I have the honour to inform you that according to all information that is true and verified, Villa is at this moment in all parts and none in particular.'

Villa won many more dashing victories but eventually he too fell victim to the weaponry that had driven cavalry from the field in Europe. The leaders of the revolution began to quarrel amongst themselves and Villa found himself fighting the forces of Alvaro Obregón. They met, on 6 April 1915, at a small town called Celaya where the latter had firmly dug himself in, placing numerous machine guns amongst a network of trenches and barbed-wire entanglements. Villa made just the same blunder as was being made by English and French generals on the other side of the Atlantic, though it must be said in his defence that he had much less experience of the real potential of these kinds of weapons. After easily overrunning some of Obregón's outposts Villa threw his cavalry against the barbed wire. Over a thousand men were scythed down, including the bulk of the *dorados*. The next morning Villa ordered another assault and this time some men did manage to break through only to be driven out by Obregón's reserves. Villa retreated and Obregón stayed put, gambling that the former's pride would force him to attempt another assault. A week later he did just this, and once again his horsemen were torn to pieces by the automatic weapons and the barbed wire. As Villa's men were reeling after the last bloody repulse, Obregón sent in his own reserve cavalry, 6000 men who had been stationed outside the town, against his opponent's flank and the latter were completely routed. They were never again a force in Mexican history.

Africa

Guerrilla horsemen were not common in Africa. Most of the resistance to nineteenth-century imperialism took the form of doomed rushes on foot against the devastating firepower of the Europeans. Very occasionally horsemen adopted similarly fatal tactics, for example, the Fulani in northern Nigeria or Samori's cavalry in Guiné in the 1880s. On at least two occasions, however, when the terrain was appropriate, horsemen used their superior mobility to keep out of the way of the heavily armed European columns, striking only when they could guarantee a local superiority of numbers, or stage an ambush from some impregnable position.

One such war was almost the last occasion on which Arab cavaliers made a significant appearance. During the period of their great conquests most of North Africa had been overrun and over the centuries numerous small tribes had made their homes in the arid plateaux. In June 1830 the French decided that the time had come to establish a new empire and an army was landed in Algeria. The Ottoman regime of the coastal strip was soon overthrown, but the invaders were far less successful in their attempts to penetrate the interior. At first they met only parochial resistance from the local tribes but their problems were greatly increased with the emergence of a supra-tribal leader, Abd-el Kader, who was able to coordinate Arab activity and make them forget their ancient feuds. Their new leader knew that he had little chance of defeating the French in open battle. Instead he set up a three-line defence and, sustaining them from huge underground granaries, sent his riders to harry the French ceaselessly, hanging on their flanks, cutting communications, seizing their baggage and transports, making unexpected attacks, and luring the enemy into ambushes with feigned retreats. As he himself wrote, in a letter to Louis-Philippe: 'It will be a partisan war to the death. I am not so foolish as to imagine that I can openly make headway against your troops; but I can harass them ceaselessly. I shall lose ground, no doubt; but then I shall have on my side a knowledge of the country, the frugality and hardiness of my troops.'

The French were unable to make any headway at all until 1840 and the appointment of Bugeaud as governor and supreme military commander. Till then they had insisted upon maintaining numerous garrisons that really controlled nothing but the ground within their walls, and sending out huge columns, loaded down with heavy equipment and bulky uniforms, that were ceaselessly harried on the march and as often as not lured to final destruction. Bugeaud had long realized that the war had no purely military solution. Abd-el Kader was out to avoid pitched battles, and any skirmish, 'like all those of this type, has not given any great material results. How is one to kill or capture many of an enemy who do not stand fast and who knows how to avoid the penalties of defeat by disappearing with astonishing rapidity?' Yet even the frugal and hardy horsemen had to live on something. Even if they could never be brought to battle and whatever engagements there were were generally inconclusive, it might still be possible to defeat them by keeping numerous sizeable columns of troops continually in the field. These columns were generally infantry because the French, like the US Cavalry, found that they moved faster than horsemen over a long period, particularly when mounted on mules as was sometimes done. They were made large enough, about 7000 men, to be immune from any Arab attack, and yet there were sufficient of them to be able to cover large tracts of territory. Their aim was two-fold: to keep the enemy on the move and deny him the opportunity to rest, recuperate and establish supply bases, and to seek out and destroy his secret crops, growing and harvested. In this way, even though the French could never hope to match the mobility of the Arab horsemen, and could rarely bring their superior firepower to bear, they did render that mobility essentially useless. The ability to escape demands that one have somewhere worth escaping to. Eventually Bugeaud denied such havens to his enemy. Abd-el Kader, like Geronimo, Cochise, Chief Joseph and other Indian leaders, was forced to acknowledge that the ability to run away was not enough. When the white man wanted your land he was indefatigable and in time ubiquity could be an adequate compensation for a lack of mobility.

Another people who learnt this lesson were the Boers of South Africa, in the very first years of the twentieth century. The Boer War had begun as a fairly conventional conflict but from November 1900 the Boers began to realize that they could no longer hope to face the British in pitched battle. After the last such engagement, at Rhenoster Kop, they decided to eschew the open warfare of Natal and to make their centres of operations in the mountains and *veld* of the Orange Free State and Transvaal. They split into their traditional bands, or *commandos*, and decided to rely absolutely on the mobility of their African ponies. Even during the Natal campaigns they had always been quite prepared to

A rather romanticized version of an Algerian Arab horseman in the nineteenth century. Such riders, in a somewhat more disreputable version, plagued the French in a twenty-year guerrilla war in Algeria.

mount up and ride away as soon as they felt that they had inflicted sufficient casualties upon the English. Like the Apaches they saw no shame in attempting to stay alive. Now they decided to avoid large-scale engagements completely and compel the British to hunt them down, turning only to make a sudden ambush on some unwary detachment, or to snipe at them from a considerable distance. Numerically it seemed that the Boers had no chance at all. In late 1900 they had only 60,000 effectives, with only a quarter of these in arms at any one time, whilst the British forces numbered 210,000. But the latter's tactics were quite inappropriate to the new conditions. *The Times* history of the war admirably summed up the futility of the operations:

> Each [column] was composed mainly of infantry, with guns, howitzers, field hospitals and bearer companies, engineers, and . . . cumbrous trains or wagons drawn by oxen and generally overloaded . . . These columns marched solemnly about the country at an average pace of ten to fifteen miles a day . . . The word had gone out that they were not to be opposed but that after their departure, the towns and districts through which they had passed were immediately to be reoccupied. Accurately informed of the British movements by their scouts . . . the burghers ran few risks of capture, and even on the rare occasions when they were surprised, simply scattered and galloped away until they were out of sight.

In 1901, Kitchener, the commander in this phase of the war, beautifully expressed the infuriated bewilderment of the European regular officer when faced with such tactics: 'The Boers are not like the Sudanese who stood up to a fair fight. They are always running away on their little ponies.' (In the fair fight against the Sudanese, British rifles and machine guns *killed* 11,000 Dervishes. Their own losses included only 48 killed.) But at least Kitchener realized that massive infantry columns could never be the answer in such open, rolling terrain and he asked the government substantially to increase his complement of cavalry. By May 1901, one-third of his 240,000 men were mounted. He then began to form special mounted columns to operate as individual raiding parties, almost totally independent of central control. These were used particularly extensively in the Free State, where commanders like Major Remington made great reputations for themselves. Later use was made of night raids. These had been initiated by Colonel Benson, who began to make long marches at night to bring himself within striking distance of a Boer *laager* just as dawn rose. Though two-thirds and more of the Boers generally escaped, this tactic greatly increased their sense of insecurity. Benson's most successful raids took place in August and September 1901 and by December General Bruce Hamilton was put in charge of organizing a much more extensive series of such raids. The cavalry was also used to support more conventional infantry columns and try to stop the Boers escaping through the gaps in the British line. As Kitchener himself said: 'The rate of captures can only be maintained by the more extended action of extremely mobile troops freed of all encumbrances, whilst the remainder of the column clears the country and escorts transport.' But even at their best, the British cavalry were never the match of the Boers in this extended game of hide-and-seek. Their traditions were entirely different. They were trained to charge shoulder-to-shoulder with sabre or lance and did not possess the initiative or open-mindedness for anything more complicated than a furious gallop across a few hundred yards. Also, as so often in this type of war, the mere possession of horse did not guarantee parity with the enemy. Conan Doyle was particularly outspoken on this point in his history of the struggle:

> Every train of thought brings the critic back always to the great horse question, and encourages the conclusion that there, in all seasons of the war and in all scenes of it, is to be found the most damning indictment against British foresight, common-sense, and power of organization. That the third year of the war should dawn without the British having yet got the legs of the Boers, after having penetrated every portion of their country and having the horses of the world on which to draw, is the most amazingly inexplicable point in the whole of this strange campaign . . . [On the one hand is] the failure to secure the excellent horses on the spot while importing them unfit for use from the ends of the earth . . . [on the other] the obvious lesson that had not been learnt that it is better to give 1000 men two horses each, and so let them reach the enemy, than give 2000 men one horse each, with which they can never attain their objective.

In fact, the cavalry war was never pursued with a vigour sufficient to permit of a military solution. Even after Kitchener's arrival many large-scale drives were organized in which it was intended to devastate the countryside and overcome the Boers by sheer weight of numbers. These 'New Model drives' were to 'clear the country systematically of supplies, horses, cattle, crops, transport vehicles and non-combatant families.' Also sufficient men were to be used such that no gaps at all were to appear in the advancing line. One such drive was organized in February 1902, when 9000 men were drawn up in a continuous cordon 54 miles long. A few Boers did manage to break through but the rest, as one correspondent saw, 'were shot like game . . . [or] fell back, stunned and bewildered, into the interior of the trap, their horses foundered, their bandoleers empty, their bodies worn out . . .' Yet, even when the Boers surrendered in April 1902, there were still 22,000 of them under arms. But the cruel lesson had

been learnt once again. Even the best horsemen in the world are powerless against an enemy, no matter how ponderous, who is prepared to harry you for years to come and who will, if necessary, destroy your country completely.

Asia

There was nothing in the nineteenth century that even approached the nomadic invasions of antiquity and the Middle Ages. Almost everywhere the great hordes had been reduced to submission by the power of the Romanov and Manchu armies. Yet here and there there occurred not inconsiderable outbursts of guerrilla activity in which elusive horsemen temporarily held powerful enemies at bay.

The Russians came up against such an adversary in the Caucasus, in the 1830s and 1840s. These were the Murids who lived in the mountains of Daghestan. Although their homeland was in parts of the most rugged and precipitous nature, they were accustomed to go around on small, sure-footed ponies which could negotiate all but the most impossible terrain. The best horsemen of all, however, were the Tchetchens, the elite of the Murid army, who inhabited the more fertile lowland areas. They were organized into units of 10s, 100s and 500s, and were clad in the Caucasian tunic, the *tcherkessa*, boots and shaggy black hats, known as *bourkas*. Their arms were flintlock muskets and swords. Many of

Australian lancers in South Africa, in 1900.

169

Members of a Boer Commando. After the early pitched battles, the Boers took to guerrilla warfare and, with very small numbers of hardy horsemen, ran rings around the British forces, infantry and cavalry.

these latter had been handed down for generations and were so sharp that they had been known to slice through the barrel of a Russian musket at one stroke. Every male was liable for service though the most successful of their leaders, Shamyl, kept the nucleus of a standing army in which one man from every ten households was maintained in constant readiness. One of the few historians to have examined these campaigns had this to say about Shamyl's strategy:

One great advantage of . . . [his] military system was that it enabled him to gather or disperse his forces at will, and in an incredibly short space of time; it allowed him also to dispense with any elaborate commissariat . . . From his central position at Dileem he threatened the enemy north, east and south, kept them continually on the move, dispersed his commandos to their homes, gathered them again as if by magic, and, aided by the extraordinary mobility of mounted troops who required no baggage, nor any equipment or supplies but what each individual carried with

him, swooped down on the Russians continually where least expected.

A Russian general, Tornau, has left a description of the tactics of these swift guerrillas as they suddenly appeared on the flanks or the rear of some Russian detachment: 'The Tchetchens had a way of handling their weapons only at the last moment. They would charge on the enemy at tremendous speed; at twenty paces they would fire, holding their reins in their teeth; then swinging back their guns they would rush right on the Russians, whirling their *shashkas* over their heads, slashing with fearful strength.'

As with the other counter-insurgency commanders mentioned in these pages, the Russians never managed to elaborate tactics that would enable them to face the Murids on equal terms. To the very end they found it impossible to track down any of the bands of mounted warriors. Once again they were obliged to attack the countryside as a whole rather than the fighting men. From the 1850s Prince Bariatinsky set in motion a huge programme of forest clearance to uncover the villages in which the Murid regulars were quartered. These were burnt down, the crops were destroyed, and the Murids were driven into the very heart of the mountains, where even their horses were of little use. Once the forests had been completely cleared the Russians attacked the mountains themselves. They built bridges across the great gorges, to avoid the necessity of tortuous ascents and descents along winding trails. Finally, when the Murids were isolated in a few remaining strongholds, Bariatinsky used dynamite and long-range artillery to blow them to pieces.

The history of China in the nineteenth century is punctuated by a whole series of uprisings and rebellions. Some of these were against the Europeans who had taken upon themselves a greater and greater say in Chinese affairs, whilst others were directed at Manchu authority itself. The greatest of the latter was the bloody civil war known to us as the Taiping Rebellion, between 1852 and 1864. The war as a whole is of little interest in terms of conventional mounted warfare. Both sides were composed mainly of infantry, though each did use some contingents of steppe horsemen. In the 1850s, however, another group became involved in the general hostilities. These were the Nien, a secret association of poor peasants, salt-smugglers and bandits inhabiting the sandy region between the Yangtse Basin and the Yellow River, in the administrative no-man's-land of the Kiangsu, Honan, Shantung and Chihli border areas. The word 'nien' means twist or roll and was used to denote the secret cells of the organization, which became openly subversive from 1853, when the Taiping rebels captured Nanking. The Nien had always been great horsemen and maintained large herds of small ponies in the interior of their domain. They now began to form numerous bands of raiders who from 1855 cooperated militarily with the Taipings. In 1857 they joined the rebels in Anhui and in 1862 it was feared that they might come to help raise the siege of Nanking. Even after the Taiping collapse in 1864 the Nien fought on and their guerrilla horsemen fought over much of northern China. An Englishman, Andrews Wilson, was in China at this time and has left the following description of Nien warfare:

> They move about in large parties . . . The women and the carts usually follow the public road while the men scatter about over the country but retreat to the wagons when danger appears. They are all pretty well mounted on good ponies and can move when necessary at the rate of 60 miles a day. Captain Coney of H.M. 67th Regiment, who went out against them with some disciplined Chinese in 1863, never saw the Nien-fei till the Nien-fei concentrated an attacked him, and when they found they were getting the worst of it they were out of range again in a few minutes. Extremely ill-armed, with spears, rusty swords, gingalls and a few cannon, they are very bad shots. They take good care, however, to send patrols out before them, and are chary of going in directions where they are likely to meet with serious resistance.

Wilson was a little too disparaging. In 1865 the Nien fought and killed the Manchus' best general, the Mongolian, Seng-ko-lin-chin in a campaign in which they wore his troops out by marching in circles and darting about this way and that like swarms of ants. In June 1865 the Manchus sent another of their more able generals, Tseng Kuo-fang against them but it took him the best part of three years to wear them down. One of his reports indicates the difficulties he faced:

> The Nien-fei suddenly appear and as quickly disappear – a hundred *li* in the flash of an eye! The reports of the spies are very uncertain. Being without definite information, I have not been able to turn and go everywhere. On the contrary there is nothing to do but take the word of each leader, allowing him to be his own spy, have full control, go or stop at will, with plans adapted to the circumstances.

A Nien guerrilla. The Nien were bandits in northern China who rose against the central government during the Taiping rebellion; for several years their horsemen easily eluded, and often defeated, all armies sent against them.

As well as allowing his subordinates to use their own initiative and operate in independent units, Tseng also mounted as many of his troops as possible, arming them with modern carbines. The Nien, too, contributed to their own defeat. In 1867, carried away with their success, they began to organize regular regiments of horsemen and infantry armed with heavy pikes. They consolidated into two main armies and gave Tseng the chance to surround them and inexorably close in. In the ensuing pitched battles his superior firepower began to tell and by 1868 the movement had been utterly crushed.

The 20th Deccan Horse waiting to be shot to pieces on the Somme, on 14 July, 1916. After almost two years of war, Douglas Haig had no better answer to German machine guns than a cavalry charge.

unwise, because in order to shorten the war, and reap the fruits of any success, we must make use of the mobility of the cavalry.' In the early evening of 14 July Haig put his theories to the test. Two squadrons each of the 20th Deccan Horse and the 7th Dragoon Guards carried out a charge against unshaken German infantry in High Wood. As they came out of the cornfields in front of the wood a German machine gun opened up. As the German commander in this sector wrote: 'The frontal attacks over open ground against a portion of our unshaken infantry, carried out by several English cavalry regiments, which had to retire with heavy losses, gives some indication of the tactical knowledge of the Higher Command.'

This knowledge was not in the least enriched by the débâcle at High Wood. In September 1916 Lloyd George himself went to France to confer with his generals about preparations for the year's last attacks. He saw what to him were peculiar sights:

I have driven through squadrons of cavalry clattering proudly to the front. When I asked what they were for, Sir Douglas Haig explained that they were brought up as near to the front line as possible, so as to be ready to charge through the gap which was to be made by the Guards in the coming attack. The cavalry were to exploit the anticipated success and finish the German rout ... When I ventured to express my doubts as to whether cavalry could ever operate successfully on a front bristling for miles behind the enemy's lines with barbed wire and machine guns ... the Generals fell on me.

Optimism about the horsemen's potential still reigned supreme in 1917. In April, during the battle of Arras, Monchy-le-Preux was captured by three tanks, and two brigades of cavalry were moved up to exploit the gap. An officer of the Highland Light Infantry witnessed what followed:

An excited shout was raised that our cavalry was coming up. Sure enough, away behind us, moving quickly in extended order down the slope . . . was line upon line of mounted men, covering the whole extent of the hill-side as far as we could see . . . It may have been a fine sight, but it was a wicked waste of men and horses, for the enemy immediately opened on them a hurricane of every kind of missile he had . . . They bunched behind Monchy in big mass into which the Boche continued to put high-explosive, shrapnel, whizz-bangs, and a hail of bullets . . . The horses seem to have suffered most, and for a while we put bullets into poor brutes that were aimlessly limping about on three legs, or else careering about madly in their agony; like one I saw that had the whole of its muzzle blown away.

Even the cavalrymen themselves began to get somewhat disillusioned. General Jack wrote in his diary on 20 July: 'High Command . . . continue to expect that infantry assaults will burst a gap in the German defences large enough for horsemen to ride through . . . The 10th Hussars, which lost some two thirds of their men at the Battle of Arras . . . do not appear to share this belief.' A breakthrough was achieved at Cambrai, in November of the same year, but once again the cavalry had to learn the lesson that even tiny numbers of well-armed survivors were quite capable of holding off such a vulnerable target. Five divisions attempted to exploit the gap but as the Official History pointed out, citing an American observer: 'You can't make a cavalry charge until you have captured the enemy's last machine gun.'

Even in the final months of the war, when the Allied advance began to gather some momentum, the cavalry never had much of a part to play. For at no stage did the Germans collapse, and there were always present sufficient strong-points to hold up any cavalry probes. When the British finally broke the Hindenburg Line into open country, in the following four weeks up to the Armistice, only twenty miles of ground were taken. Prior to that breakthrough they were even of less use. Even though the basic point had been grasped that the old-fashioned cavalry charge was now inappropriate, those refinements that had been introduced still left something to be desired. In June 1918 a unit of French lancers was sent over the top and it was acknowledged that their horses were best left behind in the rear. They related the story of their attack to an infantry unit that later took over that section of the line. 'They added that, in accordance with the orders received to maintain the cavalry spirit, they had charged on foot with their lances at the ready.' For the British the refinement was the introduction of tanks which the cavalry regarded as a convenient armoured spearhead to prelude their own dash behind the enemy lines. To the men of the Tank Corps, however, the cavalry were simply a waste of time. On 1 August 1918, during the battle of Amiens, two cavalry divisions were allotted to support a battalion of Whippet tanks. The latter's subsequent judgement was extremely scathing: 'The plan and policy of placing the [tanks] . . . under the cavalry proved a disappointment, as could have been foreseen. For when there was no fire the cavalry outstripped these tanks, and as soon as fire was opened the cavalry were unable to follow the tanks.' In its *Weekly Notes* Tank Corps HQ made the point that should have been glaringly obvious from the very first weeks of the war, four years previously: 'Being tied down to support the cavalry [the tanks] were a long way behind the infantry advance, the reason being that, as cavalry cannot make themselves invisible on the battlefield by throwing themselves flat on the ground as infantry can, they had to retire either to a flank or to the rear to avoid being exterminated by machine gun fire.'

If the experiences of the Western Front proved anything of military significance it was that armour was infinitely superior to horsemen in the horrific conditions of no-man's-land. Some men of vision also realized that one day tanks would be able to rival cavalry in mobility and quite supersede this antique arm. Yet after the hostilities were over the British only deemed it advisable to reduce the number of regular cavalry regiments from 28 to 20. One reason for this, apart from hidebound attitudes, was the somewhat misleading record of the cavalry in the Palestine theatre. There, in 1917 and 1918, Allenby succeeded in absolutely crushing the Turkish armies. His campaign was a masterly one in which secrecy, flanking movements and bold advances were used to maximum effect. A substantial portion of Allenby's forces were horsemen (12,000 sabres, 57,000 infantry and 540 guns in September 1918) and this led many theorists to believe that the victory was a complete vindication of the cavalry arm. It should be emphasized, however, that nothing could have been achieved without the infantry and artillery, and it is far from clear whether the infantry alone could not have achieved the same results. It should also be remembered that the Turkish armies were hardly first-class troops and by late 1918 they were outnumbered two to one.

Be that as it may, there were at least opportunities for old-fashioned cavalry action, some of the last

9 The Last Years 1914 to 1945

'The charge will always remain the thing in which it
will be the cavalryman's pride to die sword in hand.'
Cavalry Journal 1909

'The Soviet Republic needs to have a cavalry force.
Red cavaliers, forward! Proletarians, to horse!'
Leon Trotsky, 1919

World War I

The Boer War had shown that there was still a place for the horse in certain types of warfare. But it should also have made it obvious that, even in limited war of this kind, the mediocre firepower available to the Boers was still sufficient to prohibit the use of the old-fashioned cavalry charge. An English correspondent accompanying with the cavalry wrote at the end of the struggle:

> The cavalryman in South Africa . . . has not been able to rejoice in the tumult of the charge, to override in close knit masses the opposing squadrons of his enemy, to thunder with loose rein and bloody spur upon disorganized and shaken infantry, nor descend like a thunderbolt upon his foeman's guns, and sweep triumphantly through disordered ranks. The only part of the recognized duty of the horseman which has fallen to his lot has been . . . reconnaissance . . . the extended patrol and . . . swift and hazardous flank movements.

At the time even the most obdurate of traditional cavalrymen recognized that the latter duties were the most likely tasks of cavalry in the future, though they might have also paused to wonder whether the much greater firepower available to European armies might not render even this limited role impossible. In the event, however, pique and the brittle sensibilities of aristocratic regulars denied any opportunity for rational investigation. In the closing months of the war the cavalry was badly handled, largely because of the shortage of adequate mounts. Precious opportunities were lost and certain senior commanders were not slow to point it out. A politician at the time, L. C. Amery, showed just how pig-headed the cavalry could be when their reputation was called into question:

> [Towards the end of the war] Roberts and Ian Hamilton both issued memoranda showing that under modern conditions the old cavalry tactics were dead and that the true function of the horse in war was to convey the rifleman most swiftly to the tactically effective firing point or enable him to ride rapidly through a zone of fire [sic]. These were actually the tactics French and his Chief of Staff, Haig, had developed with such success . . . But to be told this by a gunner and an infantryman was too much! French and Haig worked themselves into a mood of opposition and, in spite of all their South African experience, convinced themselves that only the old knee to knee cavalry charge with lance or sword would decide the wars of the future.

So it was in 1913 that one British officer had the following conversation with Haig: 'I asked Haig . . . why there were four brigades in the cavalry division, more than any man can control, as the Germans had discovered. He replied, "But you must have four." "Why?" "For the charge. Two brigades in the first line, one in support, and you must have one in reserve." '

Many brave men were to pay the price of this petulance in the years to come. Not just the large numbers of horsemen who were sent to France and Flanders during the World War I; the PBI also had cause to regret the 'cavalry spirit' of their dashing commanders, who seemed to plan their great offensives as if *all* their troops were cuirassiers on some Frederickian battlefield. In fact, there were no important cavalry victories on the Western Front. As a Canadian cavalry commander put it, describing the prelude to one offensive: 'The object of this intense preparation was to use the cavalry to gallop through the breach made by the victorious infantry, and thus turn the enemy's defeat into a rout. The phrase commonly used was that we were to gallop through the "G" in "Gap".' They might as well have aimed for the dot in 'Futile'. Even in the opening weeks of the war, before the onset of trench warfare proper, little was achieved. During the British retreat from Mons the 9th Lancers and 18th Hussars attempted a flank attack near Valenciennes, only to be mown down by German machine guns. Something might perhaps have been achieved shortly afterwards when the Germans were halted on the Marne and a gap appeared between their Second and Third Armies. General Conneau's Cavalry Corps was poised for just such an eventuality but in the event it never budged. But hope lingered on. Even in October a British officer noted in his diary: 'Our advanced cavalry always ride sword in hand or lance at the "carry", and charge at sight any hostile mounted bodies within charging distance.' Almost two years of bloody stalemate still did not hammer the lesson home. In May 1916 a French infantry officer was treated to the sight of a regiment of lancers forming for the attack, lances couched. One of his fellow officers turned to him resignedly and said: 'They're holding all these fellows back for the breakthrough that we've been waiting for for two years . . . You know there's nothing like a lance against machine guns.'

Haig would not have appreciated the irony. The next month he had an interview at Buckingham Palace and was taken aback when the king suggested that the cavalry be reduced on account of the excessive cost of maintenance. 'I protested that it would be breakneck charges in the history of warfare. Ironically, none of the British regular regiments took part in this campaign. They were all locked up on the Western Front hammering away at the 'G' in 'Gap'. The Desert Mounted Corps, as it was known, was composed of English Yeomanry regiments, Indians, and Australian and New Zealand Light Horse. The latter, in particular, were not regarded as cavalry proper but as mounted infantry for whom the horse was only a means of transport. Nor were the Yeomanry archetypes of immaculate horsemen. One who fought with them has described the troopers thus: 'Dust-stained and tanned a dark mahogany, we rode without tunics, shirts cut short to the sleeves (new tennis fashion), each man carrying spare feeds and two water-bottles, and an old fruit tin or billy can.' On occasions, however, they behaved as though they were the shock troops of some eighteenth-century battlefield, though with the occasional unorthodox improvisation. The Australians, for example, captured the town of Beersheba with their horsemen.

It had been a source of great soreness with them that the Yeomanry used the sword whereas they were equipped with rifle and bayonet only. Not to be deterred by that, however, they mounted and formed into line; then fixing their bayonets and holding their rifles down under the right armpit, they galloped across the plain and charged at the remaining Turkish trenches, using the rifle and bayonet as a lance. It was a magnificent sight to see these fellows setting their horses to jump the trenches, and at the same time lunging and thrusting with this cumbersome weapon.

The charge was completely successful. Nor was it the only occasion upon which such tactics won the day. At Huj, the Worcester and Warwickshire Yeomanry actually charged two batteries of artillery across an open half mile of plain and by some miracle sufficient men got through to sabre the gunners where they stood. In July 1918, Australian horsemen counter-attacked a Turkish and German assault on the Ghoraniyeh bridgehead. The Turks retreated and left the Germans to fend for themselves. An English Yeoman recorded this account of the ensuing struggle by an Australian participant: '[The Turks] does a guy and leaves the other poor b—— up in the air. It was a shame to take the money, we just rides out bareback in our shirt-sleeves and hits a few over the head with the butt-end and one or two under the jaw. They sees its hopeless, so we brings them in . . .'

Yet many of these successes were against a demoralized enemy. Without in the least disparag-

ing the courage of those who took part, it should be realized that the Palestine experience was not a true indication of the material balance of forces on a conventional battlefield. Towards the end of the campaign, as one participant recorded, 'it had been impressed upon us . . . that, wherever possible, we were to indulge in "shock tactics"; that dismounted action was only to be employed as a last resort, and that in all cases the enemy was to be charged at sight.' An Australian cavalryman, Brigadier-General Wilson, praised the issue of sabres to his countrymen in September 1918, and allowed himself to indulge in just that same mystical speculation that had been the bane of European military doctrine at the turn of the century:

The issue of the sword was, I consider, more than justified. I consider that the sword has a great moral effect both on the man carrying it and on the enemy. One of the chief values of the sword is the spirit of progress it inspires in the carrier. He does not allow himself to be bluffed by slight opposition. He rides on feeling that he has a weapon in his hand, and nineteen times out of twenty finds the opposition only a bluff.

This was an unfortunate doctrine to hand down to soldiers who might later have to compete with self-confident troops who had carried the lessons of tank warfare to their logical conclusion. Or even soldiers who had entrenched themselves sufficiently well so as not to be outflanked with impunity. This lesson had been learnt on the Eastern as well as the Western Front. The Russians entered the war with thirty-six cavalry divisions. Their commanders made lavish claims about a new wave of Huns from the East overrunning everything before them and thrusting right into the heart of Germany. Reality was a bitter mockery of these hopes. In the first few days some Cossacks had penetrated into East Prussia and the German press began to feature lurid stories about wild Asiatics and a trail of rapine and pillage. Their success was short-lived. Hindenberg and Ludendorff surrounded the Russian Second Army and Samsonov's special guard of Don Cossacks was cut to pieces. Regular cavalrymen fared even worse. Their mobility proved a chimera for the very size of the theatre meant that they had to be transported by train and it was found that a cavalry division of 4000 men required just as many trains, – about forty – to transport it as did a division of 16,000 infantry men.

A modern historian of the Eastern Front has given an admirable account of the true worth of these obsolete and anachronistic cavaliers:

An expectant Russian lancer in 1914. Horsemen were used in large numbers by the Russians and Austrians, although they were consistently as useless as their counterparts on the Western Front.

(*opposite*) Russian Cavalry in 1915. Note the primitive steppe ponies, not very different from those of their Mongol ancestors.

There were sporadic cavalry engagements in East Prussia after 15th August but they usually ended in bloody withdrawal for the cavalrymen. Elderly cavalrymen, who had looked forward to a crowning achievement in a life of boots-and-saddles, broke down in bewilderment. The cavalry commander of I Army, the aged Khan of Natchchevan, was the nearest thing that the Russian Army came to a Hun. He was found in a tent, within a few miles of the border, weeping, out of touch with his troops, and suffering so badly from piles that he could not get on his horse at all.

The Germans and Austrians did not fare any better. The former soon stopped trying as they took account of the new battle conditions. The Austrians were forced to desist because it was found that their regulation saddle was completely unsuitable for any but horses inured to it after years on the parade

ground. All the requisitioned horses had the skin rubbed off their backs, the hot weather only intensifying the problem. Great masses of horsemen set out on raids in the first days of the war. Few even made contact with the enemy and the bulk of those riders that returned did so on foot. By the third week in August a half of all the cavalry mounts were out of action, most of the remainder nearly so.

The Russian Revolutionary Wars

It is one of the ironies of history that cavalry, the most reactionary arm in all European armies, was of more service to the Bolshevik regime between 1919 and 1921 than it had ever been to the Tsarist autocracy during the previous century. Trotsky was at first very disparaging to those who suggested that this arm could be of any use to a revolutionary army. At one stage he said: 'You don't understand the nature of cavalry. That is a very aristocratic family of

troops, commanded by princes, barons and counts . . .' His fears were not unjustified and the Russian army was no exception to the European rule. In 1912, for example, 48 per cent of the graduates of the War College were nobles, and a high proportion of these went into the elite cavalry units. But he soon had to revise his views. The Russian battlefields of the Civil War were a very different proposition from those of the fight against Germany and Austria-Hungary. The war and the revolution had brought the Russian economy to a standstill. Neither the Soviets nor the Whites could muster the munitions or supplies for large armies whilst concerted central planning was minimal on both sides. The Civil War was one fought by tiny detachments dwarfed by the vastness of the theatres of operations. Almost nowhere was it possible to establish a viable line of defence and the fronts ranged over huge distances from month to month. In such circumstances

horsemen proved invaluable. There were few heavy weapons to mow them down, no aircraft to detect their movements and a shortage of infantrymen prepared to stand their ground in entrenched positions. The fronts, in fact, were nothing more than a series of exposed flanks, a feebly dotted line easily penetrated by bands of enterprising horsemen.

Both sides formed cavalry detachments at an early date. Many of the White officers could hardly imagine another way of fighting, whilst quite a few of the Bolsheviks fell back on old Cossack traditions. Nor were all Imperial soldiers supporters of the counter-revolution. One ex-cavalryman who went over to the Reds was Semyen Mikhailovitch Budenny who, with Voroshilov, formed a squadron of horse in July 1918. But the Whites were the first to use them on any large scale and their successes with deep raiding parties forced Trotsky to reconsider his position. In June 1919 he wrote to Lenin: 'Cavalry is essential at all costs . . . All that needs to be realized is that the issue of victory or defeat turns on this.' In August 1919 he reported to the Central Committee and outlined his new viewpoint that the strategic conditions of the Civil War were such that horsemen were the most appropriate arm:

We have not had sufficient cavalry up to the present. But if, as experience has shown, cavalry is of enormous importance in a civil war of manoeuvre, its role in Asian operations would appear indisputably decisive. One authoritative military official already some months ago put up a plan for creating a cavalry corps (30,000–40,000 riders) with the idea of launching it against India.

The greatest impulse to action came in this month when the White cavalry commanders, K. K. Mamontov and Skhuro launched a massive raid. Some 7000 horsemen broke through the Red Army front and two columns swept on to Tambov and Kozlov. They did not rejoin Denikin's main army until 19 September. In the following months there was continual large-scale raiding in the Communist rear. In September Trotsky drew up an appeal for more horsemen, entitled 'Proletarians, to Horse', in which he reiterated the particular need for substantial mobile cavalry forces:

The insufficiency of her cavalry is the great weakness of the Red Army. As a war of manoeuvre, our war demands extreme mobility. The cavalry, therefore, has a great task to fulfill. In this respect, we have already fully realized our weakness; Kaledin, Krasnov, Doutov have always had the advantage over us in cavalry. At this very time, the destructive raids by Mamontov make absolutely necessary the formation of numerous units of Red cavalry . . . [Our raids] in depth will be facilitated by the fact that they take place in our own country, where the people and customs are well known by all the participants, where the same language is spoken . . . The conditions are not those of international war but of civil war. The most conservative and virtually moribund arm suddenly comes to life and becomes one of the most important means of attack and defence in the hands of the most conservative classes, at the very moment when they are disappearing. We must seize this arm from them and make it our own. The proletarian revolution must establish a powerful Red Cavalry.

Considerable success was achieved. On 2 December, Budenny was put in charge of the First Cavalry Army, the legendary *Konarmiya*, and they soon

managed to prevent the Whites raiding with quite the same impunity as before. One rather remarkable fact was that a substantial proportion of these Red cavaliers were authentic proletarians, moving straight from the factory to the saddle. In 1920, according to one source, 21·7 per cent of them were workers, a figure comparable to the most proletarian infantry division, 26·4 per cent. Budenny sought success by use of mass and surprise. Each division was allotted a march zone through which it advanced, avoiding the use of main roads. Full use was made of what modern weapons were available and it would be wrong to think of the Red Cavalry as purely traditional do-or-die horsemen. A division's advance was covered by a deployed unit of machine guns, mounted on carts, pushed well forward, whilst a battery of field guns usually formed part of the advance guard. The attacks were launched to surprise weakly held sectors of the front. While the fortified posts were blinded by intense machine-gun fire, the regiments infiltrated between them, turning the flank of the resistance.*

These tactics did not always work and the White cavalry was far from being outclassed. The Bolsheviks were completely defeated in an assault on the Bataisk Heights, near Rostov-on-Don, in October 1920, when their old enemies Mamontov and Skhuro took the laurels of the day. The independent Ukrainian anarchist, Makhno, was Budenny's other main opponent during the Civil War and he too scored many successes. One of his supporters was particularly scathing about the Reds and expressed a rather reactionary preference for the traditional tactics of the Whites:

Denikin's cavalry merited the highest praise. As Makhno declared, it was truly a cavalry that justified its name. The very numerous cavalry of the Red Army, organized later, was a cavalry in name only; it was never able to carry on hand-to-hand combat and engaged in combat only when the enemy was already disorientated by the fire of cannons and machine guns . . . The Caucasian cavalry regiments and Denikin's Cossacks always accepted combat with sabres and charged on the enemy at full speed, without waiting for him to be disorganized by cannon fire.

Be that as it may, it was units of the Red Cavalry that participated in the last cavalry versus cavalry engagements in the history of warfare. In early 1920 war broke out between Russia and Poland. Both

* In fact these tactics have much in common with those developed for infantry on the Eastern Front by the German General von Huitier, and used to great effect on the Western Front during the offensive of March 1918.

The Russian Horse Guards in 1914. Though of no use in World War I, such regiments provided the cadres of the White cavalry during the Russian Civil War. Occasionally, Imperial cavalrymen fought for the Reds, as did Semyen Budenny, who became the commander of the famous First Cavalry Army.

sides fielded large contingents of horsemen. The Russians used the trusty *Konarmiya*, now numbering 16,000 men, 304 machine guns and 48 artillery pieces. The Poles had several divisions, many of the regiments seeming to have come from another era. The 8th Uhlans, for instance, were all the sons of Galician gentry and were armed with lances and sabres. At first the Red Cavalry too seemed to think that the time had come to revert to the tactics of a bygone age. In June 1920 they attempted to storm Polish positions at Kuratov and Lipovets with head-on sabre charges. None of the attacks were successful and a conference was held on tactics. It was quickly agreed that cavalry attacks on trench positions were pointless. The delegates decided that the only feasible way of ousting infantry who had dug in was to advance in dismounted and scattered formation, to lay down heavy artillery fire and then to send small task forces against each of the strong-points. Mounted cavalry were to be used only to turn the flanks. If the enemy counter-attacked he was not to be frontally resisted but instead to be drawn into the cross-fire from the cavalry's own artillery and from its machine-gun posts.

On 5 June these tactics were successful and the *Konarmiya* broke through the Polish line at many points. In the ensuing long-range raiding there were several fights between mounted cavalry, though the only major confrontation was on 31 August when the Polish division commanded by Colonel Juliusz Rómmel ran into four Russian divisions. He concentrated upon trying to contain one sector of the Russian southern flank, around Zamość. There were two separate rounds of fighting. In the morning the Polish 7th Brigade made several charges against the Soviet 6th Division and succeeded in driving it from its positions. In the evening the 6th Brigade and the 9th Uhlans blundered into one another and the Poles immediately spurred their horses forward and charged into the Russians in the time-honoured and traditional fashion.

World War II

When the *Konarmiya* left Poland in September it meant the final end of old-style cavalry engagements. But this was not immediately apparent, least of all to the regular military establishments. At the end of World War I, as has been seen, the British made only a token reduction in their cavalry force, and right up to the outbreak of the next major European conflagration there were many who refused to believe that the age of the horsed warrior was past. In the early 1920s General Godley wrote: 'Whatever inventions and mechanical appliances there may be, you may always, in the end, have to fall back on the combination of the man and the horse.' In 1926, Haig, who of all people should have known better, reviewed a book on modern tactics that presumed to assert that there was no role for cavalry in mechanized warfare. He wrote: 'I believe that the value of the horse and the opportunity for the horse in future are likely to be as great as ever ... Aeroplanes and tanks are only accessories to the man and the horse, and I feel sure that as time goes on you will find just as much use for the horse – the well-bred horse – as you have ever done in the past.'

The 'debate' carried on in the 1930s. Discussing the Army Estimates for 1933–4, Mr Tinker wondered if too much money was being spent on the cavalry. The Conservative MP for Knutsford, Brigadier-General Makins, leapt to his feet. His testy rejoinder included the following statement: 'One thing that is very satisfactory is that the authorities feel that the day of cavalry is not done. In fact it is there just as much as ever.' Nor was this just the blatherings of a retired Blimp. The same sentiment prevailed throughout the army. An official report on the 1935 Staff College examinations stated: 'It is noticeable that a lot of sentiment is still attached to this question. For example such expressions as "The idea of the horse going is very sad" – "The horse must inevitably disappear from the Army in time, but this sad event must be delayed as long as possible".' Those in the government responsible for military matters did realize in the end that mechanization must replace the horse, but even here the transition was not viewed with wholehearted approval. In a speech in March 1936, the Secretary of State for War, Duff Cooper, reported to the House of Commons on the progress made so far. Two regiments of horse had already been mechanized and a further eight were to lose their mounts in the coming years. He congratulated the cavalry on the spirit in which they had received these changes and lamented: 'All the traditions of the regiment are bound up with their horses. It is like asking a great musical performer to throw away his violin and to devote himself in future to a gramophone. It is a great sacrifice for the cavalrymen.'

Yet the change was far from complete by 1939. Horsed cavalry were involved in at least two of the theatres of war. One was in Asia, in 1942, when part of an Indian regiment, sixty sabres of the Burma Frontier Force, was involved in the fighting against the Japanese. On 21 March they went out on reconnaissance to gather information about Japanese movements and stumbled over a force of their infantry. Though they had seen them from quite a

distance away they had assumed that they were Chinese Nationalists and as they moved towards the village of Toungoo they fell into an ambush. The commander and half his men, including a trumpeter, kept their heads and spurred their horses into a charge, yelling the traditional Sikh war cry of *Sat Sri Akal*. They were almost all killed. The other theatre was North Africa, in June and July 1941. The British found themselves opposed to Vichy French in Syria and mounted regiments were much in evidence on both sides. The British had an entire cavalry division of nine regiments, only three of them being transported by lorries. The French Army of the Levant included Legionary horsemen as well as squadrons of Lebanese and Circassian irregulars. The horsemen proved quite useful for reconnaissance operations but were hardly used at all for the offensive. The only clash between horsemen on each side took place on 14 June and was a very minor affair, in which units of the Cheshire Yeomanry brushed aside a thin French cavalry screen during the taking of Jezzine. Ironically, perhaps, the greatest disaster to the campaign involved regular cavalry who had been dismounted. These were the Scots Greys who became involved in the French counter-attack on Merdjayoun, on 14 July, and their poor performance was due to the almost complete lack of training in mechanized tactics. They broke completely and had to be moved out to 'reorganize'.

Cavalry also appeared in Europe itself, though their impact on the fighting was virtually nil. The Polish army had never been able to rid itself of its cavalry traditions and on the eve of the German invasion it included 3 regiments of light horse, 27 regiments of lancers and 10 regiments of *chasseurs à cheval*. In a book written in 1937, General Sikorski criticized those who advocated all-out mechanization, claiming that 'the horse squadron was still the arm best able to move on all terrains, to engage in regular combat, to investigate a covered zone, and to practise so-called delaying action.' But foreign military 'experts' had not done much to counteract such views. Clare Hollingsworth of the *Daily Telegraph* recorded an interview with a British military adviser in Poland, shortly before the war, in which the latter claimed that 'cavalry like the Poles' is more effective than you think. Motor columns must stop at night; then they are more vulnerable than ordinary troops. The cavalry will raid them, surprise them. They will destroy them. They will destroy some, and break the morale of the rest.' It would be difficult to be further from the truth. In one week the German tanks, lightly armoured and gunned as they were, slashed deep into the Polish lines and destroyed much of their army, reducing the rest of it to a disorganized rabble. The cavalry never had the opportunity to destroy one tank, let alone break the morale of the whole armoured corps. Nor was this their tactic. The cavalry attacked the *Panzers* virtually with their bare hands, though it is not absolutely sure whether there is any substance to the legend that lancers actually charged the tanks on horseback. The nearest I have found to an authenticated instance was near Katowice, in south-east Poland, on 3 September, when the Pomorze Cavalry Brigade found itself the only intact unit in front of the German armour. The commander gave the order to charge but not one of them even reached the tanks. Of the whole brigade, only 200 men rode back. But whether on foot or mounted the issue was never in doubt. Only anti-tank guns, aircraft or other tanks could have stopped the armoured columns and men armed with sabres and rifles had no chance at all. One source estimates that 90 per cent of the cavalry was killed. At Kutno an entire lancer brigade was wiped out by tanks and machine guns and a little later exactly the same thing happened near Chelmo, on the banks of the Vistula.

Strangely enough the cavalry did have some psychological impact on the invaders. General Guderian tells in his memoirs how on occasion the threat of advancing horsemen actually threw many German soldiers into a state of panic. At one stage he was stopped on the outskirts of a town by members of his own staff who were clad in steel helmets and busily engaged in setting up an anti-tank gun.

'When I enquired what the purpose of this was I was informed that Polish cavalry was advancing towards us and would be upon us at any minute. I calmed them down and proceeded to get on with my work at headquarters.' The same thing happened on another occasion. 'Shortly after midnight the 2nd (Motorized) Division informed that they were being compelled to withdraw by Polish cavalry. I was speechless for a moment; when I regained the use of my voice I asked the divisional commander if he had ever heard of Pomeranian grenadiers being broken by hostile cavalry. He replied that he had not and now assured me that he could hold his positions.'

Like the Poles the French had made only limited progress in their mechanization programme. In September 1939, on the north-eastern front, there were three cavalry divisions, composed of two brigades of horsed troops and only one armoured regiment. By the spring of 1940 the most frenzied efforts at re-equipping these units had produced only five divisions each of one horsed brigade and one mechanized. Militarily the horsemen achieved hardly anything and were generally used as riflemen to plug the line. Once again, however, the very threat of cavalry appearing sometimes unsettled German units. Guderian again relates one such incident on 10–11 May. 'Panzer Group von Kleist . . . ordered the 10th Panzer Division . . . to change direction at once and move on Longwy, since French cavalry were reported to be advancing from that direction. I asked for the cancellation of these orders; the detachment of one third of my force to meet the

Cossack cavalry on the Elbe in 1945. Because of the vastness of the theatre of operations, and the harshness of the climate, horsemen had several opportunities for large-scale raiding on the Eastern Front.

hypothetical threat of enemy cavalry would endanger the success . . . of the whole operation . . . [I took steps] to anticipate any difficulties that might be engendered by this curious fear of hostile cavalry . . .'

The only front on which cavalry could be said to have played an important role was the Russian, between 1941 and 1945. Throughout the interwar years the Soviets had always maintained a substantial cavalry arm, and even their progressive mechanization could not make them forget the exploits of the *Konarmiya*. In Frunze's reorganization of the Red Army, after Torotsy's dismissal in 1925, the 77 regular and territorial infantry divisions were supplemented by 11 cavalry divisions. In 1930 there were 13 divisions, in 1935 16, and by 1939 Voroshilov estimated that a further 50 per cent more horsemen had been added. The veterans of the First Cavalry Army were not immune to the same kind of traditionalism and dislike for technology that had typified the more aristocratic officer corps. At the 17th Party Congress, in 1934, he berated the modernizers and declared: 'First and foremost it is necessary to put an end once and for all to the wrecking "theories" on the substitution of men for horses, on the "withering away" of the horse.'

In the event, Voroshilov was more justified than some of his West European contemporaries, though to some extent this was because of faulty decisions by those in charge of the armoured troops. Following Pavlov's recommendations, in 1939, the armoured divisions had been broken up and distributed as separate brigades throughout the infantry army. Following the German successes in Poland and France frantic efforts were made to reorganize them back into more autonomous divisions, but only limited progress had been made. The cavalry divisions remained the only units with genuine operational independence. Terrain and climate also enhanced their value. The horses, shaggy little Kirkhil ponies from Siberia, could withstand temperatures of 30° below zero and they could easily negotiate the dense forests and muddy roads that often ground the tanks to a halt. It could hardly be claimed that these units were indispensable to Soviet victory – that was unobtainable until they had rebuilt their armoured formations – but they certainly helped to stem the German tide. Manstein wrote: 'A Soviet cavalry division can move, in its entirety, a hundred kilometres in a night – and that at a tangent to the axis of communication.' For this reason they were especially used for long-range independent raids behind the enemy's lines. In autumn 1941, Colonel-General Dovator remained

for two weeks in the German rear creating havoc wherever he went. In October Lieutenant-General Belov's cavalry corps (the corps was the standard Russian cavalry formation and consisted of three divisions, 19,000 men in all, though only about 8000 of them were actually mounted), towing their mortars and light artillery behind them, surrounded two German infantry divisions and almost completely wiped them out. In December, during Zhukov's counter-offensive, the same corps crossed the Oka on horseback, with sledges lashed to their saddles and infantrymen seated on their cruppers. In 1942 the Germans in the Pripet region were twice surrounded by Russian cavalry, and during the battle of the Dnieper–Berezina Triangle a cavalry corps advanced through the Pripet marshes into the rear of a German corps. The latter were without all contact with other units for eight days. General Halder wrote of Soviet operations in the German rear in June 1942: 'Cavalry Corps Belov is now floating around in the vast area west of Kirov. Quite a man that we have to send no less than seven divisions after him.'

Epilogue

Such was the last important appearance of cavalry in warfare. They have popped up since from time to time but in very small numbers and in fairly

A trooper of the North Frontier Tribal Police. This unit took part in the last British cavalry charge, in Kenya, in 1953, during the Mau Mau Emergency.

(*opposite*) A Khamba horseman in the 1960s. These Tibetan guerrillas, the true descendants of the nomadic Asiatic horsemen, are still fighting against the Red Chinese who now occupy their country.

unimportant roles. Their greatest usefulness since 1945 has been in anti-guerrilla operations. The British used a few mounted troops in Kenya, during the Mau Mau Emergency, hence the remarkable fact that the very last British cavalry action took place in 1953, near Isolio when a detachment of the North Frontier Tribal Police came across a guerrilla camp and successfully rode it down. The Portugese used mounted troops during the war in Angola but they achieved little, being pitted against a much more sophisticated and well-armed enemy than the Mau Mau. The Rhodesians have taken a leaf from the Portuguese book and certain of their counter-insurgency units are mounted, such as Grey's Scouts, though the latter seem to have done little but get involved in a scandal over allegations of torture. At least one force of guerrillas still uses horses to enhance their mobility. These are the Khamba tribesmen of Tibet fighting against the Red Chinese occupation forces. These are a mountain people, brigands and nomads, who are an exact modern equivalent of the Murids or the Nien. Their only modern chronicler has described them thus: 'Familiar with every crag, with every trail, with every rock, nook, creek and gully, moulded to their saddles, and accustomed to living by plunder, the so-called wild cavaliers, powered by desperation, united by blood and bone, represented a force

worthy of their great ancestors. Songsten Gampo and Genghis Khan rode amongst them.' The Chinese Communists themselves still maintain a small cavalry force, though not for use against the Khamba. Their three divisions are stationed in the north, in Kansu, Mongolia and Sinkiang, in the traditional grazing grounds of the Hsiung-nu, the Mongols and the Khitans. In the event of a war between Russia and China there might still be call for men mounted on these long-suffering ponies to traverse these vast trackless wastes. The Russians on the other hand, have finally renounced their cavalry arm. The last Cossack regiments were disbanded in the late 1950s. Ten years later, however, some of them at least got a bizarre reprieve. During the filming of the epic *War and Peace* the production executives found themselves saddled with a scratch collection of horses and riders who had no idea how to be proper lancers and hussars. A special regiment of trained horsemen was formed. Their commander, Colonel M. K. Barlio, even has Cossack blood, and since their inception they have ridden through over 200 films and TV programmes, posing indiscriminately as reactionary White Guards, Imperial hussars or heroes of the *Konarmiya*. Well over a hundred years too late the cavalry have finally acknowledged that theirs was a fantasy world.

185

Bibliography

Adcock, F. E., *The Greek and Macedonian Art of War*, University of California Press, 1957
—— *The Roman Art of War under the Republic*, Heffer, 1960
Ajayi, J. F. A. & Crowder, M., *History of West Africa*, (2 vols), Longmans, 1971
—— & Smith, S., *Yoruba Warfare in the 19th Century*, Cambridge University Press, 1964
Alfoldi, A., The Army and its Transformation, *Cambridge Ancient History*, vol 12, pp 208–22
Allen, W. E. D. & Muratoff, P., *Caucasian Battlefields*, Cambridge University Press, 1953
Ambrus, V. G., *Horses in Battle*, Oxford University Press, 1975
Ammianus Marcellinus, (trans. J. C. Rolfe), *Works*, (3 vols), Heinemann, 1950
Anderson, J. K., *Military Theory and Practice in the Age of Xenophon*, University of California Press, 1970
Anglesey, Marquis of, *History of the British Cavalry*, (2 vols), Leo Cooper, 1973–76
Appian (trans. H. White), *Roman History*, (4 vols), Heinemann, 1912–13
Arrian, (trans. A. de Sélincourt), *Anabasis of Alexander*, Penguin Books, 1958
Arshinov, P., *History of the Makhnovist Movement 1918–1921*, Solidarity, 1974
Ashdown, C., *Armour and Weapons in the Middle Ages*, Harrap, 1925
Ashtor, E., *A Social and Economic History of the Near East in the Middle Ages*, Collins, 1976
Asiaticus, *Reconnaissances in the Russo-Japanese War*, Hugh Rees, 1908
Atkin, R., *Revolution: Mexico 1910–1920*, Macmillan, 1969
Ayalon, D., *Gunpowder and Firearms in the Mamluk Kingdom*, Cambridge University Press, 1956

Bachrach, B. A., 'Charles Martel, Mounted Shock Combat, the Stirrup and Feudalism', *Studies in Renaissance and Medieval History*, vii, 1970
Baddeley, J. F., *The Russian Conquest of the Caucasus*, Longmans, 1908
Bain, R. N., *Slavonic Europe*, Cambridge University Press, 1908
Bajwa, F. S., *Military System of the Sikhs*, Motilal Banarsidass, 1964
Baker, B. G., *Old Cavalry Stations*, Heath Cranton, 1934
Banks, M., *A World Atlas of Military History*, Seeley Service, 1973
Barber, R., *The Knight and Chivalry*, Longmans, 1970
Baring, M., *What I Saw in Russia*, Heinemann, 1927
Barraclough, G., *The Origins of Modern Germany*, Blackwell, 1947
Bausani, A., *The Persians*, Elek Books, 1971
Bebel, I., 'Konarmiya', in *Collected Stories*, Penguin Books, 1975
Beeler, J., *Warfare in Feudal Europe*, Cornell University Press, 1971
Bengtsson, F. G., *The Life of Charles XII*, Macmillan, 1960
Bernhadi, F. von, *Cavalry in Future Wars*, John Murray, 1906
Blanch, L., *The Sabres of Paradise*, John Murray, 1960
Bloch, M., *Feudal Society*, (2 vols), Routledge Kegan Paul, 1965
Blunt, W., *Desert Hawk*, Methuen, 1947
Bokonyi, S., *The Przevalsky Horse*, Souvenir Press, 1974
Bond, B., 'Doctrine & Training in the British Cavalry', in M. Howard (ed.), *The Theory & Practice of War*, Cassell, 1965

Brereton, J. M., *The Horse in War*, David and Charles, 1976
Brown, D., *Bury My Heart at Wounded Knee*, Barrie and Jenkins, 1971
Brown, D. M., The Impact of Firearms on Japanese Warfare, *Far Eastern Quarterly*, vii (1948)
Brown, R. A., *The Origins of English Feudalism*, Allen and Unwin, 1973
Brownlee, R. S., *Grey Ghosts of the Confederacy*, Louisiana State University Press, 1958
Burn, A. R., *Alexander the Great and the Hellenistic World*, Collier Books, 1962
—— *The Pelican History of Greece*, Penguin Books, 1966

Caesar, J., *The Conquest of Gaul*, Penguin Books, 1952
Cahen, C., *Pre-Ottoman Turkey*, Sidgwick and Jackson, 1968
Candler, E., *The Long Road to Baghdad*, (2 vols), Cassell, 1919
Caron, L., 'The Army', in A. Tilley (ed.), *Medieval France*, Hafner, 1964
Chandler, D., *The Art of War in the Age of Marlborough*, Batsford, 1976
—— *The Campaigns of Napoleon*, Weidenfeld and Nicolson, 1967
Cheeseman, G. L., *The Auxilia of the Roman Imperial Army*, Clarendon Press, 1914
Chiang, S. T., *The Nien Rebellion*, University of Washington Press, 1954
Childers, E., *The Times History of the War in South Africa*, (vol 5), Sampson Low, 1907
—— *War and the Arme Blanche*, Edward Arnold, 1910
Chudoba, B., *Spain and the Empire, 1519–1643*, University of Chicago Press, 1952
Clark, A., *Barbarossa*, Hutchinson, 1965
Clenenden, C. C., *Blood on the Border*, Macmillan, 1969
Colin, J., *The Transformations of War*, Hugh Rees, 1912
Cooper, L., *British Regular Cavalry 1644–1914*, Chapman and Hall, 1965
Cotterel, L., *Enemy of Rome*, Evans Brothers, 1960
Creel, H. G., 'The Role of the Horse in Chinese History', *American Historical Review*, lxx (1965)
Crowder, M., *West African Military Resistance*, Hutchinson, 1971
Crozier, F. P., *Angels on Horseback*, Jonathan Cape, 1932
Cruickshank, C. G., *Elizabeth's Army*, Oxford University Press, 1966
Cruso, J., *Militarie Instructions for the Cavall'rie*, (1632), Roundwood Press, 1972
Curtiss, S. L., *The Russian Army under Nicholas I 1825–55*, Duke University Press, 1965

Das, S. T., *Indian Military* (sic), Sagar Publications, 1969
Davidov, *La Guerre des Partisans*, J. Correard, 1841
Davies, J. C., (ed.), *Pursuit of Power: Venetian Ambassadors' Reports*, Harper and Row, 1970
Davies, N., *White Eagle, Red Star*, Macdonald, 1972
Dawson, R., *Imperial China*, Hutchinson, 1972
Day, U. N., *The Mughal Government 1556–1707*, Munshiram Manoharlal, 1970
Denison, G. T., *History of Cavalry*, Macmillan, 1913
Dent, A., *The Horse through Fifty Centuries of Civilisation*, Phaidon, 1974
Deutscher, I., *The Prophet Armed. Trotsky 1879–1921*, Oxford University Press, 1954

Diehl, C., *Byzantium: Greatness and Decline*, Rutgers, 1957
Dikshitar, V. R. R., *War in Ancient India*, Macmillan, 1944
Dio Cassius (trans. E. Cary), *Roman History*, (9 vols),
 Heinemann, 1914–27
Downs, J. F., 'The Origin and Spread of Riding in the Near East
 and Central Asia', *American Anthropologist*, lxiii (1961)
Doyle, A. C., *The Great Boer War*, Smith Elder, 1905
Duffy, C., *The Army of Frederick the Great*, David and Charles, 1974
Depuy, R. E. & T. E., *Encyclopaedia of Military History*,
 Macdonald and Janes, 1977
—— *The Military Heritage of America*, McGraw–Hill, 1956
Dziewanowski, W., *Polish Armed Forces through the Ages*, Polish
 Travel Office, 1944

Eadie, J. W., 'The Development of Roman Mailed Cavalry',
 Journal of Roman Studies, lvii (1967)
Earle, E. M., *Makers of Modern Strategy*, Princeton University
 Press, 1941
Eaton, C., *A History of the Southern Confederacy*, Free Press, 1954
Eberhard, W., *A History of China*, Routledge Kegan Paul, 1975
Edwardes, M., *Everyday Life in Early India*, Batsford, 1969
Eichhorn, W., *Chinese Civilisation*, Faber, 1969
Elvin, M., *The Pattern of the Chinese Past*, Eyre Methuen, 1973
Erickson, J., *The Soviet High Command 1918–41*, Macmillan, 1962

Fairservis, W., *Horsemen of the Steppes*, Brockhampton Press, 1963
Faulk, O. B., *Crimson Desert*, Oxford University Press, 1974
Fawtier, R., *The Capetian Kings of France*, Macmillan, 1960
Fehrenbach, T. R., *Comanches*, Allen and Unwin, 1975
Firth, C. H., *Cromwell's Army*, Methuen, 1902
Fisher, H. J., 'The Horse in the Central Sudan, *Journal of African
 History*, xiii (1972) and xiv (1973)
Forde, D., & Kaberry, P. M., *West African Kingdoms in the 19th
 Century*, Oxford University Press, 1967
Formby, J., *Cavalry in Action*, Hugh Rees, 1905
Fowler, K., (ed.), *The Hundred Years War*, Macmillan, 1971
Fox, R. L., *Alexander the Great*, Allen Lane, 1973
Fraser, D., *A Modern Campaign*, Methuen, 1905
Frederic, L., *Daily Life in Japan at the Time of the Samurai*, Allen
 and Unwin, 1972
Fried, M. H., 'Warfare, Military Organisation and the Evolu-
 tion of Society', *Anthropologica*, iii (1961)
Froissart, *Chronicles*, J. M. Dent, 1923
Frontinus, (trans. C. E. Bennett), *Stratagems*, Heinemann, 1925
Frye, R. N., *The Golden Age of Persia*, Weidenfeld and Nicolson,
 1975
Fuller, J. F. C., *Armaments and History*, Eyre and Spottiswoode,
 1946
—— *The Conduct of War 1789–1961*, Eyre and Spottiswoode, 1961

Gabrieli, F., (ed.), *Arab Historians of the Crusades*, Routledge
 Kegan Paul, 1969
Ganshof, F. L., *Feudalism*, Longmans, 1964
—— *Frankish Institutions under Charlemagne*, Norton, 1970
Garlan, Y., *War in the Ancient World*, Chatto and Windus, 1975
Garthoff, R. L., *How Russia Makes War*, Allen and Unwin, 1952
Ghirshman, R., *Iran*, Penguin Books, 1954
Gibson, M., *The American Indian*, Wayland, 1974
Gibb, H. A. R., 'The Armies of Saladin', in *Studies on the Civilisa-
 tion of Islam*, Routledge Kegan Paul, 1972
Girardet, R., *La Société Militaire dans la France Contemporaine*, Plon,
 1953
Glubb, J. B., 'Arab Chivalry', *Royal Central Asian Society Journal*,
 v, (1951)
—— *The Great Arab Conquests*, Hodder and Stoughton, 1960

—— *The Empire of the Arabs*, Hodder and Stoughton, 1962
—— *The Course of Empire*, Hodder and Stoughton, 1965
—— *The Lost Centuries*, Hodder and Stoughton, 1967
Grant, M., *The Army of the Caesars*, Weidenfeld and Nicolson,
 1974
Green, P., *Alexander of Macedon*, Penguin Books, 1975
Green, V. H. H., *Medieval Civilisation in Western Europe*, E.
 Arnold, 1970
Greenhalgh, P. A. L., *Early Greek Warfare*, Cambridge University
 Press, 1973
Griffiths, G. T., *The Mercenaries of the Hellenistic World*, Cam-
 bridge University Press, 1935
Guderian, H., *Panzer Leader*, Michael Joseph, 1952
Guerdan, R., *Byzantium*, Allen and Unwin, 1956
Gurney, O. R., *The Hittites*, Penguin Books, 1952

Hail, W. J., *Tseng Kuo-fan and the Taiping Rebellion*, Yale
 University Press, 1927
Hale, J. R., *Guicciardini: History of Italy and History of Florence*, R.
 Sadler, 1964
—— 'International Relations in the West', *New Cambridge
 Modern History*, (vol 1), Cambridge University Press, 1957
—— 'Armies, Navies and the Art of War', *New Cambridge Modern
 History*, (vol 2), Cambridge University Press, 1962
—— 'Armies Navies and the Art of War', *New Cambridge Modern
 History*, (vol 3), Cambridge University Press, 1968
Halecki, O., *A History of Poland*, Dent, 1961
Hall, J. W., *Japan from Prehistory to Modern Times*, Weidenfeld and
 Nicolson, 1969
Hambly, G., (ed.), *Central Asia*, Weidenfeld and Nicolson, 1969
Hamilton, I., *A Staff Officer's Scrapbook*, (2 vols), E. Arnold, 1905
Hart, B. L., 'Analysis of Cavalry Operations in the American
 Civil War', in J. Luvaas, *Military Legacy* (op. cit.)
—— *The Soviet Army*, Weidenfeld & Nicolson, 1956
—— *The Tanks* (2 vols), Cassell, 1959
—— 'Two Great Captains: Ghenghis Khan & Subatai',
 Blackwoods Magazine, May 1924
Harvey, S., 'The Knight and the Knights in England', *Past and
 Present*, xlix (1970)
Hatton, S. F., *The Yarn of a Yeoman*, Hutchinson, nd
Herodian (trans. E. Echols), *History of the Roman Empire*,
 University of California Press, 1961
Herodotus (trans. A. de Sélincourt), *The Histories*, Penguin
 Books, 1972
Hewitt, H. J., *The Organisation of War under Edward III*,
 Manchester University Press, 1966
Heymann, F. G., *John Žižka and the Hussite Revolution*, Princeton
 University Press, 1955
Hillgarth, J. N., *The Spanish Kingdoms 1250–1410*, Clarendon
 Press, 1976
Hitti, P. K. (trans.), *An Arab-Syrian Gentleman Warrior in the Period
 of the Crusades*, Columbia University Press, 1929
Hogben, S. J. & Kirk-Greene, A. H. M., *The Emirates of Northern
 Nigeria*, Oxford University Press, 1966
Hogg, O. F. G., *Artillery: its Origin, Heyday and Decline*, C. Hurst,
 1970
Howard, M., *The Franco-Prussian War*, Rupert Hart-Davis, 1960
Hsü, I. C. Y., *The Rise of Modern China*, Oxford University Press,
 1970
Hucker, C. O., *China's Imperial Past*, Duckworth, 1975
Hughes, B. P., *Firepower*, Arms and Armour Press, 1974
Huntingford, G. W. B., *Some Records of Ethiopia*, Hakluyt Society,
 1954
Hussey, J. M., (ed.), 'The Byzantine Empire', *Cambridge Modern
 History*, (vol 4), Cambridge University Press, 1966

Inalcik, H., *The Ottoman Empire*, Weidenfeld and Nicolson, 1973
Isenbart, H. H. & Buhrer, E. M., *The Kingdom of the Horse*, Collins, 1970

Jacobs, W. D., *Frunze: the Soviet Clausewitz*, M. Nijhoff, 1969
Jankovich, M., *They Rode into Europe*, Harrap, 1971
Johnson, S., *The History of the Yorubas*, Routledge Kegan Paul, 1966
Jones, A. H. M., *The Decline of the Ancient World*, Longmans, 1966
Josephus (Trans. G. A. Williamson), *The Jewish War*, Penguin Books, 1959

Katzenbach, E. L., 'The Horse Cavalry in the 20th Century: a Study on Policy Response', *Public Policy*, Harvard University Press, 1958
Kearsley, A., *A Study of the Strategy and Tactics of the Russo-Japanese War*, Gale and Polden, 1935
Kellock, E. M., *The Story of Riding*, David and Charles, 1974
Kershap, P., *Studies in Ancient Persian History*, Kegan Paul, 1905
Kiernan, F. A. & Fairbank, J. K., *Chinese Ways in Warfare*, Harvard University Press, 1974
Kinder, H., & Hilgemann, W., *The Penguin Atlas of World History*, (vol 1), Penguin Books, 1976
Kiraly, B. K., *Hungary in the Late 18th Century*, Columbia University Press, 1969
Kitto, H. D. F., *The Greeks*, Penguin Books, 1960
Kruger, R., *Good-bye Dolly Gray*, Cassell, 1959

Lamb, H., *Ghengis Khan*, Penguin Books/Infantry Journal, 1942
Lane-Poole, S., (ed.), *Medieval India from Contemporary Sources*, F. Cooper, 1916
Latham, J. D., 'The Archers of the Middle East: the Turco–Iranian Background', *Iran*, viii (1970)
Lattimore, O., 'Inner Asian Frontiers: Chinese and Russian Margins of Expansion', *Studies in Frontier History*, Oxford University Press, 1962
Law, R. C. C., 'A West African Cavalry State: the Kingdom of Oyo', *Journal of African History*, xvi (1975)
—— 'Horses, Firearms and Political Power in Pre-Colonial West Africa', *Past and Present*, lxxii (1976)
Lawford, J., (ed.), *Cavalry*, Sampson Low, 1976
Legassick, M., 'Firearms, Horses and Samorian Army Organisation' 1870–98, *Journal of African History*, vii (1966)
Legg, S., *The Heartland*, Secker and Warburg, 1970
Léonard, E., *L'Armée et ses problèmes au dix-huitième siècle*, Plon, 1958
Levy, R., *The Social Structure of Islam*, Cambridge University Press, 1957
Lewis, A., *Knights and Samurai*, Temple-Smith, 1974
Leyser, K., 'The Battle of the Lech 955', *History*, (1965)
Livermore, H., *The Origins of Spain and Portugal*, Allen and Unwin, 1971
Livy (trans. A. de Sélincourt & H. Bettenson), *The History of Rome from Its Foundation*, (3 vols), Penguin Books, 1960–76
Lloyd, S., *Twin Rivers*, Oxford University Press, 1902
Loewe, M., *Crisis and Conflict in Han China*, Allen and Unwin, 1974
—— *Everyday Life in Early Imperial China*, Batsford, 1968
Longstreet, S., *War Cries on Horseback*, W. H. Allen, 1970
Longworth, P., *The Cossacks*, Constable, 1969
Lourie, E., 'A Society Organised for War: Medieval Spain', *Past and Present*, xxxv (1966)
Loyn, H. R., *The Norman Conquest*, Hutchinson, 1967
Lunt, J., *Charge to Glory*, Heinemann, 1961
Luvaas, J., *The Military Legacy of the Civil War*, University of Chicago Press, 1959

—— 'European Military Thought and Doctrine', in M. Howard (ed.) *The Theory and Practice of War*, Cassell, 1965
—— (ed.) *Frederick the Great on the Art of War*, Free Press, 1966

Mackintosh, M., *Juggernaut*, Secker and Warburg, 1967
McElwee, W., *The Art of War: Waterloo to Mons*, Weidenfeld and Nicolson, 1974
Maenchen-Helfen, O. J., *The World of the Huns*, University of California Press, 1973
Mallet, M., *Mercenaries and their Masters*, Bodley Head, 1974
Mann, G., *Wallenstein*, Andre Deutsch, 1976
Martin, H. D., *The Rise of Ghenghis Khan and the Conquest of North China*, John Hopkins Press, 1950
Mason, P., *A Matter of Honour*, Jonathan Cape, 1974
Maude, E. N., *Cavalry: Its Past and Future*, Clowes and Sons, 1903
Meijer, J. M., *The Trotsky Papers*, (2 vols), Mouton, 1964
Merton, C. & Munz, H., (eds.), *The Carmen de Hastingae Proelio of Guy Bishop of Amiens*, Oxford University Press, 1972
Mierow, C. C., (ed.), *The Deeds of Frederick Barbarossa by Otto of Friesling*, Columbia University Press, 1953
Millar, F., *The Roman Empire and its Neighbours*, Weidenfeld and Nicolson, 1967
Mockler, A., *Our Enemies the French*, Leo Cooper, 1976
Morczali, H., *Hungary in the 18th Century*, Cambridge University Press, 1910
Morgan, J. de, *Feudalism in Persia*, Government Printing Office (Washington DC), 1914
Mundy, J. H., *Europe in the High Middle Ages 1150–1309*, Longmans, 1973
Musset, L., *The Germanic Invasions*, Elek, 1975

Nelson, L. H., *The Normans in South Wales*, University of Texas Press, 1966
Norman, V., *The Medieval Soldier*, A. Barker, 1971

Ogilvie, R. M., *Early Rome and the Etruscans*, Fontana Books, 1976
Olmstead, A. T., *History of the Persian Empire*, University of Chicago Press, 1948
Oman, C. W. C., *A History of the Art of War in the Middle Ages*, (2 vols), Methuen, 1924
—— *A History of the Art of War in the 16th Century*, Methuen, 1937
—— *Wellington's Army*, E. Arnold, 1912
—— 'Napoleon and his Cavalry', in *Studies in the Napoleonic Wars*, Methuen, 1929
Ostrogorsky, G., *History of the Byzantine State*, Blackwell, 1968

Palmer, F., *With Kuroki in Manchuria*, Methuen, 1904
Pamenyi, E., (ed.), *A History of Hungary*, Colletts, 1975
Parry, V. J. & Yapp, M. E., *War, Technology and Society in the Middle East*, Oxford University Press, 1975
Peissel, M., *The Cavaliers of Kham*, Heinemann, 1972
Pernoud, R., *The Crusaders*, Oliver and Boyd, 1963
Plutarch (trans. I. Scott–Kilvert), *Makers of Rome*, Penguin Books, 1965
—— (trans. R. Warner), *Fall of the Roman Republic*, Penguin Books, 1958
Polybius (trans. W. R. Paton), *The Histories*, (6 vols), Heinemann, 1922–27
Powicke, M., *Military Obligation in Medieval England*
Preston, R. A. (*et al.*), *Men in Arms*, Thames and Hudson, 1962
Preston, R. M. P., *The Desert Mounted Corps*, Constable, 1921
Procopius (trans.B. H. Dewing), *History of the Wars* (5 vols), Heinemann, 1914–28

Quimby, R. S., *The Background to Napoleonic Warfare*, Columbia University Press, 1967

Quirk, R. E., *The Mexican Revolution 1914–15*, Indiana University Press, 1960

Reddaway, W. F. (*et al.*), *Cambridge History of Poland*, (2 vols), Cambridge University Press, 1950

Reed, J., *Insurgent Mexico*, Simon and Schuster, 1969

Reitz, D., *Commando*, Penguin Books, 1948

Rickey, D., *Forty Miles a Day on Beans and Hay*, University of Oklahoma Press, 1963

Roberts, M., *A History of Sweden*, (2 vols), Longmans Green, 1958

—— (ed.), *Sweden's Age of Greatness 1632–1718*, Macmillan, 1973

Robson, E., 'The Armed Forces and the Art of War', *New Cambridge Modern History*, (vol 7), Cambridge University Press, 1963

Roe, F. G., *The Indian and the Horse*, University of Oklahoma Press, 1955

Rogers, H. C. B., *The Mounted Troops of the British Army*, Seeley Service, 1960

Ropp, T., *War in the Modern World*, Collier Books, 1962

Rothenberg, G. E., *The Austrian Military Border in Croatia 1522–1747*, University of Illinois Press, 1960

Roux, G., *Ancient Iraq*, Penguin Books, 1966

Runciman, S., *Byzantine Civilisation*, Methuen, 1975

—— *A History of the Crusades*, (3 vols), Cambridge University Press, 1951–54

Rutherford, W., *The Russian Army in World War I*, G. Cremonesi, 1975

Sallust (trans. S. A. Handford), *The Jugurthine War*, Penguin Books, 1964

Schreiber, H., *Teuton and Slav*, Constable, 1965

Scullard, H. H., *From the Gracchi to Nero*, Methuen, 1951

Seward, D., *The Monks of War*, Eyre Methuen, 1972

Sharma, G., *Indian Army through the Ages*, Allied Publishers, 1969

Shaw, S. J., *History of the Ottoman Empire and Modern Turkey*, (2 vols), Cambridge University Press, 1976

Sikorski, W., *Modern Warfare*, (1934), Hutchinson, 1943

Singh, R., *History of Indian Army*, Army Educational Stores, 1963

Sinha, B. P., 'The Art of War in Ancient India 600 B.C. to 300 A.D.', *Cahiers d'histoire mondiale*, iv (1957)

Sinor, D., *History of Hungary*, Allen and Unwin, 1959

Slocombe, G., *A History of Poland*, Nelson, 1939

Smail, R. C., *Crusading Warfare*, Cambridge University Press, 1956

Smith, R. S., *Kingdoms of the Yoruba*, Methuen, 1969

—— *Warfare and Diplomacy in Pre-Colonial West Africa*, Methuen, 1976

Spuler, B., (ed.), *History of the Mongols*, Routledge Kegan Paul, 1972

Stone, N., *The Eastern Front*, Hodder and Stoughton, 1975

Strabo (trans. H. L. Jones), *Geography*, (8 vols), Heinemann, 1923–32

Sulimirski, T., *The Sarmatians*, Thames and Hudson, 1970

Tacitus (trans. H. Mattingley), *On Britain and Germany*, Penguin Books, 1948

—— (trans. M. Grant), *The Annals of Imperial Rome*, Penguin Books, 1956

—— (trans. K. Wellesley), *The Histories*, Penguin Books, 1964

Tarle, E., *Napoleon's Invasion of Russia*, Allen and Unwin, 1942

Tarn, W. W., *Hellenistic Military and Naval Developments*, Cambridge University Press, 1930

Taylor, F. L., *The Art of War in Italy 1494–1529*, Cambridge University Press, 1921

Taylor, L., *Bits*, Harper and Row, 1966

Tebbel, J., & Jennison, K., *The American Indian Wars*, Harper & Bros, 1960

Teng, S. Y., *The Nien Army and their Guerrilla Warfare*, Mouton, 1961

Thapar, R., *A History of India*, (vol 1), Penguin Books, 1966

Thomas, D., *Charge, Hurrah! Hurrah!*, Routledge Kegan Paul, 1974

Thompson, E. A., *The Early Germans*, Oxford University Press, 1965

—— *A History of Attila and the Huns*, Oxford University Press, 1948

—— *The Goths in Spain*, Oxford University Press, 1969

Tozer, B., *The Horse in History*, Methuen, 1908

Trease, G., *The Condottieri*, Thames and Hudson, 1970

Trench, C. C., *A History of Horsemanship*, Longmans, 1970

Ure, P. N., *Justinian and his Age*, Penguin Books, 1951

Varley, H. P. & Morris, I. N., *The Samurai*, Weidenfeld and Nicolson, 1970

Vegetius, 'The Military Institutions of the Romans', in T. R. Phillips (ed.), *The Roots of Strategy*, Bodley Head, 1943

Vaughan, R., *Charles the Bold*, Longmans, 1973

—— *John the Fearless*, Longmans, 1966

Vernadsky, G., *The Mongols and Russia*, Yale University Press, 1953

—— (*et al.*), *A Source Book for Russian History*, (3 vols), Yale University Press, 1972

Waley, D. P., 'The Army of the Florentine Republic', in N. Rubenstein (ed.), *Florentine Studies*, Faber and Faber, 1968

Wallace-Hadrill, J. M., *The Barbarian West 400–1000*, Hutchinson, 1967

Webster, G., *The Roman Imperial Army*, A. & C. Black, 1969

Webb, W. P., *The Great Plains*, Grosset and Dunlap, 1931

Weller, J., *Weapons and Tactics*, N. Vane, London, 1966

—— *Wellington in the Peninsula*, N. Vane, London, 1962

Western, J. R., 'Armies', *New Cambridge Modern History*, (vol 8), Cambridge University Press, 1965

White, D. F., *The Growth of the Red Army*, Princeton University Press, 1944

White, L., *Medieval Technology and Social Change*, Oxford University Press, 1962

Whitman, S. E., *The Troopers*, Hastings House, 1962

Whitton, F. E., 'The Death Ride', *Blackwoods Magazine*, May 1933

Wijn, J. W., 'Military Forces and Warfare', *New Cambridge Modern History*, (vol 4), Cambridge University Press, 1970

Wilber, D. N., *Iran*, Princeton University Press, 1969

Wilson, A., *The Ever-Victorious Army*, Blackwood & Sons, 1868

Wintringham, T., & Blashford-Snell, J., *Weapons and Tactics*, Penguin Books, 1974

Wise, T., *Medieval Warfare*, Osprey, 1976

Womack, J., *Zapata and the Mexican Revolution*, Thames and Hudson, 1969

Wood, E., *Achievements of Cavalry*, G. Bell, 1897

—— *Cavalry in the Waterloo Campaign*, Sampson Low, 1895

Woodham-Smith, C., *The Reason Why*, Constable, 1953

Xenophon (trans. R. Warner), *The Persian Expedition*, Penguin Books, 1949

Index